HOPE AND GLORY

JESUS IS COMING AGAIN

the timeless message of
1 & 2 Thessalonians

To. Dick . Jean
be encouraged!
S
2 Cor. 4v7,

SAM GORDON

AMBASSADOR INTERNATIONAL

AMBASSADOR INTERNATIONAL

427 Wade Hampton Blvd.
Greenville, SC 29609, USA
www.emeraldhouse.com

AMBASSADOR PUBLICATIONS

a division of
Ambassador Productions Ltd.
Providence House
Ardenlee Street
Belfast
BT6 8QJ
Northern Ireland
www.ambassador-productions.com

TRANS WORLD RADIO

P.O. Box 2858
Bath
BA2 5XN
United Kingdom
01225 831390
www.twr.org.uk

TRANS WORLD RADIO

P. O. Box 8700
Cary, NC 27512, USA
1 800 456 7TWR
www.twr.org

The colophon is a trademark of Ambassador

DEDICATION
to John Baines
editor extraordinaire

Truth for Today Mission Statement

'To teach the entire Bible in a warm expository style so that people's lives are influenced to such a degree that they impact their world for Christ.'

FIRST WORD

Jesus is coming again—the marvellously heartwarming theme of Paul's two electrifying epistles to the Thessalonian believers—is a stirring, rejuvenating communiqué of vibrant hope, one they desperately needed to hear. It forces us to lift our eyes to the far horizon of ultimate issues. Certainly, in today's post 9/11 world where we seemingly lurch from crisis to crisis, it is a message we do well to take on board.

Preacher Paul misses these wonderful people. His acute loss is painfully hard to bear, for a shepherd without sheep is like a leader without followers, a coach without a team, a president without an organisation, or a captain without a ship.

When that happens, as it does, there is a profound sense of emptiness and a passionate longing to be back at one's station in life. The problem is none of us can rewrite history; we cannot turn the clock back! There is no instant replay button.

The circuit-riding Paul cannot jump on a horse and go visit them; in fact, the chances of him being able to do so in the near future were pretty remote and slim. Neither can he pick up a cell phone and call them for a cosy chat.

So, not one to be beaten or scalped, the bullish apostle did the next best thing, he picked up the quill and sent them a couple of upbeat letters that echo with spirited optimism. It is not the end and, even if it was, they were on the winning team.

Join me as we reflect on this first-century text message.

Sam Gordon

TABLE OF CONTENTS

viii

x

1 Thessalonians

CHAPTER ONE
SETTING THE PACE

The Christians in Thessalonica sprinted out of the blocks on the 'B of the bang' of the starter's gun.

There was something exceptional about them—they stood out! Different. Distinctive. Distinguished. None of your average, run-of-the-mill, one-size-fits-all, plain vanilla bores in this church. These guys and gals were not content to just keep the engine idling. They were dynamic, enthusiastic, and so incredibly keen. On the ball. Super heroes!

These first-century pilgrims were excellent role models of authentic, biblical Christianity—the real McCoy! Paul even describes them, corporately, as the ideal church. A church with the right stuff. A church in a city where Paul had caused a riot. A church that turned the world upside down. This says something. Do not get carried away just yet…it was not always like that.

Before Paul arrived in town on one of his famous, highly-publicised missionary journeys, there was no church there. The reality is it was through his sterling evangelistic efforts that a church was born.

First things first

Let me take you back for a moment to Acts 17 to where and when it all began. This chapter is compulsive reading. Good stuff. Riveting. A fast-moving account of all that transpired in those early days. The big question is, what actually happened?
- Paul preaches his heart out about Jesus Christ;
- scores of people are gloriously converted;
- the locals do not like what they see and hear;

- rent-a-mob is activated and the devil fights back;
- there is pandemonium as chaos and confusion reign supreme;
- Paul and Silas come out of hiding and do a vanishing act in the middle of the night;
- they turn up in Berea, forty miles down the road, and preach the same message to a better class of people;
- wonder of wonders, history almost repeats itself.
  That is a fairly quick summary. A résumé.

Thumbnail sketch

Thessalonica was quite a city—a place of renown, a city with a reputation. It was originally named Therma from the many hot springs adjacent to it. Then in 315 BC it was renamed by Cassander, one of the top officers in the army of Alexander the Great. He called it Thessalonica because he wished to dedicate the city to a lady of that name, the half-sister of Alexander the Great.

During the next century Rome became the dominant power in the region and Macedonia was absorbed into the expanding Roman Empire. History informs us that in the early decades of the first century BC the security of the Roman state was seriously threatened by civil war. Competing generals fought to control what was then the Roman Republic.

During these turbulent years the ordinary peoples of the Empire looked on rather anxiously from the sidelines, bemused and concerned as they wondered which of the rivals would come out on top. As far as Thessalonica was concerned, they had no need to worry, for the outcome could not have been better.

She made a wise choice and sided with the eventual victor, Augustus; with victory in the bag he became the first Roman emperor. This loyalty was amply rewarded when Thessalonica was made the capital of the province of Macedonia. It was also awarded the status of a free city and enjoyed the benefits of self-government under locally appointed rulers. In fact, Lightfoot described it as 'the key to the whole of Macedonia' and then he added that 'it narrowly escaped being made the capital of the world.'

Location, location, location

As a city it occupied a strategic position because it boasted a splendid and substantial natural harbour at the head of the Thermaic Gulf (now the Gulf of Saloniki). It was situated on the Via Egnatia—the main route between Rome and the Orient. The Arch of Galerius, which spanned the Egnatian Way in Paul's day, still stands today.

It proved to be a thriving centre for trade and commerce as goods from east and west poured into the city. The shops and markets were well stocked with all sorts of consumer products. You name it, they had it; and if they did not have it, rest assured, they could get it for you!

Thessalonica had the ambience of a fashionable luxury resort.

It had so much going for it. The Olympic Games had once been held there. In terms of real estate its location was enviable. First impressions of the city would have taken the missionaries' breath away; it has, appropriately, been called the crown jewel of Macedonia. Its setting was picturesque with the majestic mountains of Greece, including the fabled Mount Olympus, rising high behind it.

Its economy was stable. There was an air of affluence permeating the atmosphere of the leafy streets of the city which, in its own way, contributed to the considerable influence of her well-to-do citizens.

Headcount

In Paul's day the population was, conservatively, estimated to be around 200,000 souls, and rapidly rising. The city and its environs attracted a potpourri of people who came from all over the world to settle there, making it a truly cosmopolitan centre.

It is most interesting to note that during World War I the city served as an exceptionally important Allied base. Then in World War II the city was captured by the advancing German army and the Jewish population of about 60,000 persons was deported. Needless to say, they were never seen or heard of again.

Today it is possible to visit Salonica in Northern Greece as part of a package holiday deal. I was there a while back when involved in some Bible teaching ministry across the border with some friends in Macedonia—a memorable visit.

Nowadays, apart from any seasonal adjustment brought about by tourism, the population hovers around the one million mark, making it a big, bustling city—second in size only to Athens. Some of Greece's most creative musicians—including Savopoulos, Tsitsanis, and Papazoglou—came from this city that is renowned as the cradle of the popular modern Greek song, 'Rembetiko' (the Greek Blues). It is also the birthplace of Greek basketball. A huge honour was bestowed on the city when it was chosen in 1997 as the cultural capital of Europe.

Head start

It was into this situation approximately two millennia ago that the trail-blazing Paul ventured on his second missionary journey. He saw it as a potential springboard for evangelising the rest of Europe. How right he was as subsequent events indicate!

How did he go about it? True to form, he went to where the people were—he made a beeline for the local synagogue. And when he got there he started where the people were. In his preaching he assumed they knew nothing. He led them through, step by step, into the great truths of the gospel.

We learn a lot from Paul's direct approach to evangelism: he used the word of God and he declared the Son of God. There were two main points in his gospel sermon—Jesus has died and the Lord has risen. What an incredibly powerful message.

There were no clever, slick programs; he had no bag of tricks; he had nothing hidden up his sleeve; there were definitely no eye-catching gimmicks to influence others. On the contrary, it was the Holy Spirit applying the word of God to extremely needy hearts. What a marvellous response, it was tremendous.

Paul simply sowed the seed, it was watered by tears in the place of prayer, then God came and, in his sovereign goodness, the Lord gave the increase. There were a number who said 'yes' to Jesus Christ for the very first time in their life.

Bringing in the sheaves

Actually, there is a trio of fascinating phrases employed by Dr. Luke in Acts 17 to focus attention on the wide range of brand new converts. He talks in verse 4 about 'some of the Jews... a large number of God-fearing Greeks and not a few prominent women.' We know the names of a couple of them from Acts 20:4—one was called Aristarchus and the other was known as Secundus. Put them all together and these folk became the nucleus of the first Christian church in this sprawling metropolitan city.

When we touch base, it is all about proclaiming the story of the Lord Jesus and then seeing people come to know him in a personal way. There is the sheer joy of evangelism: it is reaping a harvest of lives dramatically changed by the power of God.

These are the ones who would continue to turn the world upside down because they had been transformed from the inside out.

How to give away your faith

I suppose three weeks, or thereabouts, is not a particularly long time to spend in one place. Paul's time in Thessalonica was relatively short, but it was hugely significant. I imagine the apostle and his companions would have stayed there a while longer if circumstances had been more favourable.

However, Paul being Paul, he made the most of his time there, he maximised every opportunity afforded to him. He did not mess around with other people's lives! Sure, the message never changed, it was the presentation that differed on occasion.

It is instructive to note that four phrases are used by the historian in Acts 17:2-3 to underline the tactics that Paul adopted:
- 'he reasoned with them'—he engaged in some form of dialogue, a kind of question and answer session;
- 'he explained'—he opened up the word to them by exercising an

expository-style ministry;
- 'he proved'—he presented all the evidence to them clearly and distinctly;
- 'he proclaim[ed]'—as he preached the word, he was making a bold declaration of biblical truth.

Class 101

And so, having watched them come to personal faith in the living God, he begins to carefully disciple them.

We can tell by the letter Paul wrote that in nurturing them he did a splendid job. He excelled in the art of discipleship. No stone was left unturned, nothing was too much trouble. Paul invested all his energy and experience into ensuring they got off to a good start in their Christian life. He covered an awful lot of ground in the space of a few short weeks.

In fact, the lasting impression we have of them is that here was a group of people who were very well grounded in the fundamentals of the faith; they were enthusiastic and keen in their quest to know the Lord better; they were immensely grateful to Paul for his all-too-brief ministry among them; they were big-hearted and generous in giving their money to the Lord's work; they were shining brightly for their Lord in a hostile, pagan environment; they were passionate in their desire to engage in evangelism.

Knee deep in Greece

Time marches on and with it the inevitable and unavoidable changes come. Paul himself has moved on. He is redeployed in a city that tops the league in terms of sinfulness—the Vanity Fair of ancient Greece—Corinth. It has been aptly described as a sailor's favourite port, a prodigal's paradise, a policeman's nightmare, and a preacher's graveyard.

Even though the apostle finds himself knee deep in Greece in a situation which is less than user-friendly, there are many thoughts flitting around in his mind as he reflects on the infant church in Thessalonica. *How would they cope*, he keeps asking himself. *Will they*

be able to manage without him being around any longer, he wonders. *Do they have the theological know-how and get-up-and-go
to stand on their own two feet?*

Typical Paul, he does not wait to find out. He takes the initiative,
seizes the moment, strikes when the iron is hot, and sends them a
letter. Paul wrote his first epistle to them around AD 50/51. It is from
Corinth that he puts quill to parchment in a valiant attempt to encourage and quietly reassure them.

Basically, the legendary Paul wants to remind them of his continued interest in them and his prayerful concern for them. He knows
how he feels about them, but he has to communicate that message to
them, for they need to know it as well.

It was not the classic case of out of sight, out of mind. If anything,
the opposite is more accurately reflected in his thinking. How could
he forget them? After all, they are family, his spiritual sons and daughters. They matter to him because they are important to God.

A first-century stimulant

What makes this I-can't-get-you-out-of-my-mind letter so appealing and attractive? Paul writes to pep up people who are struggling—
people for whom the storm clouds are already gathering and for whom
the future appears ominous. He emboldens them—a shot in the arm.
He does it in a way that is unforgettable, unique, and one-off.

The best time to give flowers to people is when they are alive, not
when they are dead.

It is special because in every chapter he talks about the Second
Coming of Jesus Christ—the great and blessed hope of the child of God.
There is no finer incentive to living a life of holiness and no better spur
to motivate us for service. If we really take to heart what Paul is saying
and believe it with a no-strings-attached commitment, then it will lead
to a deepening of our spiritual life. We will never be the same again.

Paul never looked on the message of the imminent return of Christ
as a theory to be discussed by armchair cynics waiting for the end of
the world. He saw it as a truth to be lived out in the rough and tumble

of everyday experience. It is a clarion call to readiness, a wake-up call to live today in the light of tomorrow.

- In chapter one, it spawns assurance when our past is uncertain—a saving truth—we are saved and know it.
- In chapter two, it encourages us to get our act together—a stimulating truth—we are saved and show it.
- In chapter three, it brings buoyancy when the sea is choppy—a stabilising truth—we are saved and growing.
- In chapter four, it guarantees a light at the end of the tunnel—a satisfying truth—we are saved and going.
- In chapter five, it gives us the edge in a secular age—a sanctifying truth—we are saved and glowing.

An angle on truth

There is another way to look at the epistle when we approach it from a slightly different angle—there is a measure of interaction between the church and the gospel.

Paul shows how the gospel creates the church and the church spreads the gospel, and how the gospel shapes the church as the church seeks to live a life that is worthy of the gospel.

This is immensely helpful for, when we look at the epistle from this perspective, it opens up a significantly different outline for us to follow. John Stott expands on it like this in his commentary. In his analysis, there are five major points:

- Christian evangelism, or how the church spreads the gospel (1:1-10).
- Christian ministry, or how pastors serve both the gospel and the church (2:1-3:13).
- Christian behaviour, or how the church must live according to the gospel (4:1-12).
- Christian hope, or how the gospel should inspire the church (4:13-5:11).
- Christian community, or how to be a gospel church (5:12-28).

Irrespective of how we look at it, 1 Thessalonians opens a sparkling pellucid window on to a newly-planted church, a church filled with extraordinary promise. It tells us how it was birthed in an atmosphere of persecution; it tells us what the apostle taught it; it tells us what were its strengths and weaknesses; it tells us its theological and moral problems; it tells us how it was spreading the gospel.

Lessons to learn

When we stop and think about it, there are a number of options open to us as we reflect on our studies in this scratch-where-people-itch letter: one, we can take it contextually, as purely a letter to the Thessalonians and, therefore, miss its message; two, we can view it as nothing more than a crash course in Bible doctrine and, there-fore, miss half its message; three, we can see it as a personal letter and, therefore, get its whole message.

I know which option I am going for—not the first, nor the second. It has to be number three!

To sum up, here we have an epistle written for all those who want to live well for Jesus and who, by default, are concerned about evangelism and the end times.

- God uses homespun people—he did not send a celebrity angel to evangelise Thessalonica. He sent a converted Jewish rabbi and a couple of his upwardly mobile friends.
- There is power in the gospel of Christ—it did not take years to set up a church in this great city. God's power was enormously effective in changing lives, and a church was up and running in less than a month.
- Satan still opposes the proclamation and advance of the gospel and persecutes the people of God.

1:1 ONE-ON-ONE

Paul gives us a fascinating, behind-the-scenes look at an evangelical congregation who met together in the middle years of the first century AD, and what an eye-opener it proves to be. Paul's letter is no more than a heart-to-heart talk from the great apostle to his children in the faith. It is a fairly compact epistle, packed full with parental affection and advice.

Here was an ideal church, a church not given to extremes. They maintained their spiritual glow; they sounded out the word of the Lord; they were waiting with a sense of expectancy in their hearts for the second advent of Jesus; there was a clearly defined balance in their walk with God—those hugely positive thoughts seem to permeate the first chapter.

Sweet and sour

Did you know that the church has a fragrance? Let me assure you, I am not talking about Chanel No. 5 or some other expensive, scented perfume!

Paul referred to it as a 'sweet aroma.' This is what he said in 2 Corinthians 2:14-15 in *The Message*: 'In Christ, God leads us from place to place in one perpetual victory parade. Through us, he brings knowledge of Christ. Everywhere we go, people breathe in the exquisite fragrance. Because of Christ, we give off a sweet scent rising to God, which is recognised by those on the way of salvation, an aroma redolent with life.'

Sad to say, in the past few years, the putrefying stench of sin has invaded some high-profile ministries, obscuring the fragrance of Christ. It is inevitable, if we give the media an inch, they will take a mile as they ruthlessly exploit every whiff of scandal. They jump on the bandwagon and before we know it they have blown the whole picture out of proportion.

Unfortunately, when that happens, the man in the street who cannot see the wood for the trees writes the church off as a non-starter. Our reputation is dealt such a enormous blow that we end up severely winded. The body of Christ then becomes a punching-bag for cynics eager to poke fun. Postmodern man turns up his nose at the church. Such is life in the third millennium.

To be fair, that is only part of the story, it is not the total picture. The truth is that there are many more ambrosial churches than there are rotten ones. O yes, there are weeds, no question about that, the fact cannot be denied. But thank God, there are many flowers that are both delectably fragrant and deliciously fruitful. When I flick through the pages of the

New Testament and I come across a church like the one in Thessalonica, I very quickly realise there are some pristine lilies in a muddy pond.

They certainly had a reputation, a good one; thank God, it was for all the right reasons!

Let me introduce...

How does the apostle start the ball rolling? What are his opening comments? Is there anything that grabs our immediate attention? I think there is! The introduction! Pithy; short and sweet; straight to the point.

The intro begins with a single word: *Paul.* He just happens to be the penman of the epistle. He was, in the words of Spurgeon, the prince of preachers. As an emissary to the regions beyond he took the gospel where man had never taken it before.

Paul was Christ's flagship missionary, he sailed the world with the story of Jesus.

He held major city-wide crusades, he planted scores of churches all over the place. He was quite a prolific writer and was in huge demand across Europe, Asia, and the Middle East as a Bible teacher. It seems to me that Paul's vision for mission was as big as the world he knew. Unlike many of us, Paul was not guilty of dreaming too small. He knew he served a great God who could do great things through him if he placed his life at his disposal.

I think it is always fascinating, and not a little intriguing, to observe how a person introduces himself. It tells us something about them. It is most refreshing to read, in light of his stellar credentials, that Paul did not introduce himself as an apostle, but rather he was content just to say, 'Hi, its Paul here!'

In spite of a colossally impressive résumé, plus a long list of unbelievable achievements in his illustrious career to date, he makes no attempt whatsoever to enhance his own image. He does not need to, he does not have to. He is comfortable with himself and is most relaxed with a passing reference to his name.

He is plain Mr. Paul. What staggering, make-your-head-swim humility! There is a magnificence in his sense of insignificance. This man is a

Titan, but he is also a man with a servant heart. D. L. Moody remarked: 'The measure of a man is not how many servants he has, but how many men he serves.' True service begins where gratitude and applause ends.

Servanthood is basin theology. Whose feet are you washing?

Once seen, never forgotten

One ancient writer actually described Paul in this way, he said: 'He was a man small of stature, with a bald head and crooked legs, in a good state of body, with eyebrows meeting, and nose somewhat crooked.' Well, when we read the likes of that, I suppose we could say, once seen, never forgotten! If we met him in the shopping mall we would not look, we would stare! However, what Paul might have lacked in good looks, he more than made up for in being a willing and tireless servant of the living God.

George Whitefield (1714-70), mightily used by God, had a squint. The firebrand evangelist, Christmas Evans (1766-1838), had a false eye. Twenty minutes into his sermon his eye socket would fill up with moisture. He would pause, take out the false eye, wipe the socket with a handkerchief, and pop it back in again!

Paul, a robust preacher, stands unique in the annals of church history as one who combined the animated fervour of an evangelist-cum-church planter, with the gentle tenderness of a shepherd, the skilled diplomacy of an ambassador, and the astute intellect of a scholar.

Team ministry

Paul is not ploughing a lonely furrow, for he also includes *Silas and Timothy* in his cordial greetings to the church. They were his co-labourers.

Silas (or Silvanus, a Roman name meaning 'woodland') was a highly esteemed member of the church at Jerusalem (cf. Acts 15:22). He was one of the 'chief men among the brethren' and was credited with having a prophetic gift. Unlike some people, he was happy to play second fiddle.

On the other side of the spectrum, Timothy (meaning 'honouring God') was Paul's son in the faith. He was relatively young—late teens or early twenties—sensitive by nature, fairly raw and inexperienced. When it came to ministry, he was still in the process of cutting his teeth.

It is great to see, even though the three of them are individuals in their own right, they combine well together to form a brilliant team ministry. Each one has a distinct role to play, ensuring their gifts are used to their full potential. When Billy Graham received his Congressional Medal of Honour, the first thing he is reported to have said upon receiving the award is, 'This has been a team effort from the very beginning,' and he proceeded to name the people who had ministered unto him through the years. In closing he said, 'We did this together.'

From Paul's perspective, he is enormously grateful to the Lord for his colleagues as people. He values them for who they are and, at the same time, he treasures their warm, genial fellowship. He recognises their superb contribution to the overall ministry and is big enough in heart to acknowledge it.

Paul does not feel threatened by their gifts. This is not a one-man show. He is not into empire building; all that matters to him is that the kingdom is extended. He is not convinced of his personal indispensability. He knows he is just one among others who make up the team and who need one another's support and input.

As a servant, Paul is more than willing to reduce his own impact so as to enhance theirs. A competitive spirit and the scourge of jealousy have no place in his heart. Paul is the kind of person who does not mind who gets the credit so long as the job gets done! It goes without saying, we can be too big for God to use, but we can never be too small!

Best of both worlds

Paul addresses his first epistle to *the church of the Thessalonians in God the Father and the Lord Jesus Christ*. A double address. One tells me where I am geographically, the other where I am spiritually. Two places at once: they were here and there at the same time. Our heart is in heaven, our feet are on planet Earth. God's church was living in Thessalonica and their church was living in God.

To be sure, the preposition *in* has a different nuance in these statements, since the church is *in God* as the source from which its life comes, whereas it is *in* the world only as the sphere in which it lives. Having said that, it is still correct to say that every church has two homes, two environments, two habitats: it lives in God and it lives in the world!

The apostle wrote numerous letters during the course of his ministry, but this one is truly unique. It is the only letter that employs the phrase *the church of.* They were a company of called-out believers enjoying a remarkable sense of unity in their midst. There was a discernible bond, a wonderful feeling of affinity, a rich spirit of togetherness throughout the congregation. It was palpable. There was a beautiful atmosphere that could be felt the minute one went through the front door and entered the meeting room. Electric. Spine-tingling. What a church!

'In' the know

There is a lot more to it than meets the eye. There always is! These folk had no background; it was not a case of sporting the teeshirt—been there, done that—for they had no core of experienced members in the congregation; they are a motley crew of still-in-the-diaper Christians, freshly converted from Judaism or paganism. This God-stuff was all brand new to them. Let's face it, they have only been going for a few months, at most. Raw recruits. Christian rookies.

In a world where men wobbled like Jello, their Christian convictions have been newly acquired; in a permissive, *dolce vita* society, their Christian moral standards have been newly adopted. The nagging question is, when the tough times come, how would they handle a crisis? This actually helps explain why Paul said what he did to them in his tête-à-tête.

They were rooted in God, living in God, and secure in God.

The dynamic relationship they enjoyed with the Lord was such that it was extraordinarily close. They were *in him.* In other words, they share in his life. They may have been green and untried, but make no mistake about it, God was totally committed to them.

So it was the done thing back in Paul's day to begin a letter by telling the people whom it was from—'whoever' signed their name at the beginning rather than at the end!

Double-barrelled blessing

It was also a convention of first-century correspondence to include a prayer for the recipients. *Grace and peace* is the twofold blessing Paul offers them—the twin towers of the Christian gospel. Hey, Paul could not have wished anything better for them. This was the longing in his heart that they might know both blessings.

'Grace' and 'peace' are two of the loveliest words in the believer's vocabulary. They sparkle like lights on an evergreen Christmas tree. There is a certain pizzas about them—a vivacious dash of divine wonder.

The order is of ultra importance. We can never know peace in our heart without first experiencing the grace of God in our life. Peace is a wonderful spin-off from the grace of God. If we look at it from a different slant, grace is the fountain of which peace is the stream.

Grace is God's multiplex kindness in our life.

Grace is something that comes to us which we do not deserve and which we cannot repay. Grace stoops to where we are and lifts us to where we ought to be. John Pantry hit the right note when he penned:

> *Wonderful grace*
> *That gives what I don't deserve,*
> *Pays me what Christ has earned,*
> *Then lets me go free.*
> *Wonderful grace*
> *That gives me the time to change,*
> *Washes away the stains*
> *That once covered me.*

Peace is something that happens within us—a freedom from inner distraction; an internal rest; a feeling of well being. Spiritual wholeness. Peace is a tranquillity of soul that frees us from fear and takes the sharp edges off our anxiety. Peace is that unruffled quietness which defies the crashing, crushing circumstances of life.

- Peace with God.
- Peace with ourselves.
- Peace with our partner.
- Peace with our neighbours.
- Peace with our past.
- Peace with our present.
- Peace with our future.

A terrific greeting! A great, big, wonderful God!

Chilling with God

This God of grace and God of peace who came to the church in the first century to meet their miscellaneous needs is the same God who comes to us, two millennia later, saying, 'Put your trust in me.'

Paul's sanguine letter speaks as powerfully today as it did then. God's grace overflowed in their hearts, and God's peace reigned in their lives. Pure and simple, that is the prime reason why their marque of Christianity was so infectious and exciting.

Before we take a look at the rare qualities exemplified in the church at Thessalonica, it would be helpful to spend a moment with the apostle himself.

1:2 THEN SINGS MY SOUL...

What made Paul tick? His mindset is described, and it is abundantly clear that there are three important facets to his life.

There is praise! It is fairly obvious, even to the most casual observer, that Paul was a man with a song in his heart. Even when he found himself in a prison cell, he quickly turned it into a place where he could celebrate the goodness of God. We read all about that earth-moving incident in Acts 16.

He preached about it; he wrote about it; he practised it. Praise did not change his situation, but it radically transformed his attitude. It gave him a new outlook on life. Praise does not come easily; when we find ourselves in hot water, in trying circumstances, it is not the most natural thing to do. We are the ones who make the choice to do it or not do it. It is an orientation problem that needs to be conquered.

Another dimension is added when we realise that praise is often referred to as a sacrifice. Where we have sacrifice, we always have a price to pay; there is a cost involved. It is not just a casual, happy-clappy touch or a light-hearted, flippant singalong; it is not even someone with an overdose of charisma acting as cheerleader. In fact, praise has nothing to do with ambience or a man's personality; it has everything to do with Jesus and our relationship with him.

Thanks!

So what does Paul do? We read, *we always thank God for all of you*—a felt expression from a profoundly grateful heart, a note of glad appreciation. It is when we consciously say, 'thank you'; in many ways we see it as a debt that we owe. How that must have perked them up.

Paul writes and tells them that he feels the way he does about them—the horizontal component. His delirious praise is directed heavenward—the vertical vector.

They would be uplifted. God would be exalted.

I am sure that boosted their flagging morale and really blessed them. And so he turns to them and says, 'Thanks for the privilege of being with you.' Then he turns to God and says, 'Thanks, Lord, for letting me be there.'

How easy it is to pray for people who give us every reason to be grateful. Generally, they prove to be accepting and affirming, real instead of phoney, supportive and giving rather than subversive and grabby.

They gave Paul a host of reasons for him to be thankful. We should also give people reason to be thankful to the Lord for our presence and input in their life. There was a personal touch to his praise. He strikes a similar rich vein when he writes letters to other churches, especially Romans, Ephesians, and Colossians.

There is a practical element to it as well. Do you recall what he said about Philemon as an occasion for praise? He spoke warmly of his love for all the saints and how he refreshed the heart of the saints.

Looking at it from another standpoint leads us to see this spirit of thankfulness as a partnership. For example, in Philippians it is associated with their fellowship in the gospel; when writing 1 Corinthians, the emphasis is on the provision of God's gifts to them; in his second letter to the same church, he reflects on the fact that God's mercy reached down to him. More often than not it is linked with people, and we see this in his words in 2 Timothy when he remembers with fond affection his younger colleague. The highlight of this praise mingled with thanks is probably found in Galatians where the apostle is meditating on the death of Christ.

Praise-athon

Praise is an essential ingredient in the life of any Christian. I wonder, how often did Paul do it? It was *always*. See that?

Paul was no fool, he was not born yesterday. He was not naïve and his head was not in the clouds. He knew there were problems; he knew there were difficult people to handle; he knew there were tensions that arose from time to time; he knew there were clashes of personality. He knew all that, but in spite of all their hang-ups and shortcomings, he thanks God for each one. That, I believe, is where Paul is grounded to reality.

Pray on, brother

The second great influence in Paul's life is prayer. He is the kind of man whose praise is coupled with prayer. The emphasis here is on their fellowship in prayer. He uses the phrase *in our prayers,* and that implies they met together as a leadership team to remember the fellowship in Thessalonica. It was an early-day version of our prayer triplets concept. The American phenomenon—meet for breakfast, meet for prayer!

How essentially important it is for those in responsible positions in Christian ministry to take time out to pray. Prayer is the slender nerve that moves the muscles of omnipotence. Down on our knees is where burdens are shared, battles are fought, and victories are won. It was standard practice when they met together, par for the course. They did not think about it, they did it!

To many Christians, prayer is about as exciting as changing a flat tyre on a narrow country lane.

To Paul and his ministry colleagues, time spent in prayer was never seen as wasted time. It is astoundingly profitable, paying handsome dividends. It is quite remarkable to realise that a year down the road these folk are still lovingly upheld at the throne of grace; they remain on the apostle's prayer list. He genuinely cared for them, in the most profound way, by praying for them.

A prayer list, a prayer diary, a prayer card—these are all useful tools that enable us to tap the potential of heaven on behalf of one another. If we write a name down, or stick a photo on the fridge, we are less likely to forget to intercede for that person. So Paul thanks God for them and he talks to God about them.

1:3 A PEOPLE PERSON

The third vital factor in Paul's life is people. Now, let's be clear in our own mind, Paul was not on an ego trip, nor was he immersed in himself in his own tiny little world. Far from it! This man deeply cared for others. People mattered to him. He has a big, expansive heart. We could never say that Paul was selfish or self-centred; his attitude is above and beyond reproach.

When his eyes scan the congregation in the urban sprawl of Thessalonica, he sincerely thanks God for them. Not only a few of them, or the ones that were easy to get along with, but every single one of them: the good, the bad, and the indifferent.

This kind of love is not confined to those we like, nor is it restricted to those who like us or those we would like to have liked us. There is nothing selective about it because Paul is not enmeshed with the clique mentality. I think most of us realise that takes some doing!

No church is perfect and the folk in Thessalonica were no different from those anywhere else. They were human. Flesh and blood. Fallible specks of humanness. They had their good points and bad points. In spite of their prosaic ordinariness, they were saved by God's grace and were a real joy to his heart. A treat.

In a spiritual sense, I suppose we could say he fathered them and mothered them. To Paul, each conversion under his ministry was like the birth of a baby. And each new church was like a nursery, full of the joys and challenges of new life.

Because of this nonpareil relationship, Paul saw beyond the externals, he saw Christ in them. And because he prayed for them, he was able to thank God for them. He loved them for the sake of Jesus.

Rhapsody

We see the authentic effusiveness of his commendation as he writes about these folk who mean so much to him. There is bona fide warmth in all that he says about them. He is concerned about them; they weigh heavily on his mind. Like any doting father on the move, his heart ached for his bairns back home; you see, Paul just wanted to be with them so much, but he could not. It just was not possible!

He wanted to make sure they were getting their proper spiritual nourishment; he wanted to protect them from lurking strangers like the Judaisers who were determined to lead them astray; he wanted to soothe and allay their fears; he wanted to guide them through difficult decisions; he wanted to prepare them as best he could for the future, for he could see the storm clouds gathering on the horizon.

All these things are going through his mind, and as if he did not have enough on his plate, they are all there at the same time! So in the course of his opening remarks, he thinks about them for a minute or two longer, he knows there is so much he could say, but he refrains, he holds back, he narrows it down to three tremendous attributes.

These ace qualities underline the humongous blessing this fellowship has enjoyed and experienced. It is no wonder they are an exciting, inspiring group to be with.

Creative faith

This is what Paul means by the phrase, *your work produced by faith*. He is not speaking about the initial act of faith at the moment of their conversion to Jesus Christ—saving faith. The faith outlined here is a faith that is active; a faith that works; a faith that performs; a faith that produces fruit. True faith is not sterile. Faith that does not act is not faith at all.

Faith for them was not a wall plaque or a car window sticker, it was a life-changing encounter with Jesus Christ.

Such was their unflinching confidence in God, their total commitment to Christ, and their out-and-out reliance on the Holy Spirit that things were happening, really happening, in their church.

- Faith to move tall mountains of obstruction and difficulty.
- Faith to venture out into a potentially hostile environment in courageous witness.
- Faith to believe God for miracles.
- Faith to see that a cup of ice cold water given now in his name matters in the great scheme of things.

Holding the umbrella

No doubt about it, their faith was ingeniously creative and they had something to show for it at the end of the day. The story is told of a rural community that was experiencing a severe drought. Farmers watched helplessly as the corn crop shrivelled under the unrelenting sun. The ground cracked and dust devils swirled through the fields. Weeks passed with scarcely a cloud in the sky.

As concern deepened into panic, the little church that served the community declared a day of prayer to ask God for relief from the drought. The appointed day arrived and the community came to the church to pray. Farmers and field hands sat beside bankers and businessmen as the town united in asking God for rain.

One young girl walked into the church clutching an umbrella. 'Why are you carrying an umbrella?' some school friends asked in jest. 'Well, we *are* praying for rain!' responded the girl. She had taken to heart the Scouts motto, be prepared.

She had faith. Simple faith. Childlike faith. Faith that was willing to trust God implicitly. Faith that believed God could do and would do what he was being asked to do.

Redemptive love

The word used by Paul is important, for we need to realise that 'labour' is different from 'work.' He pays fulsome tribute to their *labour prompted by love*. The thought is of hard toil and energy expended. There was a weariness in the ministry which they felt as they broke through the pain barrier and their strength was spent. It is all about cost.

What prompted them to do it? Love! A love that is prepared to sweat, travail, and sacrifice. A love that can only be interpreted in the light of Calvary—a love that will pay anything, give anything, and do anything for the sake of the gospel. A love that counts all but loss for the making known of the message. Love is the driving force, the propelling thrust, the motivating factor.

Why? Because love always finds a way. This is an exquisite quality that sets believers apart as the children of God. This love is not something abstract and insubstantial, but tough and practical. It works wonders. For God's love truly changes everything.

Such love is not a pithy bumper sticker; it is not a misty-eyed feeling; it is not an ichthus Christian fish sign dangling pendulously from the neck; it is not a gilded silver dove decorously impaled upon the lapel. These are mere symbols of our faith. The birthmark of the Christian is love. The most powerful, four-letter word in the English language is LOVE.

'Heat makes all things expand. And the warmth of love will always expand a person's heart.' (Chrysostom)

Aggressive hope

Paul puts it eloquently when he says, *your endurance inspired by hope in our Lord Jesus Christ.*

Let me tell you what it is not before I tell you what it is! It is definitely not the grin-and-bear-it mentality, nor is it the smile-and-shrug-your-shoulders syndrome. It is not the phlegmatic resignation of a Stoic with a grit-your-teeth-and-get-on-with-it attitude.

It has absolutely nothing to do with offhand speculation; it has everything to do with resolute confidence. Triumphant fortitude. It is all about stickability. Dogged determination. It is hangin' in there because you are hangin' on to the Lord! It is like the kettle, up to its neck in hot water but it keeps on singing! It is the bounce-back factor.

When they were under enormous pressure, and they were; when they were living in abject poverty, and they were; when they experienced sore persecution, and they did—they endured. No matter what life threw at them or kicked in their teeth, they were resilient and showed a cheerful spirit.

What inspired them? Why did they not call it quits? Why did they not throw the towel into the ring? What kept them plodding on? Hope! Hope that it would quickly end, no! Hope that it would soon go away, no! Hope in the promised return of Jesus, yes!

They were looking ahead, planning for the future. They were operating with their eyes trained on the horizon. They scanned the skyline and lived their life in the future tense. They felt something was in the offing, but did not know when.

The story is told of the eminent physicist, Michael Faraday, who made no secret of his personal faith in Jesus Christ. While he lay dying, he was chided with the question: 'Where are your speculations now, Michael?' 'Speculations?' he retorted, 'I'm dealing in certainties.' So he was! So are we! They had…

- a faith alive—it was resting on the past as they looked back to a crucified Saviour,
- a love aglow—it was working in the present as they looked up to a crowned Saviour,
- a hope aflame—it was aiming for the future as they looked to a coming Saviour.

'True faith's work is never wasted, real love's labour is never lost, hope's resilience is never disappointed,' writes Philip Greenslade. Real Christianity is not benign. Someone said a church is made up of two kinds of people—the pillars who hold it up and the caterpillars who crawl in and out each week.

Improving your serve

It is interesting, but the way a person works is very revealing. Some people work because of fear of punishment, others work only for financial reward, and still others work out of a grim sense of duty.

Working because of faith makes a humble worker; in other words, we acknowledge that the Lord is the only one who can give the increase to our labours. Love makes an industrious worker since our motivation is our grateful love for the Lord Jesus. We recognise that it is his work, not ours. Hope makes a persevering worker since we know that one day we shall reap a harvest if we faithfully sow the seed and do not lose heart.

Alexander the Great, before setting out on his campaigns, divided his possessions among a few close friends. Someone asked him: *'Are you keeping nothing for yourself?'* *'O yes,'* he replied, *'I have kept my hopes.'*

When we put them all together—faith, hope, and love—they are like three legs of a stool; they need to be kept strong and balanced. You see, Christianity is not a work to be endured for duty's sake; Christianity is a person to be served for love's sake. I think that explains why this little fellowship in Northern Greece was a pastor's delight, a shepherd's dream. An ideal congregation.

An exciting bunch, they certainly are! Surely that is the reason behind Paul's ability to say, 'Thank you, Lord. There's no people in all the world like your people.'

Contagious Christianity

There are so many who embrace evangelicalism whose vocabulary is bulging with all the right words—people who give a big hug and warm handshake; the problem is, their lifestyle is shrivelled for lack of spiritual substance.

In a day when biblical Christianity was vanishing, either from Christians being hunted down and killed, or scared into silence, it is just great to meet unfeigned people who have not succumbed to the oppressive tactics of the old enemy.

Here was a little church with a big reputation, a church whose reputation was intact, a church where their red-hot Christianity was contagious. My prayer is, 'Lord, if it's infectious, I want to catch it. Let some of it rub off on me!'

1:4 PAST, PRESENT, FUTURE

Paul reminds the young believers in Thessalonica of three great facts in the opening chapter of his epistle—he shows them where they have come from, where they now are, and where they are going.

The turning point came as a direct result of the truth expounded in this verse, *For we know, brothers loved by God, that he has chosen you.* In layman's language, Paul says, we are elect! That means we can be saved and know it.

Here is the immovable ground of our assurance; the bedrock of our salvation; the unassailable proof that we belong to Jesus. This means the ebony darkness can be dispelled, the pesky doubts can be dismissed, and the tricky devil can be defeated. A gargantuan fact. An incredible statement; so incredible, it blows the mind.

God's worldwide family

The opening two phrases help us grasp the all-out wonder of our relationship with each other in the global family of God. They also magnify the mystery of God's involvement in our life. There is a word of assurance for Paul says, *for we know.* There are no doubts, no ifs, no maybes, and no buts. These few words ooze with solid certainty.

Then there is a sense of affinity for the apostle identifies them and is happy to call them, *brothers.* This would indicate they were all members of the same worldwide family. He looked upon them as his spiritual brothers and sisters.

Inside track

What does Paul know? What is he aware of? What is he convinced of? Here it is, *that he has chosen you.* This sublime doctrine is the cornerstone of our faith for it ensures that God gets all the glory for his work of grace in our heart.

A great sinner, embracing a great Saviour, always finds a great salvation.

When Paul took one look at the saints in Thessalonica, he saw the quality of their life in Christ and the fruit of the Holy Spirit in their lives, and he sensed in the depths of his own heart that they really are the people of God.

- God has called them.
- God has chosen them.
- God has claimed them.

In other words, they are elect! Simple as that! Well, is it? The moment we mention election, some people are frightened and begin to panic, others are confused, still more are thrilled with the sheer wonder of it all and joyfully declare, 'It's a smash hit!'

Be circumspect

So what do we do when we find ourselves caught between two opposite feelings, between a rock and a hard place? I realise we are walking through a potential spiritual minefield, but we will pick our steps carefully. We cannot pass by on the other side and pretend it is not there; it is! It is in the chapter, it is in Scripture, and we cannot skirt around it.

I believe we must grasp the nettle with both hands and ask the question, what does the Bible teach about election? What does the phrase *he has chosen you* mean? Warren Wiersbe has wisely observed: 'Try to explain it and you may lose your mind, try to explain it away and you may lose your soul.'

We will never plumb its unfathomable depths; it is beyond our comprehension, at least, this side of heaven. Understand it? Never! There again, do you understand how a brown cow can eat green grass and give white milk and yellow butter? We enjoy the products! That should not deter us from studying it, nor should it detract us from seeking to come to terms with it.

Election. I cannot explain it, but I can still enjoy it.

It emphasises the wonderful grace of Jesus and I am thrilled about that. It leaves me spellbound, gasping for breath. I often feel like the Psalmist in moments like these, when I just want to stand in awe and wonder and say, 'The Lord has done this, and it is marvellous in our eyes' (Psalm 118:23).

Rejoice!

* We are chosen *in* Christ.
* We are chosen *by* Christ.
* We are chosen *for* Christ.

There is the mystery of the grace of God, the marvel of the love of God, and the miracle of the salvation of God.

A threefold cord

Before we go on to think about the meaning of election, it may be helpful to realise that the Bible speaks of three kinds of election. One is God's theocratic election of Israel. The key verse in that context is Deuteronomy 7:6, and it is worth noting that this election had no bearing on personal salvation. Paul explains in Romans 9:6-7 that racial descent from Abraham as father of the Hebrew people did not mean spiritual descent from him as father of the faithful.

A second is vocational. For example, the Lord called out the tribe of Levi to be his priests, but that did not come with a *carte blanche* guarantee of salvation. It was not a blank cheque. Jesus called twelve men to be his apostles, but only eleven of them to salvation. God then chose Paul in another way to be his special emissary to the Gentile peoples.

The third is salvational and that is the thought behind verse 4. The question arises, what is the meaning of election? The words 'elect' or 'chosen' together with their variants appear many times in the Bible. Generally, they could be translated, 'to pick out, to select, to choose.'

This is a sovereign act of God whereby he freely chose certain human beings to be saved. Such an idea is applied to the nation of

Israel as suggested in Isaiah 65:9 where we read, 'This is what the Lord says, I will bring forth descendants from Jacob, and from Judah those who will possess my mountains, my chosen people will inherit them, and there will my servants live.'

Another clear link is established in that it is also used in reference to the Lord Jesus Christ in Isaiah 42:1 and 1 Peter 2:6. The evangelical prophet says, 'Here is my servant whom I uphold, my chosen one in whom I delight, I will put my Spirit on him and he will bring justice to the nations.' Peter goes on to affirm, 'See I lay a stone in Zion, a chosen and precious cornerstone, and the one who trusts in him will never be put to shame.'

Similarly in Romans 8:33 and Colossians 3:12 the term is associated with the people of God. Paul enquires, 'Who will bring any charge against those whom God has chosen? It is God who justifies.' Then we read, 'Therefore as God's chosen people, holy and dearly loved, clothe your-selves with compassion, kindness, humility, gentleness, and patience.'

It all comes together like pieces in a jigsaw puzzle—election refers to the nation of Israel, it also includes the Lord Jesus, and it specially applies to the Christian.

God is presently calling out from among the nations of the world a people for himself, a people for his praise, and a people for his name.

Loved with everlasting love

One of the most outstanding features of Paul's vision of the church is its God-centredness; as John Stott says: 'Paul does not think of it as a human institution, but as the divine society.' This is best seen in Paul's amazing turn of phrase in verse 4 where we read that they were *loved by God*. As always, the proof of the pudding is in the eating, and the evidence of the Father's electing love toward them is seen in his choice of them!

In this verse, Paul successfully unites the love of God and the election of God. That is, he chose us because he loves us, and he loves us because he loves us. He does not love us because we are loveable, but only because he is love. And with that mystery we must rest con-tent! In a word, that is what the doctrine of election is all about!

How does he go about it? What method is employed? In Deuter-onomy 7:6-8 we discover that 'the Lord did not set his affection on you and choose you because you were more numerous than other peoples, for you were the fewest of all peoples. But it was because the Lord loved you that he brought you out with a mighty hand and redeemed you.'

It was not a random choice along the lines of 'eeny-meeny-miny-mo.' He did it all in love and grace! God made all the running; he took the initiative; he made the first move.

The Father's love-gift

Take another look and fast forward to the New Testament, of some it is said, 'we are chosen in the Lord; we are chosen to be saved; we are chosen in him before the creation of the world' (Romans 16:13; 2 Thessalonians 2:13; Ephesians 1:14). To whom is Paul referring in these verses? It seems to me that he is speaking about the same ones who are mentioned in the high priestly prayer of Jesus in John 17.

Jesus speaks of them as those whom the Father has given to the Son. It is not that God's sovereign election eliminates man's choice in faith—far from it. Divine sovereignty and human responsibility are integral and inseparable parts of salvation, though exactly how they operate together only the infinite mind of God knows.

Any teaching that diminishes the sovereign, electing love of God by giving more credit to man also diminishes God's glory, and when that happens, a blow is struck at the very purpose of salvation. Charles Haddon Spurgeon (1834-92) was once asked how he reconciled God's election with man's responsibility to make a choice. Apparently, the great London preacher answered like this, 'I never have to reconcile friends.'

We should be satisfied simply to declare with the poet John Chadwick:

I sought the Lord,
And afterwards I knew,
He moved my soul to seek him,
Seeking me.
It was not that I found,
O Saviour true,
No, I was found by thee.

I appreciate the story told by Dr. Harry Ironside (1876-1951), former pastor of the famous Moody Memorial Church, Chicago. A young boy was asked: 'Have you found Jesus?' The little fellow answered: 'Sir, I didn't know he was lost. But I can tell you what I do know, I was lost and he found me!'

God's bright idea

It would be good for us to focus on the moment of election and ask ourselves the key question, when did it all take place? The answer is fairly straightforward for it all took place away back in the mists of eternity. Yes, it was born in the heart of God before time began, before the world was made.

Before the fall of man in the garden of Eden, the Lord had fallen for us in love.

Because in God's plan Christ was crucified before the creation of the world, we were designated for salvation by that same plan at that same time. Peter says as much in 1 Peter 1:20. It was then that our inheritance in the kingdom of God was determined. We compare that with Matthew 25:34 where we read, 'Then the King will say to those on his right, "Come, you who are blessed by my Father; take your inheritance, the kingdom prepared for you since the creation of the world."'

The bottom line, we belonged to God before he invented time, and we will still be his long after time has run its course. Your name and mine as believers was 'written in the book of life belonging to the Lamb that was slain from the creation of the world' (Revelation 13:8).

The more we stop and think about it, the more we realise the whole experience from start to finish is a miracle. That is certainly true when it becomes a reality in our life. This is the magic moment when we come face to face with majesty and say 'yes' to Jesus.

Succinctly put, it is planned in eternity and realised in time.

- So far as God the Father is concerned, I was saved when he chose me in Christ before the world began (2 Timothy 1:9).
- So far as God the Son is concerned, I was saved when he died for me at Calvary (Galatians 2:20).

- So far as God the Holy Spirit is concerned, I was saved on Sunday 11 February 1968 in Bangor, Co. Down (Titus 3:5).

When we draw all the strands together, it is crystal clear that in one way or another the Trinity was intimately involved in our salvation. But, as I hinted earlier, the whole process of election is shrouded in mystery.

The wonder of it all

Over the years, during the course of pastoral ministry, it was my delight and privilege to share in quite a number of wedding services. On the odd occasion and, thankfully, it has not been too often, I have had the misfortune of hearing a stage-whispered comment, 'What did she ever see in him?' I sometimes think, when I stand in glory and see the Lord in all his impeccable beauty that I may be tempted to ask myself the question, 'What did he ever see in me?'

The unsurpassed pleasure of it all causes me to reflect on the words penned by James Grindlay Small (1817-88):

> *I've found a friend, O such a friend,*
> *He loved me ere I knew him,*
> *He drew me with the cords of love,*
> *And thus he bound me to him,*
> *And round my heart still closely twine,*
> *Those ties which nought can sever,*
> *For I am his, and he is mine,*
> *For ever and for ever.*

That is what happened to the Christians in Thessalonica. But it was not a first-century wonder, nor was it a spectacularly unique phenomenon restricted to the halcyon days of the early church. Certainly not, for two thousand years down the road, in your life and mine, if we know Jesus, the same has happened!

I do not know what that does for you, but I know what it does for me, and I just want to pause, take a deep breath, and say, 'Thank you, Lord.'

When your head spins with the mystery of election, let your heart also swell with the reality of grace.

1:5 YOU GOT IT, YOU PASS IT ON

Paul sees the church as a community of ordinary people, which receives and transmits the gospel. I think it was fairly natural for Paul to move on in his mind from God's church to God's gospel because he could not think of either without the other. The plain fact is, it is by the gospel that the church exists, and it is by the church that the gospel spreads. Each depends on the other, each serves the other!

In verses 5-10, the apostle outlines in three clear stages the conspicuous progress of the gospel in Thessalonica:

- stage one: 'our gospel came to you' (verse 5),
- stage two: 'you welcomed the message' (verse 6),
- stage three: 'the Lord's message rang out from you' (verse 8).

To put it simply, Paul says it came to you, you received it, and you passed it on! I have no doubts in my mind that this sequence is God's continuing purpose throughout the world!

We unpack what Paul is saying by looking at what he writes here, *Because our gospel came to you not simply with words, but also with power, with the Holy Spirit and with deep conviction. You know how we lived among you for your sake.*

The first word *because* is a link word. Paul does that a lot! He wants to keep their attention. It joins what has gone immediately before with all that follows after. It automatically connects all that Paul has said in verse 4 with what he is about to say in verse 5. Paul says, 'I know you are numbered in the elect; I know you are loved by God; I know you are among the chosen of the Lord.'

How did Paul know? How could he be so sure in his own mind? Here is the only reasonable explanation—when the gospel was preached and the good news of Jesus proclaimed, something inconceivable happened. And it only happened because the 'gospel is the power of God for the salvation of everyone who believes' (Romans 1:16).

'The preaching of Christ is the whip that flogs the devil; it is a thunderbolt, the sound of which makes all hell shake.' (C. H. Spurgeon)

Talking the talk

When the truth of God was declared to them, it came *not simply with words, but also with power*. The gospel did not come to them with words only, but it did come to them with words! Words matter; they can be scalpels or sledgehammers depending on who wields them! Words are important. They are the essential building blocks of sentences by which we are able to effectively communicate with one another. And the gospel, as we all know, has a specific content. That is why it must be articulated and verbalised.

The implication is, in all our evangelism, whether upfront or behind the scenes, we need to take the trouble with our choice of words. I think most of us probably realise that words on their own are seldom enough, they may be disregarded or misunderstood; because of that they need, somehow, to be enforced. That is why words spoken in human weakness need to be confirmed with divine power. In all our ministry, we need God to come and do what he does best.

This potency is not dependent upon our natural ability or know-how; it has nothing to do with man's eloquence. A man may have the gift of the gab, he may have kissed (or swallowed) Ireland's famous Blarney Stone, but that is not enough. It is the work of God's Spirit that gives authority and authenticity to that which is promulgated.

Why did the Psalmist prefer to be a doorkeeper in the house of the Lord? So he could stay outside while the sermon was preached. Some preachers do not need more fire in their sermons; they need to put more sermons in the fire!

True power—divine unction in our gumption—will bring glory to God, rather than to a particular individual. This brand of power is not worked up, it is prayed down. It is not always visible, but it is promised.

This serves to highlight the powerful nature of Scripture. It is something explosive. What Semtex plastic explosive is to a terrorist, the word of God is to the sinner. Dynamite! No matter when or where the gospel is broadcast, God is actively working.

Lights on

The message also comes *with the Holy Spirit*. The bottom line, only the Spirit of God can illumine a darkened mind and quicken an enslaved will. We desperately need God to work and, when he does, he uses the medium of his Holy Spirit. Therein lies the secret to effective ministry and productive preaching.

We must never divorce what God has married, namely his word and his Spirit. The word of God is the Spirit's sword.

'The Spirit without the word is weaponless, the word without the Spirit is powerless.' (John Stott)

Paul says it came to them *with deep conviction*. It was decisive. Paul's evangelistic preaching was not only powerful in its effect, but it was confident in its presentation. He was sure of its message, its truth, and its relevance. He believed it! In consequence, he was bold in trumpeting it. The message was unmistakably clear and the unequivocal response was excellent.

There was impassioned conviction in the heart and voice of the preacher, but there was real old-time conviction in the heart and mind of those who listened. When this man preached, he looked for signs following; he expected results and he was not disappointed! Their hearts were opened; their deaf ears were unstopped; the scales fell off their eyes.

These pagans were transformed; they became new men; they came from the realm of inky-black darkness into a totally new world of light; they emerged from the tomb of death to walk in newness of life. In a split-second, they became a redeemed community. They proved the gospel actually works.

The figures speak for themselves

Paul's parting shot in verse 5 makes it clear that he is not making claims that could not be substantiated; his track record speaks for itself. So do the statistics! This is terrific, for that is how Paul knew they were a chosen people! And, wonder of wonders, the same is true of us.

So far as I am concerned, I have not the faintest idea who the company of the elect are, that is why I continue to preach the gospel of redeeming love at every possible opportunity. And when in the goodness of God some dear people respond positively to the message and turn to Christ in repentance and faith, only then am I able to say, 'Hey, welcome to the family, you're among the elect!'

The well known American evangelist, D. L. Moody, put it like this: 'The whosoever-wills are the elect and the whosoever-wont's are the non-elect.'

Glory to God

The impact of God's word upon people's lives and the ripening of the eternal purpose of God in our coming to faith and trust in him is brought out beautifully in *The Message*: 'It is clear to us, friends, that God not only loves you very much but also has put his hand on you for something special. When the message we preached came to you, it was not just words. Something happened in you. The Holy Spirit put steel in your convictions.' Fantastic!

- Salvation begins in the heart of God.
- Salvation involves the love of God.
- Salvation necessitates faith.
- Salvation coalesces the Trinity.
- Salvation transforms the life.

Those whom God chooses, God changes! They are not what they used to be, they are not yet what they are going to be, but thank God, they are what they are by God's amazing grace. The Welsh pastor, William Vernon Higham (1926-), in his great hymn sums it up better than I ever could:

Great is the gospel of our glorious God,
Where mercy met the anger of God's rod;
A penalty was paid and pardon bought,
And sinners lost at last to him were brought.

Similarly, the Methodist revivalist Charles Wesley (1707-88), revelled in this deliriously happy experience:

> *Long my imprisoned spirit lay*
> *Fast bound in sin and nature's night;*
> *Thine eye diffused a quick'ning ray –*
> *I woke, the dungeon flamed with light;*
> *My chains fell off, my heart was free.*
> *I rose, went forth, and followed thee.*

To me that is what the biblical doctrine of election is all about. Every time I stop and think about it, I am bowled over with the thoroughgoing wonder of it all. I often cry out with the apostle Paul, 'O, the depth of the riches of the wisdom and knowledge of God. How unsearchable are his judgments and his paths beyond tracing out' (Romans 11:33).

C. H. Spurgeon said on one unforgettable occasion in London's Metropolitan Tabernacle pulpit: 'If God hadn't chosen me before the creation of the world, he wouldn't choose me now!'

When George MacDonald, the great Scottish preacher, told one of his children about the glories of God's grace, the child interrupted him and said: *'Dad, it all seems too good to be true.'* A smile spread across MacDonald's whiskered face as he answered back: *'Nay, my dear, it's just so good, it must be true!'*

1:6 EXCITED ABOUT EVANGELISM

The fervid zeal and enthusiasm of these relatively young Christians hits us between the eyes. We cannot help but be impressed by the unassailable fact that they are evangelistic. These first-century believers passionately believed in outreach and were committed to sharing the gospel message with others near and far.

Outreach is 'reaching out.' WARNING: the church that does not reach out will pass away!

The members of the church in Thessalonica were overjoyed at the thought of their election; they were thrilled to bits with what God had done in their lives. By the same token, they displayed a give-all-you-can, hold-nothing-back attitude in their commitment to evangelism. They had a heartthrob for people who did not know Jesus as Lord and Saviour.

They were chosen in Christ and this is what God used to give a razor-sharp cutting edge to their zealous endeavours to win men to Jesus. Theirs was a no holds barred, pull out all the stops, let's get on with it mindset. Basically, they had a sense of responsibility to others combined with a sense of accountability to God.

The God who did so much for them, who captivated their affection, who was their everything and their all, yes, they were debtors to him; but they were out there on the frontline paying their debt to all those still outside the family of God.

We are members of the global family of God. We revel in that. We delight that we are found in such a happy, privileged position. They are not! We owe it to them to tell them of one who is mighty and strong to save. These folk were just as excited about election as they were about evangelism.

Men followers

The apostle pulls back the curtain another time and shows us three more virtues of this thriving congregation of God's people. Paul talks about their experience. It can truly be said of them that they were men followers. We read, *they became followers of us and of the Lord.*

This indicates the profound change in their life. They began to follow the example as well as the teaching of the apostles. They walked in the footsteps of Paul and in so doing walked in harmony with Christ.

Paul and his ministry colleagues lived out the gospel before them. They came with very few answers and a lot of vulnerability.

They clothed the gospel with human skin—incarnational Christianity—not, simply, verbal hot air.

That is what made the huge difference. They were glasshouse Christians—the people could see right through them, they had nothing to hide. There were no skeletons hanging in their closet. They had no hidden agenda. In computer-speak, what you see is what you get!

They emulated Paul and his associates. They mimicked them and looked upon them as role models. Amazing. It means Paul must have had an unblemished testimony—a transparency in his character. He walked a straight line on the narrow path.

I do not know how you feel when you hear something like that. I know the impact it has on me—I find it immensely challenging. Our lives are real stories that are constantly read by people milling around us.

I sometimes ask myself the question, if others were following me, where would I lead them? Am I a stepping stone, or a stumbling block? We are signposts on the highway of life, are we pointing men and women in the direction of Jesus? We are the Bible the world is reading. I cannot help but wonder, what translation they pick up when they read the book of my life?

Pointers to success

For the apostle Paul, the secret lay in his closeness to Christ. There was an intimacy to his dynamic relationship with the Lord. It was fairly obvious that he was head-over-heels in love with Jesus. His communion with Christ is superb. The channels of communication were wide open and there was no earth-born cloud between him and his God. His consecration to Christ is admirable. This man was totally sold-out to Jesus Christ. He surrendered everything to the lordship of Christ, and he had no quibbles or qualms about so doing.

There was no hint of regret, no reservation. He held nothing back because Jesus was number one on his personal agenda. Paul's priorities were sorted out on a bended knee before the cross.

It is apparent, when they looked at Paul, they saw Jesus. Paul was a leader and they gladly followed. Surely the avowed aim of any Christian leader is to win souls, but equally important, according to Hebrews 13:17, is to watch over their souls. That is the role of a pastor or elder in every local church.

Stand up, stand up for Jesus

It was not a cushy wee number being a Christian in their day. Nevertheless, they nailed their colours to the mast. They willingly counted the cost and gladly paid the price. Even though it cost them nothing to become a Christian, it would cost them everything to be a Christian. There was nothing cushioned or comfortable about their Christianity. They were not laidback in any way. In fact, the intensity of their suffering is such that Paul describes it as *severe*.

There were whopping great pressures. The psychological stress was, at times, unbearable. The constant emotional strain meant they were on the verge of cracking up. Their nerves were frayed. They felt zapped. The going was incredibly tough—an endurance test, a real struggle from dawn to dusk. It was not all plain sailing.

Actually, if the truth be told, their back was to the wall as they stood at wit's end corner. When lesser men would have given up and given in, and feebler men would have tossed the towel into the ring and called it quits, they… *in spite of severe suffering… welcomed the message*.

They received the word with gladness—a people who really loved the word of God. They rejoiced in its proclamation. Quite frankly, they could not get enough of it. What a congregation! A dream for every preacher! They were hungry for the word; they were drinking in every word that was spoken; they were sitting on the edge of their seat. And they kept coming back for more.

How were they able to do it? Well, says Paul, *with the joy given by the Holy Spirit*. Their circumstances were not conducive to such a positive response. Humanly speaking, the odds were stacked against them. The dominoes were falling. But they had joy—real joy, wonderful joy—a joy deep down in their heart.

Happiness depends on what happens to us, but come what may, there is a joy in knowing Jesus. An inward joy, an exuberance of spirit, an overflowing heart—it is the cup of our life full and running over.

'Joy is the standard that flies on the battlements of the heart when the King is in residence.' (R. Leonard Small)

Sure, the trials were there, they did not go away. The heat was on, and it was going to get hotter. But, as only the Lord can, he makes it up to them in another way. Their lives are richer. They are buoyant, even though all is sinking around them. God never short-changes his people.

These first-century believers discovered, in the words of Nehemiah 8:10, that 'the joy of the Lord [was their] strength.' I believe their experience contained the transforming power of the Holy Spirit and the living vitality of the risen Christ. That explains why they were able to hold out for as long as they did and hold on in the manner they did!

1:7 AN ECCLESIASTICAL PROTOTYPE

Experience is one thing, what about their example? They became a model church. Paul expressed it superbly when he wrote, *And so you became a model to all the believers in Macedonia and Achaia.*

This is quite something! No other church in the New Testament is referred to in this way, so let's give credit where it is due. It is an honour to be hailed as a pattern worth adopting. They got it right. First time. They were not perfect, but they were ideal. They made their mark. They left a lasting impression. They were an excellent advertisement of biblical Christianity. Theirs is an example to be embraced with open hands and open hearts.

They were not in a rut, but they had a mould.

When we read between the lines it appears that throughout the region and further afield people were sitting up and taking notice. They were looking over their shoulder and saying, 'Hey, do you see what the folk are doing up there in Thessalonica, why don't we adapt it, why don't we customise it. Let's have a go ourselves.' Or perhaps they may have said, 'If it works over there, we've nothing to lose, let's give it a try and see if it'll work down here.'

It is the nothing ventured, nothing gained syndrome. The folk in Thessalonica made all the running, and others jumped aboard the gravy train. They were pacesetters for their day and generation. They were ordinary Christians who had the vision to push the limits of faith because they themselves lived on the raw edge of faith.

This would indicate that in a constantly changing situation there was a willingness to adapt. There was a degree of flexibility in the fellowship as they geared to the times, but remained anchored to the word.

The ripple effect

From away up north in the province of Macedonia, down to the south in the province of Achaia, there was a real sense that God was doing some new thing among them. Believe it or not, but these believers were a catalyst in the wider Christian community. All of Greece was influenced in one way or another, to a greater or lesser degree, by the church that gathered at Thessalonica.

There was something exceptionally special about them. They were a beacon of light, for theirs was a radiant testimony and a shining witness as they impacted their peers. Shimmering saints. Luminous believers.

The thinking that governed their strategy could be summed up in two familiar words, *shake* and *shine*. The same philosophy is expressed in Matthew 5:13-16 where Jesus challenges us to bring out the 'God-flavours' of this earth and the 'God-colours' in this world.

It is marvellous to see the beneficial effect of the gospel on all those who receive it. Four new relationships are implied:
• the militant opposition of the world,
• the indescribable joy of the Holy Spirit,
• the imitation of the Lord and his servants, and
• being an exemplary model to the rest of the church.

John Stott writes: 'If the preachers were marked by truth, conviction, and power, the converts were marked by joy, courage, and obedience.' Let nobody say that the gospel is devoid of positive effects!

1:8 SHARING YOUR FAITH

What did they do? They had a message to share, a story to tell. Let me tell you what they did not do—they did not do what most of us probably would have done—form a committee and organise a special big-money, star-studded event with some big-name preacher.

Instead, they rallied the troops and got on with it themselves! We read, *the Lord's message rang out from you*. They were partisan to evangelism. The *you* is personal—it is as individual as it can be, and at the same time, it is corporate, for none are left out. There is no exclusion clause. There was no way any of them could opt out if they did not feel like it or feel up to it.

They were reaching their friends, neighbours, and colleagues with the greatest story ever told. The old adage remains relevant to this day, across the street, across the world. Their faith was believable and they knew how to give it away.

They all had something to say. O yes, they could blether about the weather, the rate of inflation, and the escalating price of all kinds of consumer goods—they could rattle on about everything under the sun—but they also had plenty to say when it came to talking about the Lord Jesus. Every member of the body of Christ was functioning efficiently and effectively. To a man they were mobilised in the army of the Lord.

Churches grow when Christians evangelise.

Sometimes we act as if we do not really believe that! It is estimated that 75-80% of new converts are brought to faith in Christ by the favourable influence of someone they already know. It is about building bridges, rather than constructing high-rise barricades. It is about making friends with people so that we can introduce them to the best Friend of all. It is making sure that our actions match our words, for what we do speaks louder than what we say.

Take a moment, think outside the box of the possibilities and potential in your church if something similar were to take place. The won't-go-away fact is, God loved Thessalonica and so did they!

Transmitting the truth

- It involves a measure of preparation—we have to learn how to do it, and we cannot beat on-the-job training.
- It involves a degree of partnership—we are in it together. It is not individuals blowing their own trumpet.
- It involves a hint of progress—the idea is to go forward and not stand still or mark time.
- It involves a note of purity—when the trumpet sounds, clarity is of the essence.

Let's be realistic, we may choose to make the presentation more upmarket by bringing the style that we adopt into the 21st century. There is wisdom in going down that road; there is nothing wrong with adopting that approach. It makes a lot of sense, for we must be relevant!

Paul said elsewhere that it is by all means that we save some. Having said that, the gospel message is just the same now as it was then. The story of Calvary is timeless, changeless, and eternal. They were sharing *the word of the Lord.*

They could not keep it to themselves. They caught a vision of a world without Jesus—a vision that first captured their imagination then conquered their heart.

No uncertain sound

The thought inherent in the phrase *rang out* is the noise which comes from a resounding gong or a roaring sea. It can also be likened to the sound of a loud trumpet or the noise generated from a great thunder. This is the only time this word appears in the Greek New Testament.

The implication is, at all events, whether Paul is thinking of thunder or trumpets, the gospel proclaimed by the believers in Thessalonica made an incredibly loud noise, which seemed to reverberate through the hills and valleys of Greece.

Actually, they did such a splendid job that no matter where Paul went he was sure to hear from someone, 'Some Thessalonians already gave us that message; they have told us about your Jesus.'

There is a hugely important lesson for us to grasp. We are a media-conscious, media-savvy generation. We know the power of the mass media on the public mind—talk to any advertising agency—so we seek to use it to its fullest potential. Nothing wrong with that!

By the same token, there is another way, and it is a route implicit in Paul's wise comments in this verse. The chances are this way is even more effective than blanket coverage of the message on a global scale. This way requires no complicated electronic gadgetry, it is unbelievably simple. It is neither organised nor computerised. It is spontaneous. It is not hugely expensive; in fact, it costs precisely nothing. We might call it, holy conversation.

God's gossipers

It is the excited transmission from person to person of the impact that the good news of Jesus is making on people. It is the kind of thing that happens when Mrs. Jones meets Mr. Brown and they strike up an animated conversation at the bus stop or supermarket checkout, or when Sally and Dave get together for a confab and cappuccino.

It sounds like this, 'Have you heard what's happened to so-and-so? Did you know that such-and-such a person has come to believe in God and has been completely transformed? I tell you, something extraordinary is going on in Thessalonica. It's all-change! People are different. Their attitude is different, they're into faith, love, and hope in a big way.'

The result of such gratuitous publicity was enough to blow the mind. Comprehensive. Beyond their wildest dreams. As J. B. Phillips translates: 'We do not need to tell other people about it, other people tell us...' Not only was the media redundant, the missionaries felt redundant too! The bottom line—the message was spreading like wildfire without them!

Up-and-at-em

It was an all-hands-on-deck kind of evangelism! How quickly the gospel would spread today if each Christian would simply do what these folk did two millennia ago. When it comes to witnessing, sometimes we are like goldfish, we open and close our mouth and nothing comes out! So, says Paul, watch this space; watch what is happening, for near and far they shared the word of the Lord.

Like a mighty oak, the church of Christ at Thessalonica stood strong against the harsh winds of chilling persecution and cold apathy. She spread her branches of faith throughout the then-known world. They were getting the word around. They were top-class witnesses telling others they knew Jesus saves because he had done it for them. It is the I-was-there-when-it-happened-so-I-ought-to-know mindset. They rehearsed their own story and nobody could refute or deny it. These folk were highly effective in their outreach because they themselves were infected. Each one, reach one.

What about the message they passed on? It was:

- a pure gospel—Christ and nothing else,
- a full gospel—Christ and nothing less,
- a plain gospel—Christ and nothing more.

It was sensationally good news in a mad, bad, sad world. It was the gospel as it really is. It rang out, sure; but first they started where they were—they commenced at home in their own back yard. Only then did they venture further afield. Sounds like the Acts 1:8 principle put into practice—the ripple in the pond syndrome.

Talk of the town

Their ministry of propagation transcended their own city, region, and nation. Its tentacles reached out far beyond their geographical boundaries to, ultimately, have an international scope. It has been well said that 'in just about one year, a new church with first-generation believers was experiencing a ministry whose proportions matched those of Christ's great commission.'

I have no doubts in my mind that God intends every local church to be like the church in Thessalonica. As John Stott says, the risen Lord wants us 'to be like a sounding board, bouncing off the vibrations of the gospel, or like a telecommunications satellite which first receives and then transmits the message.'

Across the land, all over the nation, people were passing comments about the wee church at Thessalonica, chatting about their faith in God. That was the focal point of many an enlightened conversation from up north to down south. They had put Jesus on the front page of all the newspapers in the region.

Why? Because they were fired-up in Thessalonica. They heard the word of God and they could not wait until they passed it on to others. They were not sitting up in the bleachers, they were down on the field of play, not sitting on the bench but in the starting line-up. They were boundless in their energy; their heart was burning with the life-changing message of Jesus Christ. Saints with loads of vim and a good dose of sanctified panache!

Such hostile persecution as they endured could so easily have smothered the flame of Christ. Instead it was like pouring gasoline on a burning match. Their suffering fuelled a fire that exploded into even greater evangelism. They were evangelical and evangelistic. Their united testimony was an expression of vibrant, authentic Christianity in action.

'Faith is like calories. We cannot see them, but we can always see the results.' (Anonymous)

The onus is on us

If we were willing to adopt a similar attitude to theirs, before long our church would be renowned as a hotbed of evangelism. We would be the talk of the town for all the right reasons, when we reach out and sound out, and with the Lord on our side, get up and go out.

Never forget that God has placed us where he has placed no one else! As Elsie Yale's song says, 'There's a work for Jesus, none but you can do!' As long as one person does not know Jesus, our work is not finished. With a vision like that we cannot afford to fold our arms and permit the so-called professionals do the evangelism. We do not have the luxury of resting on the laurels of past success. It is a case of every church, every member, every hand reaching the lost. There is no other way to reach the world for Jesus.

God's heart beats with a passion to save the lost.

From that first dreadfully dark day when sin separated him from his creation, a loving and gracious God has been reaching out to a lost mankind. Faithfully. Persistently. Like a distraught father searching for a wayward child, he has been calling out to the world ever since.

He does not speak through a temple in Jerusalem or a nation *in situ* today. He speaks through a redeemed people—us. We are the mega-phone through which he lovingly pleads with the world to be saved. In light of all we have seen of the early church, let's remember, the same

God who fanned the flame in the first century can ignite a blaze in our heart in the twenty-first century. Are we willing to let him?

1:9 BONDSLAVE

Paul pulls no punches when he writes, *They tell how you turned to God from idols to serve the living and true God.* In one sense this is a paradox for they were set free in order to find perfect liberty in serving Jesus. Their goal in life is God. Born of God, blessed by God, now they show how enriching it is to be bound to God.

The hymnwriter, Frederick Brook, expressed it well:

> *My goal is God himself,*
> *Not joy, nor peace,*
> *Nor even blessing,*
> *But himself, my God:*
> *'Tis his to lead me there,*
> *Not mine, but his,*
> *'At any cost, dear Lord, by any road.'*

For them, the price was high—the suffering, intense and severe; the cost, king-sized; the pressure was really piling on, thick and fast. The bumpy road down which they travelled had many twists and turns and a plethora of obstacles strewn across it. Yet their number one goal in life is unchanged, God.

Why is that their upbeat attitude to life? When bad things are happening to good people, why are they still on track? Why have they not lost their keenness to serve Jesus?

The answer is found in a delightful story told by Jesus where the punchline is, 'The man who is forgiven much is the man who loves much.' The more we stop and think about it and the more we look at the Christians in Thessalonica, the more we realise this was certainly true of them.

47

Emancipation

Conversion is not worth the paper it is written on if it is not a life-changing experience—a transformation, an internal revolution. It is something so radical that it causes men to march to the beat of a different drum. An about-turn, a change of direction. A personal encounter with the living God, and when man meets God on a one-to-one basis, he can never be the same again.

Their conversion bears dramatic testimony to the miraculous touch of God upon their life. Mind-blowing. Enough to take the breath away. Someone has said it is 'an experience which happens in a moment that lasts for a lifetime.' This was unquestionably true of the people who made up the church in Thessalonica.

We read that *they turned to God*. That is what theologians refer to as repentance, regeneration. We go on to read in the next phrase that *they turned to God from idols*. That is separation.

Initially they made a choice, followed by a change—a change of heart, a change of mind, and a change of will. It was a change of life coupled with a change of lifestyle.

There was a plus factor in that they turned their hearts toward the Lord. There was a minus factor in the equation when they turned their backs on idols. By and large, these folk were converts from paganism. The idols in question will have been images of a tangible and obvious kind—manmade statues intended to represent the deities who were supposed to reside on Mount Olympus. So when these heathens turned in childlike faith to the Lord, they repudiated their former allegiance to such fatuous vanities.

Burning bridges

These folk did not turn to God because they were disillusioned with life, nor because they felt they had suffered enough, nor because they were fed up with all that life was throwing their way, nor because they were at the end of their tether and living their life on the flip side. Certainly not!

It was the unimpeachable character of the one true God that won them over. It is always that way. Before him everything else pales into insignificance. Into nothingness. In limbo. He is unrivalled. Peerless.

In his 24-carat light all else fades into oblivion.

Salvation does not begin when we give up something, it begins when we receive someone. And that is precisely what they did!

- They turned to the *living* God—he is not dead, he is alive!
- They turned to the *true* God—he is not deceitful, he is real!

The Psalmist reminds us in Psalm 115:5-7 that idols have eyes, but they cannot see; they have ears, but they cannot hear; they have feet, but they cannot walk; they have hands, but they cannot touch; they have bodies, but they cannot feel.

It would be difficult to exaggerate the impact the gospel had on these folk. The contrast is unreal: idols are dead, God is living; idols are false, God is true; idols are many, God is one; idols are visible and tangible, God is invisible and intangible, beyond the reach of sight and touch. In the wider sense, an icon—a sacred cow—could easily be defined as a God-substitute. An injection of God-replacement therapy.

The fallen imagination is so fertile that man down the centuries has invented tens of thousands of fetishes. The number of things that a sophisticated person may put in God's place is legion. Whatever we spend most of our time thinking about becomes our god! Some of us make an idol of a career, others make an idol of their home. The fast car, the latest technology, the jet set lifestyle, or for that matter, any other designer label, must-have accessory—all these can easily be promoted in our mind to the status of deity, a god we lovingly and adoringly worship. In that sense every convert to the faith of Jesus turns away from idols.

A. W. Tozer said that the essence of idolatry is thinking thoughts of God that are unworthy of him. If we are honest, at one time or other, the overwhelming majority of us have been guilty of making idols which dominate our devotion, idols which govern our duties, idols which influence our decisions, idols which dictate the things we like and dislike when, all of the time, in our life, in our ministry, in our church, in everything, it should be God plus nothing!

That was a lesson they learned well in Thessalonica. This may be an opportune moment for us to pray along with William Cowper (1731-1800):

The dearest idol I have known,
Whate'er that idol be,
Help me to tear it from thy throne,
And worship only thee.

Things are different now

Look what happened to them! See the stupendous difference. They were dead in sin, now they are alive in God. They were living in pitch-black darkness, now they are walking in translucent light. A brand new creation. A spiritual metamorphosis. For them and for us, it is new life in Christ.

How true it is that no testimony is quite so compelling as that of a changed life. People can argue theology and dispute translations of the Bible until they are blue in the face, but they are rendered speechless when confronted with the reality of a transformed life. It is 'the unarguable apologetic.'

'It's hard to be a Christian, but it's too dull to be anything else.' (Brennan Manning)

Their testimony is summed up in the words of Rufus Henry McDaniel's (1850-1940) song:

What a wonderful change in my life has been wrought
Since Jesus came into my heart!
I have light in my soul for which long I had sought,
Since Jesus came into my heart!

The emphasis here is on a God who is *living and true* and, when we compare this with a host of other comments dotted throughout the New Testament, we can say that Christians are children of the living God; their body becomes the temple of the living God; they are indwelt by the Spirit of the living God; they become an integral part of the church of the living God; and for it he is preparing even now the city of the living God. Wow!

We joyfully sing with Rob Hayward, 'I'm accepted, I'm forgiven, I am fathered by the true and living God.' Or again, we gladly affirm with Dave Bilbrough, 'I am a new creation, no more in condemnation, here in the grace of God I stand.'

Saved to serve

Saved, they definitely were. But why? Well, their motto is summed up in the well-worn cliché, saved to serve! That was their primary occupation, their labour of love. They were captivated by Christ. Enraptured with Jesus.

The thought behind the word *serve* introduces the picture of a bondslave—one so devoted and dedicated to his master that he wants to be his servant all his days. He loves the Lord as his Master. It is in slavery to Christ that he finds true liberty and freedom. A paradox, but gloriously true.

George Matheson (1842-1906) echoes a similar sentiment when he writes, 'Make me a captive, Lord, and then I shall be free.' The bondslave declares by his actions: I have no rights, it is all down to the plan of my master; I have no will, except it is one with his.

That goes against the modern trend. It is not in vogue. It takes an awful lot of assiduousness to go down that road. Too often we are like the young man who poured out his heart's devotion in a letter to the girl of his dreams. He wrote: 'Darling, I love you so much that I would climb the highest mountain, swim the widest stream, cross the burning desert, die at the stake for you. By the way, I'll see you on Saturday, if it doesn't rain.'

Commitment! Regrettably, one word rarely found in Christianspeak in the third millennium. Ask any pastor. It embraces a firm dedication to each other in the family of God, a lifelong devotion to the Lord Jesus and his great service, and a total loyalty and diligence to the local church and her various ministries.

Commitment says 'no' to me and 'yes' to Jesus!

1:10 A GROWING SENSE OF EXPECTANCY

Here is the climax of our personal faith in the living and true God. This is, unquestionably, hope with a capital H. It is the moment for which we have all been chosen, the ultimate experience for all the redeemed of the Lord—future grace.

The question needs to be asked, what on earth are they doing? It is worth noting from verses 9 and 10 that serving and waiting go hand-in-hand in the experience of converted people. Indeed, this is at first sight a little surprising since serving is active, while waiting is passive. In Christian terms, serving is getting busy for Christ on earth, while waiting is looking for our Lord to come from heaven. And yet these two are not strange bedfellows. They are buddies!

Each beautifully balances the other. On one hand, however hard we work and serve, there are limits to what we can accomplish and achieve. We can only improve society, we cannot perfect it. We shall never build Utopia on this earth. For that, we have to wait for Christ to come. Only then will he secure the final triumph of God's reign of justice and peace.

On the other hand, although we must look expectantly for the advent of Christ, we have no liberty to wait in idleness, with arms folded and eyes closed, indifferent to the needs of the world around us. Instead, we must work even while we wait, for we are called *to serve the living and true God.*

John Stott summarises this concept well when he writes: 'Working and waiting belong together. In combination they will deliver us both from the presumption which thinks we can do everything and from the pessimism which thinks we can do nothing.' The Thessalonian believers did not serve the Lord without an imminent hope, nor did they wait inactively without an urgent mission to do the Lord's work.

Worth waiting for

It is most interesting to note that Paul says, they are *wait[ing] for his Son from heaven.* The Greek word translated *wait* is used only here in the entire New Testament; in that exclusive sense, it has the thought of anticipation or expectation associated with it. A similar idea is found in Paul's insightful comments in Philippians 3:20.

It rings with the idea of the prophetic hope that things on earth will not always continue the way they are currently; that is another angle on the phrase *patience of hope*, which Paul used at the top of the chapter in verse 3.

This is what makes the Christian life really worth living, for we have something to live for today, and we have so much to look forward to in all our tomorrows. In that sense, we have a distinct edge over the average man on the street.

When tomorrow comes, and it will, we expect it to be a bright one and a better one. We know the best is yet to be. We are convinced that one day, sooner rather than later, we shall see the Lord in all his flawless beauty. One glorious morning the clouds will be swept aside, the shadows will have flown, and we shall rise to be with Jesus. What an exhilarating, mouth-watering prospect!

We live every day knowing that Christ could be back before another day dawns. Today, grace; then, glory. Today, we see a poor reflection as in a mirror; then, face to face. Paul writes in 1 Corinthians 13:12 in *The Message*: 'We don't yet see things clearly. We're squinting in a fog, peering through a mist. But it won't be long before the weather clears and the sun shines bright! We'll see it all then, see it all as clearly as God sees us, knowing him directly just as he knows us!'

Looking out, looking up

These first-century believers were not hanging around on every street corner idling the hours away, nor were they sitting back on a leather chair twiddling their thumbs, nor were they relaxing on a deck chair waiting for it all to happen. 'They were not just part of a religion locked out of time and space, drifting aimlessly across the landscape of humanity,' writes David Jeremiah. Far from it!

Their future orientation to life is what energised their present service. They were zealously working flat-out for the Lord. Like John Wesley they wanted to be 'up and doing for Jesus.' They really believed in their heart that the Lord's return could happen at any moment. Impending. Imminent. Yes, for them, it was just as close as that. For us, two thousand years further down the road, how much nearer it is. The reality is, like the village clock that kept on chiming, it has never been so late before!

They looked forward with a real sense of expectancy to the advent of Jesus Christ. They were watching for the appearing of the Lord from heaven. They were passionately longing for him to break through the clouds. They avidly read the signs of the times and the cry went up from fast-beating hearts, 'How long, O Lord, how long?'

The fact is, Jesus Christ is coming. Coming soon! Coming suddenly! We do not know when, but we do know it will happen. Guaranteed. John Ross Macduff (1818-95) voiced those sentiments when he wrote:

> *With that blessed hope before us,*
> *Let our joyful songs be sung;*
> *Let the mighty advent chorus*
> *Onward roll from tongue to tongue.*
> *Christ is coming!*
> *Come, Lord Jesus, quickly come!*

Up, up, and away

When Christ returns he will, as Paul says, *rescue us from the coming wrath*. His is a rescue mission that will not be botched. No matter which way we look at it, it will be eminently successful. Deliverance is the order of the day.

The *coming wrath* could refer to a couple of significant events. Number one, it could speak of the frightening eternal judgment of God. Number two, it could refer initially to the period of seven years tribulation upon planet Earth. This is what Joel called 'the great and terrible day of the Lord.' Jeremiah described it as the 'day of Jacob's trouble.' Jesus spoke of it in his highly acclaimed Olivet discourse of Matthew 24 as 'the great Tribulation' (cf. Revelation 6-16).

It is cosmic. Global. All hell is let loose. It is the devil and his angels on the rampage in a reign of terror. It is one calamity hard on the heels of another, a classic case of going from bad to worse. A vortex of evil. A downward spiral of sin.

Yes, Christ will come and snatch us away. The one who in a moment of time plucked us as brands from the burning will, at the end of the day, return for us to take us safely home to glory. That implies the true church of God will not enter or go through the period of Tribulation. I believe this is alluded to elsewhere in 1 Thessalonians where Paul says in 5:9 that *we are not appointed to suffer wrath but to receive salvation through our Lord Jesus Christ.*

All's well that ends well

So far as the people of God are concerned, Christianity is the religion not of the dead-end street, but of the happy ending. These early believers were working, watching, and waiting. The word used by Paul is in the present tense which means they were living today in the light of tomorrow. Eternity was etched on their heart and the thought of it occupied their every waking moment. They lived for it and were prepared to die for it.

These folk were numbered among those, of whom John speaks, who 'love his appearing.' They were sitting on the edge of their seat, standing on the tiptoe of expectancy. They were waiting up for him, for he could be back at any moment. They were watching out for him, peeking behind the curtains.

Like them, our future is as bright as the promises of God.

What a delightful group—an evangelical fellowship where people believed in the Second Coming of the Lord Jesus. Believe it or not, they were excited about eschatology (doctrine of last things), for all the right reasons. Samuel Trevor Francis (1834-1925) captured the mood and mystique of that moment when he wrote:

I am waiting for the coming
Of the Lord who died for me;
O his words have thrilled my spirit,
'I will come again for thee.'
I can almost hear his footfall
On the threshold of the door,
And my heart, my heart is longing
To be with him evermore.

Perhaps today

A tourist was exploring the sites of Lake Como in northern Italy and came to a beautiful castle, the Villa Asconiti. Feeling brave, he pushed open the ornamental iron gate and ventured inside. To his delight, everything was elegantly A-1. Flowers were blooming in a rainbow of extravagant colour. The shrubbery was luxuriously green and magnificently manicured to precision.

Over to the side, the man noticed a gardener on his hands and knees clipping nearly every blade of grass. He asked: 'May I walk around and have a look at the gardens?' The gardener replied: 'Sure, you're welcome. Come right in. I'm glad to have a guest.'

The visitor began to tour the expansive grounds and asked the gardener: 'Is the owner here today?'

The gardener replied: 'No, I'm afraid not. He's away.'

'When was the last time you saw him?' he asked.

'About twelve years ago,' said the gardener.

'Twelve years? You mean, this idyllic place has been empty for twelve years?' exclaimed the tourist.

'Yes,' said the unruffled gardener.

The inquisitive tourist asked: 'Who tells you what to do?'

The gardener explained that the owner had an agent in Milan.

'Do you ever see him?' enquired the tourist.

Still clipping, pruning, and trimming, the gardener answered: 'Never. He just sends instructions.'

The tourist could not believe his ears. 'But you have everything so pristinely beautiful. It is perfect. It looks like you're expecting him tomorrow.'

The gardener replied: 'Today, sir. I expect him to come at any time—perhaps today.'

CHAPTER TWO
SWINGING FOR THE FENCES

The young pastor had just announced to his congregation that he was leaving. He was standing at the door after the service, greeting his congregation, when one of the elderly saints approached him, her eyes swimming with tears. She sobbed and said: 'Pastor, I'm so sorry you've decided to leave. Things will never be the same again.' The young man was flattered, but was equal to the situation. He clasped her hands in his and replied most graciously: 'Bless you, my dear, but I'm sure the Lord will send you a new pastor even better than I.' Choking with emotion, she said: 'That's what they all say, but they keep getting worse and worse.'

Postnatal care

Any parent will tell you, it is one thing having a baby, it is quite a different matter seeing that kid grow up! That is what this chapter is all about—a church being nurtured in the faith. We saw Paul in the role of evangelist in chapter one, and now we meet him in a pastoral capacity.

The abiding value of this chapter (and the next) is the remarkable insight it gives into Paul's heart; it is a crystalline window on what makes him tick. In these chapters, more perhaps than anywhere else in his letters, Paul discloses his mind—what he thinks—his prime reason for getting out of bed in the morning; he expresses his emotions—the joys and sorrows of ministry—for he wears his heart on his sleeve; and he bares his soul as he shares some of his most intimate dreams and fears.

Paul saw himself as an undershepherd of the flock of God—someone to look after the lambs and share Christ with the sheep and to, ultimately, bring every one into a deeper understanding of the means of grace.

Every pastor to God's flock is given the command, 'do the work of an evangelist' (2 Timothy 4:5). From reading between the lines, it is clear that Paul was not only good on theory for he practised what he preached. There is a weight of clear-cut evidence amassed in his favour that it was through his faithful biblical preaching that the church in Thessalonica was founded. To his credit, it was through his faithful shepherding that this infant church progressed as well as she did, and as far as she did, down the road to spiritual maturity.

'The conversion of a soul is the miracle of a moment, the manufacture of a saint is the task of a lifetime.' (Alan Redpath)

Therein lies the difference between commitment to Christ and consecration to Christ. We all know it is one thing to start a race, but it is quite a different matter to keep on track and with arms aloft to cross the finishing line. Sadly, the long and chequered history of the church confirms that so many fall out on the last lap.

As we begin to carefully unpack the teaching in this chapter, we discover some unbelievable insights into the lifestyle of the apostle. This true servant of God was characterised by integrity, devotion, and total allegiance to Christ—all harnessed to a life of discipline. The missionary statesman, Hudson Taylor, has written: 'A person may be dedicated and devoted, but if he is ill-disciplined, he will be useless.'

2:1 A MINISTRY DRIVEN CHURCH

The apostle, with both hands, seizes the opportunity to remind them of the kind of ministry he exercised among them. He paints five pictures—a thumbnail sketch—of his overall ministry on the canvas of Scripture.

- His rejoicing as a reaper (verse 1).
- His purpose as a preacher (verses 2-6).
- His nature as a nurse (verses 7-8).
- His saintliness as a servant (verses 9-10).
- His faithfulness as a father (verses 11-12).

In so doing, Paul has given us a vignette of the role he occupied when he was with them. He exercised in the familiar words of an outstanding Baptist preacher of a bygone era, C. H. Spurgeon, 'an all round ministry.'

Handling his critics

Paul is stepping up to the plate and the reason why is not too hard to see. No defensive batting for Paul, he is swinging for the fences!

Some of these fifth-columnists were pointing an accusing finger at him, others were spreading scandalous stories about him, a few were trying to undermine his entire ministry—whatever way we look at it, some were so determined to discredit him that they launched a malicious smear campaign against him.

'The preacher man ran away,' they sneered, 'and, wonder of wonders, he hasn't been seen or heard of since. He's just another one of a long line of phoney teachers who tramp up and down the Egnatian Way. This guy's in the job only for what he can get out of it in terms of sex, money, prestige, and power. So when red-hot opposition arose and he found himself boxed in, he took to his heels and ran, you couldn't see him for dust. He doesn't give two cents for you; he's left you to fend for yourselves. Don't be so naïve, he's much more concerned about his own skin than your welfare!'

There is no way that Paul was going to take that scurrilous nonsense on the chin. They were not going to treat him like a doormat. Hating people is like burning down your own house to get rid of a rat. As soon as he became aware of the rumblings, he went into fire fighting mode and moved quickly to extinguish the flames. He wants to do all that he can, as fast as he can, to quell the ridiculous rumours and bolster the church.

The chances are that some of the more gullible, easily-led folk in the congregation were being carried away by this torrent of abuse. The twin facts of Paul's abrupt departure and his failure to return seemed to fit the accusations being levelled against him. On the surface, their case sounded pretty plausible. Fairly convincing.

Paul must have found this personal attack extremely painful and unnerving. In all fairness, he does not allow it to colour his thinking, nor does he permit it to cloud his perception. He knows he has to respond to the charges, and when he does, it is not out of pique or vanity, but it is because the truth of the gospel and the future of the

church were at stake. He voluntarily goes on the record and says, 'Let the facts speak for themselves...'
- Their impeccable character (verses 1-7).
- Their unimpeachable conduct (verses 8-12).

Cooking the books?

Hey, what a thrilling story. Front page news. Inches of editorial column. I mean, this is really sensational! This first-century Billy Graham spent three weeks, give or take a day or two, with them and, as a result of his noteworthy efforts, a church was started. Paul oozes confidence for he knows his track record speaks for itself. He does not juggle the statistics to make them look better than they really are; he does not have to, and he does not need to.

He says quite categorically that, in spite of what other people might say, including the cynics and critics sniping from the relative safety of the sidelines, they all know in their heart of hearts that his visit to them was a runaway, rip-roaring success. All in all, it was a resoundingly positive experience. By no stretch of the imagination was it a failure.

A God-blessed ministry

No sooner has Paul cleared his chest than he turns on his accusers by asking them a penetrating question. Pointing to those who had been converted under his anointed ministry, he asks, what's that? There is only one possible answer, it is God giving the increase.

Paul's labours were well and truly rewarded. Famously so. He could look back with no tinge of sadness and no hint of regret. This preacher was buoyant because the Lord performed a series of miracles in northern Greece. His visit had not been unfruitful or unproductive. It had a measurable goal, and with God's deluge of blessing, that was achieved and accomplished. You see, our obligation is to do the right thing; the rest is in God's hands.

In moments like these, it is opportune to recall the sentiments of the saintly Samuel Rutherford (1600-61) writing from his prison cell in the granite city of Aberdeen. He was reflecting on his pastoral charge in Galloway in southwest Scotland when he wrote:

Fair Anwoth by the Solway, to me thou still art dear,
E'en on the verge of heaven, I drop for thee a tear,
O, if one soul from Anwoth, meet me at God's right hand,
My heaven will be two heavens, in Immanuel's land.

2:2 NOT ALL SUNSHINE

Paul gives us a breathtaking glimpse into what life was like for a travelling evangelist in the first century AD. Any preacher worth his salt with an expanding and fruitful itinerant ministry was often hunted and hounded. Frequently beaten up and left lying in a ditch at the side of the road, they were just another statistic on the missing persons list. More often than not they were hauled before the courts to face trumped-up charges. Regularly they were thrown out of city and town with the label 'undesirable' attached.

If we were to trace Paul's journeys it would be like tracking the path of a wounded deer running from a hunter, leaving one bloody trail after another. It is maybe convenient, but sometimes we are inclined to forget that this was Europe two thousand years ago.

Paul talks openly and honestly about his persecution. He does not embellish it in any way; he does not exaggerate; he tells it for what it is. With clinical precision, he explains and exposes what happened at Philippi.

He and Silas had been stripped and savagely beaten, then unceremoniously thrown into prison, with their feet fastened in the stocks. It had not only been an extremely painful experience, but humiliating as well, since they were flogged naked in public, without trial, in spite of their Roman citizenship.

Both men had been physically abused; they had suffered badly at the hands of others; they had been grossly insulted; they endured and experienced deprivation; they underwent systematic mental torture—

these men went through the proverbial mill. And, again, Paul says to them, *as you know.*

'No event ought to prevent a soldier from obeying.' (Napoleon)

In spite of all the harassment and belittlement he encountered, he pressed on. He battled on. Soldiered on. He resolutely moved ahead, nothing daunted or deterred him. It winded him for he had been treated like a punchbag, but when he recovered his breath, he was back on the road! Battered, bruised, and bleeding, it would take a lot more than that to put him off. It proves the point that he was no self-serving religious fraud, rogue preacher, or charlatan with ten suits and ten sermons.

Déjà vu

In the providence of God that is how the missionaries happened to find themselves in Thessalonica where it was a case of more of the same! History repeats itself. Paul did not simply arrive in town because it was a port in a storm, nor because it was a convenient place to hole up and lick his wounds. It could never be said of him that he was a piece of human flotsam washed up in Macedonia by a tidal wave of events.

There was an explicit purpose behind it all. This guy believed in the sovereignty of his God—a God who overrules. He came as a man with a mission, and for him, as well as the locals, this was a defining moment. In Acts 16:40 he brought a measure of comfort to the saints at Philippi and encouraged them; in Acts 17:1-10 he brought Christ to the sinners in Thessalonica and evangelised them.

How was Paul able to keep going? What was his secret? I believe the answer is seen in a fresh new light in the middle of verse 2 where the main beam is on divine power—*the help of our God.* He was not trusting or relying on past success or academic ability, nor was he depending on the arm of flesh. His strength lay in the Lord enabling him to be what he wanted him to be. God undertook for him. And so, with bravery and boldness, he preached Jesus.

The wonderful thing about it is that God never let him down. Not twice; not even once! When all is said and done, how could he? He is God!

Dare to be a...

There is a mighty phrase employed in this verse that reinforces the kind of man that Paul really was. It says, *we dared to tell you*. That simply means, he dared for the Lord Jesus. He was bold in jail and out of jail. He took his boldness in God into every arena of his life—such is the calibre of this man. He was no Johnny-come-lately. He was no theorising professor in a six-feet-above-contradiction ivory tower. He was in the thick of it, down where the action was.

The odds were stacked high against him; he was deep in enemy territory, in the trenches, operating in a stronghold of Satan. Still he dared. He faced the opposition head-on in an eyeball-to-eyeball confrontation. Paul and his team pulled no punches as they squared up to them. They took their hands out of their pockets, rolled up their sleeves, and knocked the enemy out cold. No messing around here, for there is a job to be done! Alistair Cooke reminds us that 'the great need for anyone in authority is courage.'

Feisty, yes. Courageous, yes. Spunky, yes. Pertinacious, yes. Men—ordinary men—yes. But they were men with a big heart for the Lord and a burning passion aflame in their breast. Their philosophy is summed up in the familiar adage—no gain, no pain; no crown, no cross. Paul and his colleagues saw their today in the light of God's tomorrow.

2:3 TOO MANY INDIANS, NOT ENOUGH CHIEFS

There is a great premium on godly leadership these days. Most people realise, in the average congregation, there are fewer leaders than are needed and fewer faithful leaders than are expected. We also know that leadership is colossally difficult. As they say, many of us have been there and done that!

In soccer, for example, when the team fails to win because they cannot put the ball in the back of the opposition's net, the board of directors sack the manager; in business, when the employees do not deliver the goods, the shareholders call an extraordinary general meeting and fire the chief executive. Pronto!

I venture to suggest that the vast majority of us realise the tremendous need for capable, enthusiastic, inspiring influence, which is the primary role of Christian leadership. No matter where we look, there is a leadership crisis prevalent in today's evangelical church. The failure of many Mr. Big's—who are involved in gospel ministry—seems to be a daily occurrence; it really is that common. It is not systemic I know, it just appears that way. The tragedy is there will be more such high profile failures in the future!

The question is, knowing the subtlety of the enemy, how can spiritual leaders excel in competence? How can they have a genuine, lasting impact on other people's lives? How can they influence and shape their generation for God and good? How can they be history-makers?

The answer is found in these first half-dozen verses of chapter 2; they are marvellous verses, for in them Paul shares some timeless principles for conducting an effective ministry! When it comes to doing church, there is a handful of five ingredients that God signally honours and significantly blesses; each of these relates to Paul's view of a wondrous God. He was...

- confident in God's power—giving him a gritty tenacity and a sense of being unbeatable;
- committed to God's truth—giving him integrity and a sense of awesome responsibility;
- commissioned by God's will—giving him authority and a sense of vocation;
- compelled by God's knowledge—giving him accountability and a sense of security; and
- consumed with God's glory—giving him humility and a sense of eternity.

The truth doesn't lie

If the enemy cannot destroy us by relentless opposition, he will do the next best thing: he will wage an all-out war on our character. He will undermine our integrity so that people begin to question our sincerity. He will do all in his power to shatter people's confidence and trust in us as individuals.

That is why Paul pleads with these young believers in the manner he does. He urges them, appealing to them to accept him as a man, imploring them to accept the message. Actually, what he says is a triple negative.

Paul pulled no punches when he elaborated on point number one; he more or less said, 'Look, the facts are there, the facts are true, the facts speak for themselves!' Basically, what he shared with them in the course of his ministry *did not spring from error.* In other words, he preached the truth of the gospel, the whole truth of the gospel, and nothing but the truth of the gospel. He faithfully preached the Lord Jesus Christ even if it appeared unpalatable to sugary sermon connoisseurs.

The truth is absolute. It always was non-negotiable—at least for God and Paul.

He was not a peddler of lies or a purveyor of falsehoods. He was not a scam artist. I was intrigued to discover that the thought behind the Greek word for *error* is the word *plane* from which we get our English word *planet.* The word means 'to wander, to roam' like the planets in the ancient sky. Not like the stars, which behaved more predictably. Error, therefore, is roaming from the truth—it is wandering without any standard, without anything to contain or control us! It is not too difficult to ascertain what they were saying about Paul; we do not have to be rocket scientists to work that one out!

The plain fact is, as a Christian first, and a preacher second, he was totally committed to God's truth; Paul was not deceived, neither was he a deceiver. The gospel that Paul preached was both accurate and authentic.

Modeling the message

Paul was not only committed to proclaiming the truth; he was equally committed to living the truth. Here is a preacher who modeled his message. There were no sensual undertones in what he said or did. There were no *impure motives,* for everything he did was above-board and open to public scrutiny.

He was not guilty of any indiscretions; he was never caught in a position of compromise. No matter where he was, no matter what he did, no matter who he was with, Paul was a brother above and beyond reproach. No one could point a finger at him! There were no sexual connotations contained in his message and no innuendo in his conversation.

This is one area where the enemy often attacks the servants of God and, in recent days, there have been many such scandals that have rocked the foundations of not a few Christian organisations. Mind you, it is nothing new. In Paul's day the same was true!

You see, some of Paul's accusers said he was winning converts in return for sexual favours. And the fact that Luke records in Acts 17:4 that a significant number of well-known, well-heeled women were saved only adds fuel to their fire—it gives street credibility to their side of the story! Well, if we believe that malarkey, we will believe anything!

The truth is, Paul is no filthy dreamer; he is no fornicator; he is not hopping in and out of bed with every pretty woman convert; he is not a man of dubious standards, living a double life!

Straight as a die

Paul never attempted to pull the wool over other people's eyes. He was able to say, *nor are we trying to trick you.* There was nothing in his demeanour or conduct that even remotely smacked of the unscrupulous. So far as his evangelistic ministry is concerned, he was not a wolf in sheep's clothing! The Thessalonians had not been lured towards Christ with a false hope.

One commentator notes: 'The gospel had not been set out as a decoy to attract potential converts to their own slaughter. Christ was not the bait used to hook the people on some cult.' There was absolutely nothing devious about his methods. He made no attempt to induce conversions by dangling a juicy carrot in front of people, for example, either by concealing the true cost of discipleship or by offering fraudulent blessings.

Here, then, is a threefold claim—Paul insists that his message was true, his motives were pure, and all his methods were open and aboveboard. In each of these his conscience was entirely clear. Paul had no qualms about anything; he had no niggling doubts lurking in the front of his mind, absolutely none! In what he said and in why and how he said it, he was free from anything underhand.

These first-century gospel preachers were men of the highest proficiency. They were men of truth—true to their Lord, true to their word, true to their calling, and true to their message. It goes without saying that they were holy men and honest men!

2:4 HONOUR

Paul has a profound feeling of privilege that leaves him stunned and seriously overwhelmed. He sees himself as a steward entrusted with a priceless and valuable treasure. He was a steward of that which God allocated to him, and so should we be. For example:

- our time—by redeeming it and using it wisely;
- our talents—by refusing to bury or hide them under a bushel;
- our tithes—by bringing them into the storehouse to be used for the advance of the gospel;
- our treasure—by knowing how to effectively handle the word of God.

Paul, bless him, cannot understand it fully, nor can he explain it satisfactorily; it leaves him spellbound. Lost for words. He says something similar when writing to young Timothy, 'I thank Christ Jesus our Lord who has given me strength, that he considered me faithful, appointing me to his service. The grace of our Lord was poured out on me abundantly, along with the faith and love that are in Christ Jesus' (1 Timothy 1:12, 14).

To think that God handpicked him and counted him worthy to put him into the ministry, well, the sheer thrill of it never left him. He has a great sense of awe and wonder at his calling in life. *To be allowed and approved of God* is something that leaves him out of breath. He passed a rigorous divine selection process having been thoroughly vetted by the Spirit of God. He enjoyed the backing and blessing of the Lord. He was tested times without number and on every occasion he passed with flying colours.

He knew how to handle himself when disappointment came and John Mark left him for greener pastures. He often encountered danger and not infrequently diced with death—e.g. the stoning at Lystra. He knew the constant pressure of dealing with internal wrangling and disputes—church politics—and came out the other end untainted and untarnished. Remember the council at Jerusalem.

Paul was a man who had been sorely tried, but here was a man who could be trusted. He was given the benefit of God's approval. We cannot get a better commendation than that—the living Lord Jesus was with him, and for him.

God endorsed him and gave him a glowing reference.

He can face the enemy and walk down the Main Street with his head held high. Come what may, he knows that God has vindicated him as a man and wonderfully blessed his ministry. He is not on an ego trip; he is not flaunting himself; he is not a superstar. He is still Paul, famed for his humility. Just plain Paul, a man whose trust is fixed in God.

The old, old story

What about his preaching? Anything Paul proclaimed in the course of his spoken ministry he is happy to stand over. It was the gospel of God's dear Son. There was no other message, no other theme, no human rhetoric or opinion. The gospel was the sole foundation upon which the apostle built his exhortations and reproofs.

It was, and still is, the most vital news in the world, and at all costs, it must be placarded to a watching world, shouted to a listening world, and lived out before a world that rarely sees reality. Paul never once got sidetracked by allowing other well-meaning individuals to lead him off the beaten track. For Paul, the main thing was to keep the main thing the main thing! All he told them from day one was the gospel of the sovereign, saving grace of God. Good enough for him, good enough for me!

God-pleaser

In the early 1990s when President George Bush had fiery John Sununu as his White House chief of staff, a reporter asked Sununu if his job was difficult. He quickly answered, 'No.' The reporter thought

SWINGING FOR THE FENCES

Sununu had misunderstood the question, so he asked again, and got the same reply. Sununu, a former governor of New Hampshire, then explained why he felt his job was easy, 'I have only one constituent.' He knew his job was to please the President.

Paul has not finished with them yet for he goes on to affirm that, so far as he is concerned, men did not matter—*we are not trying to please men but God, who tests our hearts.* Paul was people-oriented, that is true, but he is definitely not a man-pleaser. He never attempted to play to the gallery and be of all men most plausible. He had no desire, half-hearted or otherwise, to impress them. There was nothing silvery and smooth about his tongue. Bill Cosby was right when he said, 'I don't know the secret to success, but the key to failure is trying to please everybody.'

These thoughts come out so clearly in *The Message*: 'We never used words to butter you up. No one knows that better than you. And God knows we never used words as a smoke screen to take advantage of you.' In other words, so far as his memory bank can recall, Paul never flattered them on any one occasion.

Flattery is a form of callous exploitation. Someone defined the difference between flattery and gossip as:

- flattery is what we say to someone's face which we would never dream of saying behind their back, and
- gossip is what we say behind someone's back which we would never think of saying to their face.

Flattery is telling people what they want to hear so they will do what we want them to do.

Flattery is based on the premise that everybody's ego loves to hear good things about themselves. We can look at it like this: if we say a good thing about a person and we have no intent other than to say good about them, that is not flattery; however, if we say a good thing about a person and have in our mind some purpose for that which will come to our benefit, that equals flattery! It is down to motive, ulterior or otherwise.

It is when we set someone up for our own deceptive purposes. We read in Proverbs 29:5 that 'whoever flatters his neighbour is spreading a net for his feet.' On a similar note, the wisdom of Solomon in Proverbs 26:28 says, 'A lying tongue hates those it hurts, and a flattering mouth works ruin.'

We all know how it works. Because the average person is so egotistical, the minute someone fires off a volley of nice things about him, his head swells and, in no time at all, he cannot handle the hype. He gets sucked in! That is not communication; quite frankly, it is nothing short of people manipulation.

I heard about the new pastor who had just preached his first message. The people were coming up to him and saying: 'Wow, that was a wonderful message, it did my heart good.' Finally, this man, with a scowl on his face, came up and said: 'That's the worst sermon I've ever heard. Who told you that you could preach? If you're a preacher, then I'm the President of the USA.' One of the elders could see that the new pastor was visibly upset so he came over, put his arm around him, and said: 'Don't worry what that man says, anyhow he just repeats what everyone else is thinking.'

Flattery is like perfume: OK to smell, but not to swallow!

2:5 The mighty $

Money did not matter to Paul for he writes, *nor did we put on a mask to cover up greed.* Paul was not in it for what he could get out of it—he was no rip-off merchant out for a quick buck. He never attempted to fleece the flock or meanly exploit them in any way. Even the thought of taking people to the cleaners appalled him and scared the daylights out of him. Paul, therefore, did not have one hand around their shoulder while his other hand was deep in their pocket. Put another way, Paul and his team did not give the appearance of being poor in order to get rich.

It is a harsh fact of life that, from the beginning, money and ministry have generally appeared to clash; they are more often than not on a collision course. George MacDonald has wisely observed: 'For every hundred people who can handle failure, there is only one person who can handle success.' Every one of us involved in any aspect of Christian ministry is to be above suspicion in the whole area of finance—we are accountable to the Lord.

At this point Paul flies in the face of convention and calls on God as his witness. A brave thing for any man to do! But the apostle has no quibbles; he knows he has not let the Lord down in any of these areas. He knows the Lord God is the perfect witness, for he knows everything—he is omniscient—and, unlike fallen man with his prejudices and jaundiced opinions, he cannot lie.

'It is impossible for God to perjure himself, thus his witness is the apex in reliability.' (Richard Mayhue)

It is worth noting that those who preach the gospel of Jesus Christ are not primarily responsible to the church, nor to a mission board, but to the glorified Lord himself, as Head of the church. The chain of command may tell us where to go and what to do but, ultimately, God is our boss. We are answerable to him as our divine CEO.

There are two sides to this coin: on one side, this is an extremely disconcerting fact because God scrutinises our heart and its hidden secrets, and his standards are incredibly high—he knows us better than we know ourselves; on the other, it is a marvellously liberating truth since God is a more knowledgeable, impartial, and merciful judge than any human being, ecclesiastical court, or committee will ever be—he knows us better than they know us.

I agree with John Stott when he concludes: 'To be accountable to him is to be delivered from the tyranny of human criticism.' Had Paul not been absolutely sure of his assertions and totally confident of his own position, how foolish it would have been to call God as his witness! No matter what we think of Paul, he is not that crazy! I saw a bumper sticker that said: 'If you don't believe in God, I hope you are right!' Make no doubt about it, God will eventually call us all—including Paul—to account.

2:6 NO BROWNIE POINTS

Paul writes with candid openness and razor-sharp honesty, *we were not looking for praise from men, not from you or anyone else.* The fact is, Paul was not interested in being centre stage; he did not want to hog the limelight. He had no hidden agenda, either for them or himself. He is on the level.

This man was the epitome of transparency as he stood before them in all his vulnerability; he was not afraid to confide in them his king-size struggles; he was not ashamed to share with them his many weaknesses. He knew that his humanness was the very avenue through which Christ's work in him would be revealed to them.

Paul knew full well that at any time he could have pulled rank on the Thessalonians. He could even have used his position as an apostle to intimidate and browbeat them into giving him anything he desired. In all fairness he did not abuse his authority by taking advantage of them. Instead he came to them as a servant whose ultimate goal was to meet their needs in the best way possible.

His was not a mercenary mentality; his tactics were not those of a guerrilla soldier. He was not a shady back street character from the underworld. His was not the hit and run mindset. His was not a covert deployment. Certainly not! This man did not look for esteem or honour; he did not squeeze all the juice from the lemon, for he was no Diotrephes! He was not interested in their admiration nor did he seek their rapturous applause; he did not expect them to show their appreciation in any way or at any time.

Paul had a wonderful understanding of human nature, and because of that, he was not too disappointed if it did not happen. If they did show it, he was immensely thankful and he accepted it with a sense of profound gratitude to the Lord. Even then, he was conscious of his deep indebtedness to the grace of God in his own life—that is what kept him on the right side of humility!

He had no compulsive desire to be top dog; he did not want to occupy the best seat at the top table; he did not have to be the big shot! Paul never forgot who he was in the eye of God. Here is one preacher, and I love this about Paul, who never forgot his roots!

What would Jesus do?

When we take time to analyse Paul's defence, it is abundantly clear that he was not preaching just for the good of his health, nor was he in the Christian ministry to line his own pockets. There was no trace of more-faces-than-Big-Ben hypocrisy in his character and no over-the-top hype in his message. He was not preaching for anything or anyone but Jesus Christ—to him the Lord was all that mattered. God's verdict was all that counted to him.

Here is a man who cared supremely what God thought of his ministry. It seems to me that is the reason why Paul is the man he is. When I think of Paul I think of a dear brother who loved the truth and a man who loved the task in hand. Someone once introduced Hudson Taylor as a great missionary who had given his life to the Orient because he loved the Chinese. Mr. Taylor slowly shook his head and answered thoughtfully: 'No, not because I loved the Chinese, but because I loved God.'

Paul passionately embraced the word of the Lord and he was totally dedicated to the Lord of the word.

It is the 'clean hands and pure heart' syndrome that we read of in Psalm 24:4. Perhaps we need to pray using the words of Sylvanus Dryden Phelps (1816-95):

> *Give me a faithful heart,*
> *Likeness to thee,*
> *That each departing day*
> *Henceforth may see*
> *Some work of love begun,*
> *Some deed of kindness done,*
> *Some wanderer sought and won –*
> *Something for thee.*

2:7-8 BREAKING THE MOULD

A nurse, a servant, and a father are how Paul sees himself in relation to the young church in Thessalonica. In 2:7-12 he develops each of these ideas in a most intriguing way. This is where good leadership is terrifically important. If this is your forte—your field of expertise—you will know that you can attend many conferences, read a wide variety of books, watch an enormous selection of DVDs and videos, and you can do so much and hear so much all on the subject of spiritual leadership and how you can be a better leader.

A good leader, according to Paul,

* inspires influence—he galvanises people,
* seizes the moment—he is up for it,
* takes the initiative—he goes for it,
* sees the need—he is awake when others are asleep,
* delegates responsibility—he shares the load, and
* ensures the job gets properly done—he does not quit.

With the passing of time many churches lose their vitality—the sparkle goes, the excitement wanes, the thrill evaporates, the shine and lustre fades off their fellowship. Their zing goes ping and their pep goes pop!

Instead of allowing God to stretch and shape them into a living, vibrant community of believers, many congregations petrify and mummify into a state of traditionalism.

When maintaining status quo programs becomes intrinsically more important than ministering to people, the result is an ingrown, inward-looking, stagnant clique. In these few verses, Paul takes the lid off by showing us how we can keep our ministry fresh and alive in Christ. As well as that, Paul gives a few more desirable qualities for those immersed in leadership:

* an ability to feel where people are at (2:7),
* a real heart-affection for people (2:8),
* a kosher lifestyle (2:9-10),
* an eager enthusiasm to hand out bouquets (2:11), and
* a genuine gifting to affirm others (2:12).

A mother's touch

The picture is that of a mother and her children where the underlying thought is one of gentleness. Here we see the tender loving care Paul showed towards them in a dignified manner. The use of the word *among* conveys much more than we possibly realise. It suggests that he was in there with them in a heart and life involvement.

The word *gentle* is a beautiful word; in the Greek it is *epios*. It is used only here and on one other occasion in 2 Timothy 2:24 in the New Testament. It simply means to be kind to someone. Paul says, as we moved among you, we were kind to you! We did not come to abuse you, or take from you, or exploit you, or ride roughshod over you, or manipulate you; on the contrary, we moved among you with kindness.

This is a spiritual leader caring for his all-sorts congregation, someone genuinely concerned about their wellbeing and sensitive to their personal needs. It implies that he accepted them for who they were; he respected them; he extended compassion to them; he displayed a tolerance of their imperfections; he exercised patience in all his dealings with them; he showed a sense of loyalty to them.

Gentle giant

How gentle is gentle? We do not have to look too far for the answer for we read at the end of verse 7 that his presence and ministry among them was like *a mother caring for her little children.* Most of us appreciate how a mother feeds her young child is almost as important as what she feeds him.

We can do so much harm, and in the process, cause irreparable damage by force-feeding truth down unwilling throats. Thankfully, Paul was not like that—he showed consistent care and compassion appropriate to the needs of those in the church.

Paul was obviously respected as a man of his time and, for better or worse, people tended to take him rather seriously. The Average Joe felt inhibited when he was around—he was just so incredibly gifted. He was not the kind of bloke with whom they could crack a joke. They felt jittery with a sense of unease when he was within earshot. That is a shame because they did not have to, or need to, feel inferior. Paul would be horrified if he thought they felt like that.

Because right here, he says, 'we mothered you.' In other words, it was tender love! Soft-hearted love. One translation uses the term 'cherishing' which means 'to warm.' Paul warmed their heart; he ignited a spark in their life.

Warm—do not scald—people with the truth.

Bird talk

Another picture is hinted at in Deuteronomy 22:6 where we read of the mother bird covering her young. These young converts were in his arms, ever so close to his heart. One writer has suggested that what we have depicted here is a mother who fondles her children—she comes down to their level, uses their language, and plays their games. As it were, she becomes childlike with her children.

It is a picture of a brand of care that is protective and knows the right moment to step aside. It is not domineering, but is always under-girding. This side of Paul's character does not always shine through in his letters, but we cannot miss it here. Sounds a bit like the words written in the flyleaf of the Bible of John Watson, the Scottish preacher: 'Be kind, you don't know what battles people are fighting.'

It shows us the kind of man he really was in public and behind the scenes. He is not aloof or distant, nor is he unapproachable. As the Lord's servant, Paul was never patronising or condescending. He is in there with them, loving them, throwing his arms around them, and that is what he enjoys most. It is a devotion that is truly selfless and totally sacrificial. Far from using them to minister to himself, he gave himself to minister to them. Paul is fully aware of their needs and sought to meet them as best he could. He is a man with a mother's heart!

'The pulpit shouldn't be a stainless steel milk dispenser but a rocking chair where the pastor lovingly nurses the church.' (Charles Swindoll)

A mother's love

Paul develops his argument further when he unfolds the role of a mother in the full beauty of its metaphorical meaning. Here we see a real mother in her true colours when he writes, *we loved you so much, you had become so dear to us*. No matter how cynical we may be about Paul's approach to ministry, or how critical we may be of Paul's attitude to these young believers, these selected words from verse 8 speak volumes—here is affection at its finest and best.

Paul yearned for them with a big heart, just like a young mother hankering after her child (cf. Job 3:21). It is like a mother being irresistibly drawn to her child, so powerfully strong is the emotional pull. When Paul looked at his spiritual children in the crèche in Thessalonica, there was a bond—a heart connection—between them; they were his pride and joy.

It is significant that Paul did not turn them over to baby sitters or child minders by choosing to care for them and look after them himself. Paul felt so deeply for them because they genuinely won his heart. Please do not get the idea from Paul's loving language that he is a spiritual softie, for he was not; this man was a warrior for the gospel.

Paul had a tough exterior and a soft inside!

Paul had enough spiritual perception to distinguish between the enemy and those hurting and lost in darkness. He knew these good folk were imperfect like himself and, because they often suffered from the dreaded collywobbles, regularly needed a helping, supportive hand along life's way.

Yes, he was more than happy to share the gospel with them, but even surpassing that, Paul was willing to wrap his life up in theirs. He was so motivated and constrained by love that nothing was too much trouble to him. He gave everything, holding nothing back in unreserved abandonment—he was two hundred percent committed to them.

Paul was more than just a put-your-dime-in vending machine for the truth. He did not only dispense candy, he actually imparted his life to them for he valued them; he gladly acknowledged their worth before God, and he appreciated their worth in his own life. He stayed with them and fleshed out the gospel that he preached. His whole life incarnated the love of God. The nineteenth-century British Prime Minister Benjamin Disraeli noted that 'the greatest good you can do for another is not just to share your riches, but to reveal to him his own.'

An authentic biblical ministry is not one that lobs instructions from the trenches like hand grenades to those struggling in the game of life. Paul did not bark commands at them like a sergeant major on the parade ground. It is not the classic scenario of them-and-us, sitting on opposite sides of the same room, waiting for someone to carry out the necessary introductions. A warm relationship like this, within the family of God, is one that cannot be carried out at arms length.

2:9 TENTMAKER

Surely you remember, brothers, our toil and hardship; we worked night and day in order not to be a burden to anyone while we preached the gospel of God to you. It is apparent that Paul knew exactly what he was doing, and it shows itself in many different ways. Paul got it absolutely right from at least three angles—his preaching, his priorities, and his profession.

His preaching is spot on. The only message Paul shared with them is what he calls *the gospel of God.* In short, the good news, the best news, the only news worth listening to—the evangel. Such a message incorporated three fundamental truths: Christ died for our sins, was buried, and raised again on the third day (cf. 1 Corinthians 15:3-4). It was, therefore, solidly biblical.

If we had been there, sitting on hard wooden benches alongside the worshippers in Thessalonica, we would have heard the clear, consistent declaration of God's word—a message pregnant with truth. We would be spared the agony of listening to the idle ramblings and whimsical opinions of a preacher man.

His priorities were also right. Paul did not want to be a financial burden to them so he plied his arduous trade as a tentmaker by day and, when the sun was down, he preached the gospel by night.

Paul did not arrive in town as a gospel virtuoso and demand celebrity treatment.

He was not like Diotrephes (cf. 3 John 9), or the Pharisees (cf. Matthew 23:4), or Simon Magus (cf. Acts 8:9-24)—all of whom acted like pastoral prima donnas. Instead, he was tireless in his efforts as he expended monumental amounts of energy, working himself to the bone.

O yes, it was a real hard struggle at times; there were many gallons of tears, but he did it all for them. It was not an easy option, for this was no cheap alternative lifestyle. It certainly was not a cop-out. Paul did not adopt the attitude that says, 'Stop the world, I wanna get off!' All of this is an unmistakable indication that his priorities were on target. Paul knows what he is doing is right so he gets on with it; he knows where he is going and gets there. Oswald Chambers makes the point: 'If we are going to be used by God, he will take us through a multitude of experiences that are not meant for us at all; they are meant to make us useful in his hands.'

2:10 RIGHT PROFESSION

You are witnesses, and so is God, of how holy, righteous and blameless we were among you who believed. Paul is a brave man. What a staggering claim for any mortal man to make! He says they know it. That is fine, we have no qualms about that, there is no need to hesitate there; but Paul does not leave it there, he takes a breath, leaps forward and says, God knows it. He is a man of unquestioned probity as he tells them how it was when he was privileged to be with them.

• He is holy—his conduct in relation to God.

He is a man of piety. The Old Testament speaks of the 'beauty of holiness' and, when we look at Paul, we see something attractive about his demeanour. There is a glow to his personality, something that only comes when a person is walking close with the Lord. He and Jesus are on the same wavelength, in touch and in tune with one another.

In Paul we see someone who knows to whom he belongs and is, therefore, perfectly satisfied. He was single-minded in that he was sold out to Jesus. His all is on the altar; he has kept nothing back for himself.

- He is righteous — his conduct in relation to his fellow man.

He is a just man who behaved himself in such a manner that his whole life was above and beyond reproach. He did not leave himself open for criticism; he was upright in all aspects of public ministry. No man could point a finger at him. They would try and have a go, but they were on a hiding to nothing. There were no chinks in the armour of his character. No matter where he was, it did not matter who he was with, for he was always above-board in all his dealings.

From Paul's vantage point, nothing was conducted under the counter; no business was done behind closed doors in clandestine hush-hush meetings. Before other people his life was an open book. He had no hidden agenda for plugging his latest autographed epistle, or touting his success as a church planter, or begging for money to keep his ministry alive.

- He is blameless — his conduct in relation to self.

We all know that Paul was not sinless, and we are very much aware of the fact that he was not perfect, he had his faults — plenty of them — like the rest of us. He never said he was any different! We have lifted him on to a parapet and elevated him six feet above contradiction. Whatever we say, this man was the real McCoy!

One of the lads

A lovely feature in Paul's life is that he has no airs or graces — he is one of the lads. In our enthusiasm to applaud our boyhood hero, we are guilty of lifting him up to a level that is much more than he ever aspired to. We have put a halo on top of his head, almost given him the status of a celebrity, and hung a do-not-touch notice around his highly polished neck.

Paul was no pin-up or cultic personality.

Nothing could be further from reality; if we see him in that light, we are either looking at the wrong man or else we have a caricature image of him in our mind. This man was a very ordinary man — open, honest, and transparent. In public, blameless. In private, blameless.

This peripatetic preacher is a man of renowned integrity. If he said he would do it, he did it. He kept his promises. He never scampers into the shadows when the light is switched on. He does what is right even when no one else is looking, and he does what is right even when others are compromising all around him. Martin Luther King Jr. has observed that 'the ultimate measure of a man is not where he stands in moments of comfort and convenience, but where he stands at times of challenge and controversy.'

For Paul, old-fashioned decency is not just a convenient prop or something for him to lean on when he needs a character reference; it is something that comes from deep within. It does not fade or fluctuate with the passing of time or depend on the company it is in. It remains intact whether the test is the worst of times in adversity or the best of times in prosperity.

When we think of what happened to Paul in a miscellany of situations, it is good to realise that here is a guy who walked away unscathed in terms of personal uprightness. Some people in today's world are so twisted they could hide behind a corkscrew. Not Paul, he is as straight as a gun barrel! Winning or losing, passing or failing, his integrity shone through.

2:11-12 PATERNAL INSTINCTS

We have a beautiful picture emerging when Paul's relationship is likened to that of a father with his children. John MacArthur says of the apostle at this point: 'Paul acted like a man. There was a side of him that acted like a mother, but there was another side of him that acted like a man, like a father with strength and courage. And he never flinched from the immeasurable risks of life and the challenges that he faced because one, he was assured of God's presence; two, he knew the cause was just; and three, he trusted an unfailing sovereignty.'

Paul has a definite paternal instinct, and he ensures that each one receives the very best of individual attention. Each one was vitally important to him. They mattered. What did he do? He modeled the message before them. But he did a lot more for it goes beyond pattern to precept.

- He *encouraged* them.

He lifted their hearts. He picked them up when they were on a real downer. People get discouraged so easily so his ministry to them was one of reassuring, ongoing support. He gave them the priceless gifts of a listening ear and an understanding heart. He came alongside them and made them feel so much better. It is the Barnabas factor being worked out in the context of a local church family. He excelled in motivation.

- He *comforted* them.

He certainly did not pamper or mollycoddle them. Because of his unique style in ministering into their situation, he made them want to do better in themselves. He counselled them to keep on trying, to hang in there, to hold on tight. He sought to bring out the best in them while others, with the gift of agitation, often bring out the worst in us.

- He *urged* them.

He testified to them from his own experience — it is the empathy principle established by Paul in 2 Corinthians 1:3-4 being put into practice. He shared with them what happened to him. He followed the shining example of the prophet Ezekiel; he sat where they sat.

Remember Corrie Ten Boom? When her dear sister Betsy was dying amidst the unthinkable horrors of Ravensbrück concentration camp, she uttered a sentence that has travelled all around the world. She said: 'There is no pit so deep that Christ is not deeper still.' Another profound statement of equal worth came from her lips when she said: 'They will listen to us because we've been here.' So true.

God has no problems, he only has plans.

Paul could identify with them. He could relate to them. That is why he urged them. It is as plain and simple as that! Here is a leader at work — leading by example and encouragement. Here is a man with the ability to carry out a good resolution long after the excitement of the moment has passed.

Being what God wants us to be

Why did he do it? What was his ultimate goal? It was, as he says himself, so that they might *live lives worthy of God*. Here is the big difference between the mother and father traits in Paul. The 'mother side' wants to provide what is needed at a given moment; the 'father side' wants to produce the product at the end—a delicate balance that needs to be, somehow, maintained.

The mother wants to cherish, and nurture, and love, and hold, and affirm. Perfectly natural for that is the motherly instinct coming to the fore. Then the father comes along and says, 'That's all very well, in fact, it is wonderful; but we want to be sure at the end that he is living according to God's standards.'

Both—mother and father—actually complement each other beautifully. It is all about modeling, mentoring, motivating, and then moving them on to the next step. That is where the involvement of a father is mega important, for any father worth his salt wants each of his children to walk in a manner worthy of the God who has called them. And that is what they needed to do; they needed to learn how to walk.

In those early stages of finding their spiritual feet, Paul was constantly available to them as a father. He was at their beck and call. The importance of this experience is underlined with the reminder that the Lord is the one *who calls you*. That phrase is in the present tense. They have been called to salvation. Now God is calling them to a life of obedience and holiness.

Whether we preach from a pulpit on Sunday morning or sit behind a computer monitor or stand in front of a kitchen sink on Monday morning, God wants to blend our vocation with our calling. Your vocation is special, and your calling is sacred, regardless of whether you wear a clerical collar, a blue collar, a white collar, or no collar at all. No matter what job pays your household bills at the end of the month, he wants you to come to terms with your calling and use your 9-5, Monday through Friday berth to further his kingdom. Down here we are an integral part of his kingdom. One day we will leave this world behind when we enter his eternal kingdom and share his glory forever. What a day that will be!

This is the bones of godly leadership—intelligent leadership by God's design—it is giving people hope.

On one hand, a concern for the whole person; on the other, a concern for the process. On one hand, a concern for kindness; on the other, a concern for control. On one hand, a concern for affection; on the other, a concern for authority. On one hand, embracing; on the other, exhorting. On one hand, cherishing; on the other, challenging.

Where there is that healthy and proper balance, God can work in a glorious way in our life. If we have a generous mix and match of all these components we have the makings of a biblical leader—a leader who stands head and shoulders above everyone else.

In fact, we have a Paul and, because we have a Paul, we have a church in Thessalonica. That proves the point! Our friend Paul fulfilled that role admirably. He was a leader and servant at the same time—servant leadership. A businessman once asked Lorne Sanny, president of Navigators, how he could know when he had a servant attitude. The reply, 'By how you act when you're treated like one.' The words of Graham Kendrick's song, *The Servant King*, spring to mind for they say it so well and come as a fresh challenge:

So let us learn how to serve,
And in our lives enthrone him,
Each other's needs to prefer,
For it is Christ we're serving.

2:13 GROWING PAINS

Growing pains can be a problem—perhaps that is an understatement. When we look at the final verses in the chapter, there is copious evidence to suggest that the relatively young believers in Thessalonica were going through something similar. They are stretching, developing, maturing, and growing; and for all of us who have been there and done that, we know there are times when it can be horrendously painful. For them it certainly was.

They faced so many trials and so much trouble. They suffered. Their only crime was their sincere love for the Lord Jesus. When we stand back and look objectively at their situation and try to analyse what was happening, one inescapable fact emerges — it was tough living for Jesus in the first century.

Paul chose his words carefully as he summed up their egregious predicament. He speaks of *severe suffering* and that means pressure from circumstances. He says they have *suffered* which is the same word that is used for the sufferings of Jesus. He then says they *drove us out* which means to be rejected by those to whom you seek to minister. Another word employed is *hostile* which is used of chilling winds that blow against us. Then he says they were *stopped or hindered* which pictures a road so broken that travel is well nigh impossible. Welcome to the real world! This was life as it really was. Life in the raw.

Remarkably, though, they still possessed a joy in their heart (cf. 1:6). It is a fair comment, but Paul was an extremely worried man. He was deeply concerned about their welfare — would they make it through another day? Yet he similarly displays a real joy in his life. Happiness depends on what happens to us but even when life falls apart, there is a real joy in knowing Jesus.

No matter how adverse the circumstances, or on which front the enemy is attacking, the Lord is always with us. He goes through it with us. We are not on our own. Paul shows them three resources that they have and on which they can depend when life is lived in the hostile, relentless environment of a pressure cooker.

- We have the faith — God's word in us.
- We have the family — God's people around us.
- We have a future — God's glory before us.

A right attitude

Paul thanks the Lord for them because of their splendid attitude to the precious word of God. W. Clement Stone makes the point that 'there is little difference in people, but that little difference makes a big difference. The little difference is attitude. The big difference is whether it is positive or negative.' Paul says, *And we also thank God continually because, when you received the word of God, which you*

heard from us, you accepted it not as the word of men, but as it actu-
ally is, the word of God, which is at work in you who believe.

That simply means they accepted it not as the word of men, but as it is, the oracles of God. It is the living word of a God who is alive, a message unchanged, unchanging; timeless truth which is never dated. The word of God is God's words to us.

The Bible is 'God's best gift to man.' (Abraham Lincoln)

When we read the Bible for ourselves we quickly discover it speaks to the major issues facing every generation. A good working knowledge of Scripture is the master key to understanding the vital problems of our day. Back in the first century, how did they see it?

Appreciation

They knew it was so much more than the words of mortal men. Far from viewing it as some concoction of his own, they had no doubts in their mind that they heard the word of God every time Paul opened his mouth. 'Preaching,' said Phillips Brooks, 'is truth through personality.'

Their enthusiastic and positively openhearted reception of the word of God gives us an insight into what made Paul tick as an apostle of Jesus Christ. His language in this verse is strangely reminiscent of the Old Testament prophets who would often preface their message by saying, 'The word of the Lord came to me' or 'Thus says the Lord.'

This goes a long way to explaining Paul's dogged persistence in the face of massive odds. He always believed it was much too soon to quit. He was not a self-publicist peddling pet notions of his own. If that had been the case, persecution would have knocked the conceit out of him long before he ever reached Macedonia.

This man was a spokesman for the Almighty, a herald with the king's message and the king's commission. So when Paul started to speak, people sat up and listened. They were riveted to the spot. They took notice. We often contrast words and actions as though words are empty, worthless things that compare badly with deeds. On one hand, some people are all talk, while others get things done! What Paul said as he declared the whole counsel of God was a force to be reckoned with. It produced results.

These dear friends in Thessalonica, whose lives were radically changed, passionately believed it to be the living word of the living Lord. The Bible is not like any other book. It stands alone and above all other volumes and weighty tomes found in every library throughout the world. It is significantly different—different in origin, character, and content.

The Bible is the word of God, inspired by the Spirit of God, for all the people of God.

When we hear it or read it, we are receiving his message, listening to his voice, and considering his thoughts. I just wonder, what is our attitude to God's word right now? Do we treasure it like Job who reckoned it was worth more than his daily food; or like David who said it was of more value than money, even more to be desired than fine gold; or are we like the Psalmist who felt it was even of greater importance than sleep. They appreciated it!

Appropriation

There are two words that Paul uses which combine to show their intelligent response to the proclamation of biblical truth. The first word is *received* and the second, *accepted*. The first means 'to accept it from another.' The second means 'to welcome it warmly.' One has the idea of hearing with the ear; the other implies a hearing of the heart.

They not only heard the word but they took it and made it part and parcel of their life. They assimilated the truth—personalised the truth—and they did it to such an extent that it became an integral part of their spiritual makeup. The word of life became a way of life to them! As the old preacher was heard to say, 'They went through the Book and the Book went through them.' It penetrated down deep into the inner sanctum of their life.

We can look at it from a slightly different angle when we borrow the analogy from a well-known parable; because of their upbeat response we are able to affirm that the living seed was planted in the exceptionally fertile soil of a willing, responsive heart. When Jesus was communicating with his followers, he often focused attention on their attitude to the word of his Father. In three different Gospels he says:

- 'He who has ears let him hear' (Matthew 13:9).
- 'Consider carefully what you hear' (Mark 4:24).
- 'Consider carefully how you listen' (Luke 8:18).

To put it simply, the time has come when we need to learn again the profitable art of meditation—ruminating—chewing the cud of Scripture. We could make a comparison and say that meditation is to spiritual life what digestion is to physical life. If we did not digest our recommended daily intake of food, eventually we would die. It takes time to meditate, but it is the best way I know to appropriate the teaching of Scripture and thereby grow in our relationship with the Lord. It has nothing to do with getting sound bytes from the Lord.

It is not the mentality that says, *'Lord, speak to me. You have sixty seconds, starting now!'*

There is an awful lot to be said for quietly waiting upon the Lord as we ponder his message to our heart. We should approach our daily portion of Scripture with an intense longing to hear God speak to our heart and mind. And when he does address us we should take time to let it sink in, allowing it to soak our heart and flow through our spiritual veins. We then become a people saturated—permeated—with the word of God.

The reality of Christ suffuses our life so deeply and so completely that it changes the very chemistry of our being. It was C. H. Spurgeon who said in his inimitable way: 'A Bible which is falling apart usually belongs to someone who is not.'

Application

So far as the young Christians in Thessalonica were concerned, they had no problems in this respect. They not only appreciated and appropriated biblical truth, but they went one step further and applied it. In other words, they put it into practice. They knew that between saying and doing many a good pair of shoes are worn out. Good listeners! Good livers!

They were 'doers of the word' (James 1:25) and that is where real spiritual blessing is found. Therein lies the age-old secret; it is all about living it out in the rough and tumble of everyday life. In the comfort of our home, in the college lecture hall or university campus, at the supermarket checkout with a week's groceries in the trolley, standing in the bus line when the rain is lashing down, in the world of business, down on the factory floor—wherever we are, whoever we are, it is all about living out the word of God.

God's word changes people and, if we let it, it will change us too. 'With the heart we appreciate the word of God, with the mind we appropriate the word of God, and with the will we apply the word of God,' notes Warren Wiersbe. When the whole person is controlled by the word, we evolve into men and women of the word. Exciting!

2:14-16 THE ENEMY FIGHTS BACK

When trouble knocks at our front door, how do we handle it? If we are scrupulously honest, when the enemy strikes, sometimes we go down and under, or we cave in and collapse under the intensity of the relentless pressure, or we feel hurt and badly let down, or we feel particularly vulnerable and isolated. At times we are prone to feel as though we are very much on our own and that we are the only ones going through a rough patch. The abiding fact remains and it cannot be emphasised enough, we are not!

For you, brothers, became imitators of God's churches in Judea, which are in Christ Jesus: you suffered from your own countrymen the same things those churches suffered from the Jews, who killed the Lord Jesus and the prophets and drove us out.

Paul's words are less than complimentary but they amount to sober reality. In the cold light of a new day they are a substantiated fact of life. The harrowing and traumatising experiences of all those in Thessalonica were more or less a carbon copy of what was happening to those believers further east in the environs of Judea.

This is a fascinating way to describe this particular piece of real estate. Judea is the Greco-Roman name for the land of Judah and comes from the word *Jewish* which was used of the Babylonian captives who returned to Israel during Persian rule. The finer detail is submerged in the writings of men like Ezra and Nehemiah. Basically, it extends from Gaza on the coast, north to Caesarea (where the Judean governor lived in Paul's day), and from the Mediterranean on the west, to the Dead Sea in the east.

Samuel Johnson, famous literary giant of the eighteenth century once said: 'I never think I have hit hard unless it rebounds.'

In the same way, the antagonism that the early believers faced was an unassailable proof of the transformational power of the Christian gospel in their life. Christianity made a massive enough difference to leave their contemporaries well and truly rattled.

There was nothing strange or sinister about their misfortune. In fact, it was to be expected. Sooner or later it was bound to happen. In a providential sense, they were destined for it. The Christian life was no manicured bed of perfumed roses. It was not all plain sailing into an orange sunset; they quickly discovered that. They would be stronger and better for it at the end of the day.

Facing tough times together

They were only human with roller-coaster feelings, but they were definitely not on their own. That is one of the great values of being part of God's international community. We stand together in our darkest hours. When the storm clouds gather, we cling to the Lord and hold on to one another. In the family of God we should be able to find in each other a measure of help and encouragement. A touch of empathy. They were stressed out, but they were strengthened!

It was when Elijah isolated himself from the others that his heart sank to an all-time low, and he wanted to quit. The lesson is, lonely saints are easy meat for the enemy. Whether we realise it or not we desperately need each other. We cannot do it alone. In the battles of life, in the vicissitudes of life, in the mixed fortunes of life, in all the comings and goings of life, we can survive if we stay together.

Who killed Jesus?

Paul does not beat about the bush when he points an accusing finger at the Jews for their fiercely hostile attitude to the Lord Jesus. It is worth noting that some Bible teachers have argued that Paul's language in these verses betrays a spiteful streak that was unworthy of him. It has even been suggested that he was in a stinking bad mood because of his treatment at the hands of Jews in Corinth.

Let's remember that Paul was a Jew himself and had every reason to be proud of his heritage (cf. Philippians 3:4-6); he longed to see the people of his race won to saving faith in Jesus Christ (cf. Romans 10:1). He even said on one memorable occasion that he would willingly contemplate the loss of his own salvation if that would act as a catalyst to bring theirs about (cf. Romans 9:1-5).

Just because Paul was a man of high moral principles and remarkable intelligence and gifting, that did not cloud or colour his thinking, it did not dull his mental capacity or deaden his critical faculties; in fact, the opposite is probably the case. He was alert to all that was going on, he did not stand with his tail in the air and his head buried ostrich-like in the sand. So when he picks up his quill and writes on the parchment, there is a reason for it. It is not what they necessarily wanted to hear, but it had to be said nonetheless.

Paul is definitely not on a charm offensive when he writes in the scathing manner he does. He actually says quite explicitly, in a matter-of-fact kind of way, you *killed the Lord Jesus*. In a politically correct era when such grave matters are regarded as highly sensitive, it could be regarded as a very reprehensible, anti-Semitic statement. But like so much in Scripture, there is a lot more to it than first meets the eye.

It is also true to say that the Romans were implicated in the death of Jesus. The one will-not-go-away fact is that so were all of us — it was for our sin that he died. Your sin. My sin. Indeed, Paul included himself personally in this (cf. Galatians 2:20); he never forgot that he had once been a blasphemer and a persecutor (cf. 1 Timothy 1:13). Nevertheless, the Jewish people as a whole shared in the blame and said so (cf. Matthew 27:25). While implicating ourselves, we cannot exonerate them!

91

On the charge sheet

The second charge Paul lays at their feet is that they *killed the prophets*. Actually, Paul was not the first to do this; Jesus himself had accused them (cf. Matthew 23:29-31; Luke 13:34). The third charge levelled against them is that they *also drove us out* which seems to put the apostles on a level with the prophets. For more on that score we read his erudite comments in 1 Corinthians 4:9.

Number four is when Paul draws attention to the fact that *they displease God* especially by rejecting his Messiah. The last one is when he says they *are hostile to all men*. This phrase has reminded many commentators of the famous saying of Tacitus when he described them thus: 'Towards all other people (i.e. except their fellow Jews) they feel only hatred and hostility.'

Gagging God

In the succeeding verse Paul adds fuel to the fire when he explains their hostility to the human race in terms of their attempt to stop the apostles from preaching the gospel and so to stop the Gentiles from being saved. An echo of this less-than-friendly attitude is found back in Matthew 23:13.

Paul saw this policy for what it really was—appalling. The Jews had not only savagely killed the Lord Jesus and ruthlessly persecuted the prophets and apostles, but they were also obstructing the spread of the gospel and so the work of salvation.

They attempted to silence God's spokesmen.

What could be more distasteful and horrible than withholding a life-saving message from people who otherwise will die? It was God's express will and desire that all men be saved through the gospel of Christ, but the Jews wanted no one to find salvation in Jesus, even though he specifically came to save them from their sins. In effect, they did not like what they saw, and they did not like what they heard, so they resorted to the old tactic of attempting to gag the living God. Paul exposed it like this, *They displease God and are hostile to all men in their effort to keep us from speaking to the Gentiles so that they may be saved.*

Payday coming

Paul gives it to them straight from the shoulder. He could not have spelt it out any clearer. What a serious indictment to make against any people group! It should be enough to cause them to shudder in their boots and shake like leaves on a windy autumn day. Needless to say that did not happen for Paul goes on to say, *in this way they always heap up their sins to the limit.*

As a direct consequence of their crass arrogance and blatant antagonism they sinned at the most severe level, so much so that their cup of transgression and guilt was filled to the brim with their heinous and despicable sins. The God who acted before is the same holy God who will not hesitate to act a second time! Just as God's judgment fell on the Amorites when their sin 'reached its full measure,' so it would fall on the Jewish people when they had filled up the measure of their sins and those of their forefathers (cf. Genesis 15:16; Matthew 23:32).

Someone has ruefully said: 'Nothing could do this more directly or fully than persecuting the preachers of the gospel.' God does not sit idly by while men try to outwit and pull a quick one over him; he does not stand back and act as if nothing has ever happened.

If the truth be told, they get their comeuppance, for Paul says *the wrath of God has come upon them at last.* Reading a statement of intent like that sends shivers down the spine, and we break out into a cold sweat. What kind of wrath is this? Down through the years many Bible commentators have come up with all sorts of weird and wonderful ideas. Generally speaking, there are four main views:

* Historical—it could refer to the Babylonian captivity in and around the sixth-century BC.

However, I think that dateline is too far removed from Paul's day and generation; it is much too obscure for it to carry any real clout.

* Prophetical—it could refer to Jerusalem's destruction in AD 70.

It is difficult to see how this would affect Jews outside the region of Judea. The damage limitation would be restricted to a given geographical area and would not necessarily impinge on those living beyond those borders.

- Eschatological—it could refer to Christ's coming in judgment.

The proponents of this view see it as a reference to events surrounding the second advent of Christ. It has to be said that such a strike at the heart of Judaism would be confined only to the Jews alive at the time.

- Soteriological—it could refer to God's eternal wrath in exactly the same way as the apostle John spoke of it (cf. John 3:18, 36).

This view is my preferred option. One where the outcome is so certain, it is guaranteed. There is no last minute reprieve letting them off the hook that Paul sees it as a present reality.

According to 1:10, God's wrath is future, but here it appears to be past. The use of the words *has come* is clearly indicative of the fact that, so far as God is concerned, the whole judgment scenario has already happened (cf. Romans 8:30 for a similar use of this tense). Basically, it conveys the sober and solemn idea as outlined by J. B. Phillips that 'the wrath of God is over their heads.'

Richard Mayhue, in his fine commentary, has this to say by way of summary: 'Those who reject the gospel or refuse to let it be preached will know the eternal wrath of God to the extreme, while those who believe the gospel will be rescued altogether from experiencing God's wrath.'

2:17-18 TANGLED EMOTIONS

In these last few verses, Paul gives the inside story of his tangled emotions. I am just so glad that Paul was as honest as he was. There were times when he was scared stiff and other occasions when he bubbled with joy. I sometimes wonder where the misguided idea ever arose that Paul was a stern, cold individual. We cannot read this letter without sensing the genuine warmth of his heart and the voluminous depth of his love.

At the time of writing, Paul was ministering alone in sin city, promiscuous Corinth. He was feeling the incredible loneliness of that moment. His mind was working overtime as he thought about his very dear friends further north in Thessalonica. It gave Paul no pleasure leaving the city, for he had not gone voluntarily. On the contrary, he was dragged out of the place kicking and screaming.

Paul was not in the least ashamed to admit that he loved these folk, they meant so much to him. He felt a sense of bereavement because he could not be with them. His heart was with them and he wanted his body to return to where his heart was. They may have been out of sight, but they definitely were not out of his mind.

He felt deprived because he did not have a chance to say a proper goodbye, so he longed to return. From his perspective he was on the receiving end of an enforced raw deal, the rough end of the stick. It was a brutal experience and not one that he would have chosen in the normal course of events.

He felt like an orphan as he hinted quite openly by using the word *bereft*. It speaks of an unnatural kind of separation, both forcible and extremely painful. The prefix on the original Greek term intensifies it so that it literally means 'to be torn away from.' Perhaps a better translation of this word would be 'kidnapped.' When Paul left the Thessalonians, he felt shanghaied.

Between a rock and hard place

It was an unbelievably difficult experience for him and it must have had a distressing influence on them; if it was traumatic for him, it must have been unthinkably tough for them. Paul desperately wanted to stay and minister to them but the enemy drove him out. Events were outside his control and there was little or nothing he could do about them. He tried to return but, again and again, his path was solidly blocked, there was just no way through. Humanly speaking, it was impossible!

There were many obstacles strewn across the road and Satan effectively stopped him from making any headway. Some of the translations prefer to use the word 'hindered' in this context. Such a word is used in a military sense of breaking up or cluttering up a road so as to make it impassable to the opposing army.

So far as Paul was concerned, this was intense spiritual warfare and the enemy was lying in ambush to attack him. He was in serious danger of being caught in the crossfire. Paul lays the blame fairly and squarely at the devil's door when he says that he is the one responsible for thwarting his valiant and persistent attempts to make contact with them. There have been many opinions offered as to the precise reason for this minor inconvenience, a hiccup in Paul's well laid plans—a blip on his travel schedule.

At the end of the day the reason why is down to pure conjecture on our part; the indisputable fact is that it happened and that was that! It has been well said: 'When God is at work, Satan is surely alongside.' What Christ was building in terms of the church, the devil was committed to destroying. It is not surprising then to see Satan so visible and with such a high profile in so many local churches in the New Testament.

Satan is alive and well

A quick look at Scripture indicates that Satan's chief activity and goal in our life is twofold: he'll do all in his power to get us to think differently to biblical truth and, consequently, to act disobediently to God's will. He attempts to accomplish this end through four basic strategies:

- by twisting the truth of God's word (cf. Matthew 4:1-11),
- by tarnishing the testimony of God's people (cf. Acts 5:1-11),
- by trashing a believer's zeal to accomplish God's work (cf. 2 Corinthians 12:7-10), and
- by thinning down the effectiveness of God's church (cf. Luke 22:3-6).

Those are four hugely effective pincer movements on the part of the devil! The encouraging fact is that Paul has been able to discern between God closing a door to ministry and Satan blocking the way.

That is true but it still leaves one question lurking in the front of our mind, how can we explain such a terribly frustrating incident? There is only one possible explanation—the overruling providence of the Lord. As Philip Arthur writes: 'Although his movements are circumscribed by the sovereign purposes of God, Satan has an objective reality and is permitted, in measure, to hamper the servants of God.' The Lord sees tomorrow, we only see today.

Our disappointments are his appointments.

A pupil in God's school of hard knocks

It goes without saying that God had something better, much better, for him; there was something around the next curve on life's road that he could not yet see. We need to always remind ourselves that God permits Satanic opposition.

An obvious example is the moving story of Job — a man who lost everything: his family, his home, and his health. But God allowed it to happen. It was true of Job and it is certainly true of Paul that God gave the go-ahead for this to take place but he ultimately used it to bring Paul closer to himself.

Paul learned a whole range of vital lessons through this traumatic and devastating experience. God in his wisdom used this distressing episode to teach Paul some unforgettable lessons in the school of life, lessons which he probably could not learn any other way. So what did he do?

He did not look back and pine and give in to guilt feelings of regret and remorse. Rather, he looked forward with anticipation, he looked ahead with a keen sense of expectancy in his heart, and rejoiced. Paul is not deterred, he is not put off; the thought of throwing the towel into the ring does not even enter his mind.

2:19-20 TOMORROW'S WORLD

He has a joyful hope that is undiminished by all the seemingly insurmountable, immovable problems. He scanned the distant horizon and saw his dear friends from Thessalonica in the intimate presence of his Lord in heaven. One writer says: 'In a sudden burst of energy, Paul breaks out in hallelujahs over the Thessalonians. To demonstrate the ultimate in commitment and love, Paul asks one question in three parts.'

For what is our hope, our joy, or the crown in which we will glory in the presence of the Lord Jesus Christ when he comes? Is it not you? And then he gives us the answer we've all been waiting for when he affirms, *Indeed, you are our glory and joy.*

Moffat's Law

Robert Moffat (1795-1883), Scottish missionary to Southern Africa, when asked to sign a young woman's autograph book, wrote the following:

> *My album is a savage breast*
> *Where tempests brood and shadows rest*
> *Without one ray of light.*
> *To write the name of Jesus there*
> *And see that savage bow in prayer*
> *And point to worlds more bright and fair,*
> *This is my soul's delight.*

Moffat does not anticipate a crown for his work with them—they are his crown!

We'll meet again...

I think most of us realise that Paul had many spiritual hopes which were all bound up in the will of the God of hope (cf. Romans 15:13). In one way or another all these hopes relate to the believer's progress towards our ultimate salvation of being with the Lord. For example, Paul hoped in:

- the glory of God (cf. Romans 5:2),
- righteousness (cf. Galatians 5:5),
- salvation (cf. Colossians 1:5),
- Jesus Christ (cf. 1 Timothy 1:1),
- eternal life (cf. Titus 3:7), and
- the Second Coming of Christ (cf. Titus 2:13).

But right here, Paul's hope is specifically focused on God's unique work in their life. He and others paid a dear price personally for their spiritual progress and he had high hopes that one day salvation's work would be completed in a final sense.

They brightened his day

They were a source of unparalleled joy to Paul and his colleagues. In fact, Paul is singing from the same song sheet as John when he writes in his tiny third epistle that he found no greater joy than seeing his children walk in truth (cf. 3 John 4). Paul speaks of the believers in Philippi in much the same way (cf. Philippians 4:1). Paul often found occasion to rejoice in the Lord (cf. 1 Corinthians 1:31); he revelled and rejoiced in the hope of the glory of God (cf. Romans 5:2); there was never a day went by when he did not rejoice with a sense of profound gratitude for the cross of Christ (cf. Galatians 6:14); and he often rejoiced in the lives of those to whom he had the rare privilege of ministering (cf. 2 Thessalonians 1:4; 2 Corinthians 9:2).

To crown it all…

They not only brought unsurpassed joy into his life, but he also sees them as his crown! The crown we are talking about here is not the royal diadem which we read of in Revelation 19:12, that is reserved for the head of the sovereign Lord Jesus, the King of kings. It is more like the simple garland or wreath worn by the victor as the top prize in some athletic contest—the equivalent of winning a gold medal in the Olympic games of the modern era.

The Greek word *stephanos* indicates various aspects of our 'so great salvation.' A concordance will show there are five key references to this crown in the Bible: one, the imperishable wreath that celebrates salvation's victory over corruption (cf. 1 Corinthians 9:25); two, the righteous wreath that celebrates salvation's victory over unrighteousness (cf. 2 Timothy 4:8); three, the unfading wreath of glory that celebrates salvation's victory over defilement (cf. 1 Petet 5:4); four, the wreath of life that celebrates salvation's victory over death (cf. James 1:12; Revelation 2:10); and, five, the wreath of exultation which celebrates salvation's victory over every kind of persecution of believers (cf. 1 Thessalonians 2:19-20).

Seeing events through the lens of eternity

What a breathtakingly beautiful vision the Lord in his tender love and grace gave to Paul. It was just what he needed; it changed his outlook giving him a brand new perspective on life in the here and now because he caught a glimpse of the there and then. The truth of the matter is that troubles and trials will come; they are par for the course for every one of us who love the Lord.

In such moments we need to take a long view of things. We need to view them from the vantage point of heaven. That is how Paul lived.

He wanted to shape tomorrow, so he started today.

He planned not for the short term, but for the longer term. Paul mapped out clear goals for himself and his ministry and he went for them one by one. Obviously, all these activities were subject to the overruling will of God in his life; nevertheless, Paul's actions today were governed by what God may do tomorrow.

In spite of what some of them were saying about him in the church at Thessalonica, he knew that one day Christ would return to reward him. That is what kept him going, it was all the incentive he needed.

The real saints in the church would bring glory to the Lord and, at the same time, bring immense joy to his heart. They would become his crown of rejoicing, something he would gladly lay down at the feet of Jesus. It is on this wonderful event that Paul could hang his hope.

Pastor and people

We have seen in this lengthy section how Paul responds to his critics. In the course of his many comments, he has illustrated his pastoral ministry by four superb metaphors: the steward, the mother, the father, and the herald.

- As a steward, he was faithful in guarding the gospel.
- As a mother, he was gentle in caring for his converts.
- As a father, he was diligent in educating them.
- As a herald, he was bold in proclaiming God's truth.

Paul referred to his message three times in this chapter as *the gospel of God* and two times as *the word of God*. He had no doubts in his mind that his message came from the Lord; he knew that 'his' gospel was in reality 'God's' gospel. He did not invent it, he did not concoct it, and he did not put it all together. In fact, it had little or nothing to do with him; he was only a steward entrusted with it and a herald commissioned to proclaim it.

Above everything else, he must be faithful to this calling. I believe John Stott hits the nail on the head when he writes: 'Every authentic Christian ministry begins here, with the conviction that we have been called to handle God's word as its guardians and heralds.'

There is no way that we can ever be satisfied with 'rumours of God' as a plausible substitute for 'good news from God.' For as the great theologian reformer John Calvin put it: 'The gospel…is as far removed from conjecture as heaven is from the earth.' It is true that we are not apostles of Christ in the sense that Paul was, but we do believe that the baton has passed from them to us. We are, therefore, trustees of this apostolic faith which is the word of God, and which works powerfully in those who believe. Our primary task is to keep it, study it, expound it, apply it, and obey it.

We also have a high level of commitment to the people of God. We have seen how Paul expressed his deep love for them, he felt and acted towards them as if they were his own children; he was like a mother and father to them. He fed and taught them; he earned his own living so as not to be a burden to them; he was concerned to see them grow into maturity; he was gentle and sacrificial in all his dealings with them.

When we put them both together, we discover that we are ministers of the word of God and ministers of the church of God. Another way of expressing the same thing is that the two chief characteristics of pastoral ministry are truth and love.

Truth is hard if it is not softened by love, and love is soft if it is not strengthened by truth.

Danger of losing out

It is interesting to note that when we become so intense in fighting our battles that we become grim and forlorn, we can lose three things. One is our hope. As we come to believe that we will never make it through the struggle, we begin to feel defeated and we end up with the Monday morning blues that last a lot longer than a single day.

We also lose our hunger for God's word. As our joy decreases, so our desire to read, study, and believe his truth diminishes. In the middle of all this we also lose our sense of humour. We begin to take ourselves too seriously and we fail to take God seriously enough. It is imperative that we face all our struggles with a joyful hope that no person or thing can take away from us. Such a wonderful prospect should spur us on. It should put the sparkle back into our life, rejuvenating us, recharging our spiritual batteries. What a tremendous motivation. Jesus is coming again!

O yes, we will have our ups and downs, we will have our problems with people, we will have many hassles down here, but take heart, get excited, the Lord is surely coming. And until that day dawns and the shadows flee away, we have three resources—a biblical faith, a wonderful family, and a fantastic future.

CHAPTER THREE
UP IN A DOWN WORLD

In chapter 3 Paul gives some assurances about affliction that are neither bland nor blasé, but biblical; and, in the second half of the chapter, where he focuses on truth about the tempter, we will discover some fascinating insights into our age-old enemy—our adversary, the devil.

Basically, it is all about finding our feet and learning to stand on them. We need to be grounded—established—in the faith so that when the stormy winds of trial blow in our face, we do not fall flat. Consequently, Paul shows us the path to spiritual maturity, the road down which we must go to attain spiritual advancement.

'Mere soul saving is easy—what is difficult is making those converts into soldiers, saints, and soul-winners!' (C. T. Studd)

The key word in this chapter is located in verses 2 and 13—*strengthen*. The key verse is verse 8: *For now we really live, since you are standing firm in the Lord*. There is one little phrase which appears five times in the space of ten verses—*your faith*—that is both significant and suggestive:

- the profession of your faith (verse 2);
- the examination of your faith (verse 5);
- the proclamation of your faith (verse 6);
- the consolation of your faith (verse 7);
- and the additions to your faith (verse 10).

3:1 ABSENCE MAKES THE HEART...

It is patently obvious that Paul's heart pined for them. He knew a measure of felt pain because he could not be with them—he was distraught. In fact, it became so bad that he was buckling under; it seemed as though he could not stand the strain one minute more. The sound of silence was far from golden; it was unbearable and the suspense of wondering how things were going was proving too much for him to handle. The whole experience was pushing him over the edge.

Paul was much more than cheesed off. He was so frustrated he found himself at breaking point. About to snap, he longed for a measure of release and relief. Let's remember, he could not pick up the phone and call them for a chin-wag, nor could he jump on his Harley and drive north. Poor Paul, he could not even send a fax or communicate by email!

Imagine life before Internet broadband (DSL) and Outlook!

The preacher was in Athens and on the verge of going further south to Corinth, but his heart was up north in Thessalonica. He knew where he preferred to be—where he wanted to be—because they meant so much to him. They were his baby! That explains why he feels totally overwhelmed with an abject sense of inconsolable desolation. Abandoned. Deflated. Alone.

The thought behind the Greek word for *left* is that it describes what happens when parents die and their children are left as orphans. The implication behind his refreshingly honest comment is that Paul is passing through something akin to a bereavement. In other words, a big part of him is missing. So what does he do?

3:2 ALL ALONE IN ATHENS

Well, rather than go himself—the easy option—Paul stays where he is and, instead, sends young Timothy on his behalf. Not an easy decision for a man in his sandals to make. On past experience, Athens was not Paul's favourite location. He had been alone there once before. On that occasion, his escort left him to find his own way about town—a very painful and unnerving experience it proved to be (cf. Acts 17:15).

Such a city was a demanding place for any evangelist—it was a hotbed of intellectual activity, and his whole being felt oppressed and provoked by the unbelievable idolatry that prevailed in the place. It was a cesspool of iniquity. That said, his sermon on Mars Hill at a meeting of the Areopagus is quite brilliant. Preacher Paul took them on using their own intellectual games and beat them hollow (cf. Acts

17:22-34). He started where they were—the unknown God—but he quickly took them right to the heart of the Christian gospel—God in Jesus Christ can be known. Paul had a handful of converts in Athens, but it was not overly encouraging—no wonder there is no epistle to the Athenians!

Paul did not have any realistic alternative—he was suffering from information underload; so, bearing in mind his insatiable thirst for news, this was the best plan he could come up with. Even though he shrank from it, it was the lesser of two evils. He knew that Timothy would be able to see them, and when he got there, he could enquire as to their spiritual health.

Paul is not unduly concerned about their comfort; he is not too alarmed about their welfare; he is not stressed-out about their prosperity. Those things are important, but not all important. It is their faith that he is most interested in; it is their day-by-day relationship with the Lord that matters most to him. Surely that is symptomatic of a father's love for his spiritual children.

Short-term missionary

He could not have chosen anyone better than Timothy. As they say, he was a chip off the old block, a man after his own heart. Actually, what the older man Paul has to say about the much-younger Timothy in Philippians 2:20 speaks volumes about him, 'I have no one else like him who takes a genuine interest in your welfare.'

In one sense, he was Paul's trouble shooter, an emissary, a kind of special agent. Paul reckoned if something was broken in their local fellowship, this young man would be the ideal person to fix it.

It is intriguing to see how Paul describes someone a number of years his junior; after all, Paul was old enough to be his father and, more often than not, he treated him in a very fatherly way! This microchip description stores a world of priceless information about Timothy's character. Paul gives him a superb reference.

• Our brother

He was a saved man in the family of God. It is obvious they enjoyed a sweet relationship with each other. It was a sheer joy and genuine delight for Paul to have him as his right-hand man. We see something here of the dignity of his role in life for he is the Lord's. In spite of his youth, he had a stable relationship with the Lord.

- God's fellow worker

He was a team player—they were fellows! He was a servant, unafraid of hard work. This man had the sterling qualities needed to effectively minister to young believers. He had patience, and lots of it, for Timothy realised you get the chicken by hatching the egg, not by smashing it. His first-rate dedication to whatever assignment the Lord entrusted to him was combined with a measure of love and grace in his heart.

Timothy would become Paul's protégé and one of the early church's first pastors.

What was his task? It was twofold. One, it was to strengthen the believers as they were weak at the knees. The Greek verb *to strengthen* was an almost technical term for the consolidation and building up of new converts; it means 'to shore up, to buttress.' These good folk needed built up.

Two, he was also to *encourage* the church because they were low in spirit. They needed a boost and he was despatched in order to comfort them and cheer them up.

3:3-4 THE ROUGH WITH THE SMOOTH

The primary objective of Timothy's mission was so *that no one would be unsettled by these trials.* Paul yearns for them to stand firm—stand fast—in the Lord. He has a fair idea what they are passing through and he is all too aware of the devastating consequences such difficult times can bring in their wake. He knows it could make or break them.

The Greek word *unsettle* was used at first of dogs wagging their tail and so came to mean 'flatter, or fawn upon' and, therefore, 'deceive.' Satan is more dangerous when he flatters than when he frowns. Paul was extremely worried that their sufferings might lead them astray from Christ. John Stott suggests: 'Perhaps the best way to protect people from being upset by tribulation is to remind them that it is a necessary part of our Christian vocation.'

Nagging away at the back of Paul's mind was the ugly thought that they might have succumbed to this unrelenting pressure. Would they be shaken to the core by their experiences? Would they be persuaded to abandon their Christian profession? If they did, life in the short term would be a whole lot easier for them!

Perhaps, like the followers of Jesus in every period of history, they were tempted to jump to unwarranted conclusions about the character and nature of the Lord himself—either he does not have the power or the will to prevent the suffering, or he is not strong enough to shield me from tribulation, or he does not care what happens to little me anyway! Paul's unqualified response is that suffering is an integral part—an essential component—of the unfolding purpose of God for all his children.

It's hurting, Lord

Paul moves on to deal with the perplexing problem of affliction. *You know quite well that we were destined for them. In fact, when we were with you, we kept telling you that we would be persecuted. And it turned out that way, as you well know.*

The apostle handles troubles, as we would expect from a man of his calibre, when he combines a sensitive heart with a common sense approach. He is both tactful and tender. Paul gives them a word of assurance by informing them that affliction and trial is inevitable for the Christian. There is no getting away from it.

The Christian life is not a Sunday School picnic nor is it one big spiritual Disneyland.

It was never intended to be. Following Jesus is not an easy alternative to life. The chances of us being 'carried to the skies on flowery beds of ease' are nil. Rather, says Paul, troubles and trials will come, and when they do, they will hurt. We cannot avoid them; we cannot play hide-and-seek with them. They are part and parcel of every believer's experience.

They are our portion, according to Philippians 1:29, where Paul says, 'For it has been granted to you on behalf of Christ not only to believe on him, but also to suffer for him.' In a different sense, they are a privilege, according to Philippians 3:10, where Paul describes them as 'the fellowship of sharing in Christ's sufferings.' And in a strange kind of way, they are our power, as in 2 Corinthians 12:9, where Paul confirms that '[God's] grace is sufficient for you, for [his] power is made perfect in weakness. Therefore I will boast all the more gladly about my weaknesses, so that Christ's power may rest on me.'

Divine intruder

Paul talks about our attitude, our mindset, by saying that we were *destined* for such times of disquiet. If you like, we had them coming to us, they were coming our way, come what may. It is not the luck of the draw, nor is it a question of pulling the shortest straw. These traumatic experiences were not just sheer bad luck or even an uncontrollable conspiracy.

When trials intrude into our life and invade our privacy, they are not accidents waiting to happen. Rather, they are sent to us by divine appointment. A trial in court is a royal commission.

'God's love letters are often sent in black-trimmed envelopes.' (C. H. Spurgeon)

Nothing happens to us by chance, and there is nothing that can be slotted into a pigeon-hole labelled 'coincidence.' Everything—the best of times, the worst of times—what we like, what we do not like—is a vital part of the outworking of God's plan for our life. If anything, they are a God-incidence. They are well within the scope of the perfect will of God and can all be attributed to the sovereign providence of a loving heavenly Father.

My Father planned it all

When we find ourselves with more questions than answers in our mind, we need to recognise God's purpose in it all. In God's goodness he has something to teach us; there is always a timely lesson to be learned. Remember Joseph! His brothers meant it for evil, but the

Lord had a few other ideas up his sleeve (cf. Genesis 50:20). From the divine vantage point, it would ultimately be for Joseph's good and benefit. And it was! It is Romans 8:28 being activated as a powerful principle in our life. When we rise to the occasion on a plane, we find that behind the dark threatening clouds, the sun still shines brightly.

We also need to realise his perfection. David was thoroughly convinced of this. After he was hunted and hounded by his enemies, he was able to write, 'As for God, his way is perfect' (Psalm 18:30). It was not the easiest way for David, far from it; but it was the best way.

And we need to rest on the divine promise. When we compare Romans 8:18 with all that we are going through at this point in time, everything is brought sharply into focus. Paul says, 'I consider that our present sufferings are not worth comparing with the glory that will be revealed in us.' The problems remain, but they last only for a brief moment in the light of an eternity spent in the near presence of the Lord. It may be devastating and demeaning down here, but it cannot be compared to the glory that will be ours when we reach the other side. The hurts of this life will be followed by hallelujahs in the next!

Bespoke trials

When we do all of that, we can rejoice in God's gracious provision. The Lord knows how much we can take, and he will send us no more than we can bear. Our trials are tailor-made—personalised—for God in his infinite wisdom deals with us individually.

F. B. Meyer expressed this truth well: 'The sweetest scents are only obtained by tremendous pressure; the fairest flowers grow amid Alpine snow-solitudes; the rarest gems have suffered longest from the lapidary's wheel; the noblest statues have borne most blows of the chisel.'

The Lord does not make the back for the burden—he makes each burden to suit the back.

'Til the storm passes by

Paul makes an assessment of the situation. The Greek word Paul used for *persecuted* speaks of intense pain; it conveys the idea of crippling heartache and enduring hardness. It has the basic thought of being often found in a perilous situation where the pressures come from both without and within. It is when we feel buffeted from every possible direction. It does not matter where we turn, we cannot run away from it. When the troubles come, our comfort zone gets the squeeze. We know all about it when it happens.

I take immense comfort from the fact that God is not in the least bit interested in watching our faith get torpedoed by all sorts of trials; the fact is, every test is designed by God to elasticise our faith. When real faith is stretched, it does not break, and when it is pressed, it does not fail.

As Paul himself admitted, we may be knocked down, but we will never be knocked out. Not for us the shame of being counted out on the canvas (cf. 2 Corinthians 4:9). Perhaps the moving words written from the heart of Andraè Crouch (1950-) sum it up best:

> *I thank God for the mountains*
> *And I thank him for the valleys,*
> *I thank him for the storms he brought me through.*
> *For if I'd never had a problem,*
> *I wouldn't know that he could solve them,*
> *I'd never know what faith in God could do.*

He continues:

> *Through it all, through it all,*
> *O I've learned to trust in Jesus,*
> *I've learned to trust in God.*
> *Through it all, through it all,*
> *I've learned to depend upon his word.*

3:5 TRUTH ABOUT THE TEMPTER

Paul then reminds them of his prime reason for sending Timothy on a special fact-finding mission to them. *For this reason, when I could stand it no longer, I sent to find out about your faith.* In other words, it was all becoming too much for Paul—he had had enough. He could not stand the heat so it was best for him to get out of the kitchen! In moments like that, we think we have to justify our feelings, and Paul in this instance was no exception. He is a man like the rest of us!

Paul changes tack when he writes along these lines, *I was afraid that in some way the tempter might have tempted you and our efforts might have been useless.* Paul bares his heart as he opens up and shares with us the major concern that has gripped him. The Greek word translated *tempt* can be neutral in the sense of 'test,' or negative in the sense of 'lure.' God tests, Satan lures! Because it is obvious that Paul is talking about the devil, the avowed intent of the enemy is to disable their faith by deceitfully drawing them into sin; he wants to disarm them by testing them with a host of malicious intentions.

Paul did not at any time underestimate the power of Satan. He knew only too well that what had earlier occurred in the idyllic setting of the garden of Eden could also repeat itself in their little church fellowship. Paul reminds us with some straight talking that the devil is alive and kicking.

If we have any lingering doubts, we need only ask the good folk in the church at Thessalonica for their considered opinion; they are in a position to respond because they are the ones who have been on the receiving end. Day after day the devil made a nuisance of himself in their extremely delicate situation. No matter where they turned, no matter what they did, he never seemed too far away. He was ever loitering with intent. A real pain in the neck; a thorn in their flesh.

His overt aim was always to make them stumble. The devil was only happy when they were the epitome of misery.

The devil was committed to wiping the smile off their face.

Ring fencing the devil

God's policy is unmistakably clear and concise with regard to the tempter. Three unassailable facts:
- his scope is God-determined—he can go so far and no further,
- his sphere is God-defined—he can go so near and no closer,
- his strength is God-dictated—he can do so much and no more.

Each of these truths is vitally important to our understanding of the work of Satan in relation to the Christian. Having said that, we rejoice at this point in time that, because of Calvary, the tempter's power is broken.

Ever wondered, what is the devil's line of attack? How does he strike at us? Paul said elsewhere in one of his epistles, 'I write so that Satan might not outwit you, for we are not unaware of his schemes.'

It was the humorist Oscar Wilde who quipped: 'I can resist everything except temptation.'

On the Wilde side

The story is told of the little boy whose mother told him not to go swimming as he had a bad head cold. The doorbell rang and Johnny went off with his friends. Later on his mother passed the spot where the boys were splashing around in the pond. She could not believe her eyes when she saw her son in the water alongside them. She stopped the car and shouted for him to come and explain himself.

Dripping wet, he blurted out to his mother: 'Mum, I'm sorry, I didn't mean to disobey you.' She retorted: 'Well, if you didn't mean to disobey me, why did you bring your swimming trunks with you? Why didn't you leave them at home in the bottom drawer?' Johnny thought for a moment and then he said: 'I'm really sorry, mum, but I brought them with me just in case I was tempted...'

It goes without saying but temptation is the oldest of all the internal conflicts that rage in the heart of man. Sometimes, like little Johnny, it seems we tempt ourselves, or at least put ourselves in harm's way. It does not matter who we are, it stalks every single one of us. None of us is immune! I am as vulnerable as the man next door.

Oscar Wilde was not the only one who had to cope with that particular weakness, as the same was true of Mark Antony. He was known as the silver-throated orator of Rome. He was credited with the accolade of a brilliant man, as well as being a strong leader and a courageous soldier. Having said that, he had one gaping hole in his armour—one chink—he lacked strength of character. On the outside, he was powerful and impressive; on the inside, weak and vulnerable.

His tutor is reputed to have been so enraged on one occasion that he shouted at him: 'O Marcus, O colossal child, able to conquer the world but unable to resist a temptation.'

Most of us know the sequel to the story, for his most widely known and costly temptation sailed up the river to him on a barge. Cleopatra captured his unguarded heart, and their sinful relationship cost him his wife, his place as a world leader and, ultimately, his life.

Surprise, surprise

Now, when it comes to our door, the enemy may choose to surprise us. The classic example is David and Bathsheba. It was the most unlikely moment when David was caught napping. His guard was down. He was torn apart in a moment of time when least expecting it. It only took a split second for him to court spiritual disaster.

The devil may use the siege method. His intentions are crystal clear from Daniel 7:25 where we are reminded that 'he shall wear out the saints.' Constant pressure can crack us. We break up, then break down, and he breaks in. He tells us that our circumstances are far too difficult, and our past failures have weakened us too much. He highlights our inability to overcome some besetting sin. His tactics are to wear us down until we can take no more. The devil is no fool; he knows our weakest point and he can always locate with pinpoint accuracy the chink in our armour.

Satan knows our Achilles heel.

Another tactic is for him to use the subtle line of attack. The wily devil is the past master of disguise. When he approaches us, dressed as an angel of light, he makes sin look innocuously innocent. Remember our first parents, Adam and Eve, in the pacific Garden of Eden? Instead of fresh fruit they found toxic poison; instead of a contented smile of satisfaction they found hang-your-head shame; instead of immense pleasure they found intense pain.

In Matthew 4 he attempted to trip up the Lord Jesus by adopting similar scare tactics. He told him to turn the stones into bread and go before the will of God; he told him to throw himself down from the pinnacle of the temple and go beyond the will of God; he told him to bow down before him and see the kingdoms of the world and go behind the will of God. We know the sequel! Thank God, the adversary was unsuccessful on all three counts.

> *Trust God when the tempter is near,*
> *Trust in him for grace to turn aside,*
> *Trust God mid the billows of life,*
> *A refuge to provide.*

Now we see why Paul did what he did by despatching young Timothy as his special envoy. Like pieces in a jigsaw, it all fits neatly into place. It all comes together, and when it does, it makes a lot of sense.

3:6 JUST WHAT THE DOCTOR ORDERED

At this juncture Timothy has returned, his important assignment ably carried out. *But Timothy has just now come to us from you and has brought good news about your faith and love. He has told us that you always have pleasant memories of us and that you long to see us, just as we also long to see you.*

Evangelist Tom Hayes notes that faith and love run side by side in Timothy's report:

- they go together (verse 6);
- they grow together (verse 8); and
- they flow together (verse 9).

Timothy has done the job Paul asked him to do and the news he brings back could not be better. The phrase *good news* is the same we use when we speak of the glorious gospel of Christ. Glad tidings. I was intrigued to find that this is the only time the word is used in the New Testament when it does not specifically refer to the gospel. When Paul heard Timothy's glowing report, he felt as if he was being saved all over again. Such is the Damascus Road effect it had on him.

Without any hyperbole, or any stretch of the imagination, or any hint of exaggeration, Paul is like a brand new man—euphorically ecstatic, deliriously jubilant, and totally rejuvenated. This was the morale booster he desperately needed; as they say, it was just what the doctor ordered! It was like a proverbial tonic to his soul, it really thrilled him. It was comparable to him being drenched with a refreshing spring shower.

Heart of gold, feet of clay

We are inclined to forget that Paul was made of the same material as the rest of us. We elevate these men into super saints, when the fact of the matter is they are made of exactly the same stuff as we lesser lights. We put the Lord's servants on a pedestal when in reality their feet are standing on the same old world as ours.

When we read between the lines, it would appear that Paul was having one of his off days; he was on a real downer. The blues! He was utterly depressed and extremely disheartened. Discouraged to the nth degree. His outlook changed, however, when he heard the brilliant news from Timothy. It did the trick. With his battery recharged, it set the adrenaline flowing through his veins. Now he is back to his usual good self. To Paul, dumped right in the middle of his arid wasteland of personal loneliness, Timothy's report was a lush oasis of hope. What an encouragement!

The preacher man got a second wind.

Like cold water to a thirsty soul

Timothy has talked about their faith and love and given a clear indication that they were really going on well with the Lord. They were enthusiastically reaching out to others in the community. In many areas of gospel ministry, they were like the pioneer of modern missions, William Carey, in that they lengthened the cords and strengthened the stakes. They were tirelessly active in the work of God. People on the go, running and gunning for God.

On a spiritual level, they were alive and well. It appears they were standing firm against the world's erosion. They had pleasant memories of Paul and his brief visit with them. It meant so much to Paul because at this point he was feeling low and rejected, dejected and forgotten. You see, Paul had his moments when he wondered, is it really worth it?

There were many times in Paul's life when he felt as though he was well past his sell-by date. His mind was in overdrive on the fast lane of life where so many issues were blown out of all proportion. Mind you, the longer he wallowed in his deep slimy pit of despair, the more introverted and self-conscious he became. He felt as if he had really blown it, big time, and that he was just a wretched failure coming apart at the seams.

Now Timothy reassures him that the folk remember him with fond affection and they, likewise, hoped that their paths would cross again. Whether we are a Paul or not, we all need to feel accepted and sense that our ministry is appreciated. The best of men are only men at their best! The question is, what impact did this all have on the apostle? I think it was like a bridge in that it helped him reach the other side.

3:7-8 IRON SHARPENS IRON

Paul is enormously encouraged for he writes, *Therefore, brothers, in all our distress and persecution we were encouraged about you because of your faith.* The apostle talks openly about his personal distress; the idea wrapped up in that Greek word is the kind of trouble that has a crushing effect on a man—he felt as though he had been submerged to such an extent that all talk of keeping his head above water was nonsense. The way he felt, even snorkelling was well nigh impossible.

He then speaks of his persecution, which means the kind of mitigating pressure that has a choking effect on us—he felt strangled. Suppressed. Both words are used together in Job 15:24 where they speak of one who is so terrified and overpowered that their hair stands on end. We find that paralysing combination in the LXX (shorthand for the Septuagint—the Greek translation of the Old Testament).

He was left breathless, as it were. He felt stifled. Muffled. His blood ran cold. But this was the best news he could have possibly heard. Why did Paul feel the way he did? As I hinted earlier, he is in Athens which is not the most user-friendly place to be if you happen to be a preacher, and to make matters a million times worse, the poor guy is very much on his own. Paul has had one harrowing experience after another of apparent defeat since he set foot on the soil of the continent of Europe. His situation seemed to spiral from bad to worse.

Sure, he promptly responded to the Macedonian call, but he got a lot more than he bargained for; it was one trial hard on the heels of another. Any clear thinking man would automatically question all this in his own mind. He could be forgiven for asking himself:

- did he get it wrong?
- did he misread the leading of God?
- did he mistake what God was saying to him?

So…this fantastic news from Timothy was just the pick-me-up he needed. His life was wrapped up in theirs to such a degree that he was one with them. That is the gist of his comments in verse 8 where he seemingly shouts at the top of his voice, *For now we really live, since you are standing firm in the Lord.*

No matter what angle we view it from, this is body ministry, pure and simple. Paul is energised to such a degree that it would appear as though he has been given a total new lease of life — a heavy burden has been lifted off his sagging shoulders. That little phrase speaks volumes for it tells us that a troubled, tension-filled servant of Christ felt able to relax one more time. To breathe normally. Perhaps he also felt that, after all, his life was not in vain, that in laying it out for the sake of the gospel he was not spending himself to no purpose.

3:9-10 LOST FOR WORDS

Because of this welcome development, he is able to break forth into a paean of praise. Paul asks a rhetorical question, *How can we thank God enough for you in return for all the joy we have in the presence of our God because of you?* He says a sincere thank you to the Lord for them and it is worth noting that this is his first reaction to the uplifting news that Timothy has shared with him. It naturally leads him into praise and thanksgiving mode. It not only seemed the proper thing to do, but it was the right thing to do! The Thessalonians mean more to him than words can tell.

He is not speechless, but he is lost for words when he thinks about them. He says, *how can we thank God enough for you?* It would have been so easy for Paul to have taken a different line. He could, for instance, have congratulated the young believers on their staying power. For that matter, he could have patted himself on the back and waxed lyrical in personal congratulation, 'See what a great church I've planted!'

In fact, the approach adopted in this passage was typical of the apostle Paul. It illustrates the fact that he understood the reality of the prevailing situation. God made these believers what they were; the credit was his, and his alone. The Lord enabled them to step up to the plate.

As a direct result, Paul pours out a never-ending stream of prayer, adoration, and thanksgiving as an offering to God, knowing that he will never be able to fully repay the obligation. God has blessed him more than tongue can tell and the folk in Thessalonica bear eloquent testimony to that. The Psalmist in Psalm 116:12 expressed the same idea when he posed the leading question, 'How can I repay the Lord for all his goodness to me?'

Furthermore, there is profound pastoral sense in Paul's accentuating the positive kind of approach. To be assured that a mature believer like Paul sincerely thanks God for us, I imagine, is a tremendous crank up to most of us. Simply wonderful. It introduces the feel good factor back into our life, but there again, that is the genius of grace. It is mightily encouraging to us without pandering to our innate tendency to self-promotion.

In passing, I believe that Paul was immensely gladdened by the spiritual quality of his friends. As someone has said: 'Christian excellence is a great help to others, for it reminds them that the power of God is at work in a human life. Thus it is not only a source of encouragement but a spur and a challenge.'

Four habits of a successful pray-er

'Prayer does not just enable us to do a greater work for God. Prayer is a greater work for God.' (Thomas Chalmers)

Paul prayed earnestly for them. He did not get down at the side of his bed every night and say, 'Lord, bless my friends away up there in Thessalonica, period.' Many people pray like the man who said,

'Lord, bless me and my wife, our son John and his wife, us four and no more!' On bended knee, Paul considered seriously what these people were going through. He set the problem before the throne of grace and he reminded the Lord of his many promises. Paul took time to reflect on their many needs, both corporate and individual.

Paul prayed frequently for them. We read it was *night and day.* That means while he was working on his goat hair tents and while he was walking the dusty, pot-holed streets of the city, his prayers flowed freely out of a heart of concern and love.

Paul prayed specifically for them. He was definite in his prayer requests. He knew what he wanted for them; he wants to see them again. That is the deep longing of his heart, as there was a refreshing spontaneity about their relationship. They always brought a smile to his face, never a frown. They were number one on his priority list.

A sense of belonging

It shows how much the church meant to him. That is the dynamic relationship—the bond—we should all be pursuing in our regular place of worship. When we meet one another, it is wonderful to say, 'Thank you, Lord, he's my brother, she's my sister.' It is not a back slapping service, nor is it a mutual admiration society. It is a simple realisation that, since we belong to the Lord, we really do belong to each other. Maybe we should take a few moments even now and pray, 'Bind us together, Lord, bind us together with cords that cannot be broken.'

At the end of the day and at the end of his prayer, his all-consuming passion for them is that they might grow in grace and go on well with the Lord. He wants them to make spiritual headway, and that by leaps and bounds. To progress. To develop. Back-pedalling puts us in reverse. And there is no mileage gained by standing still.

Faith in working clothes

Faith is like a muscle, we either use it or lose it!

It is equally true to say that the more we use faith, the stronger it becomes. Faith must be exercised or it will atrophy. Perhaps the best example of that principle is enshrined in the life of the patriarch Abraham:

- he believed God when he had no idea where he was going to end up (cf. Hebrews 11:8);
- he believed God when he did not have a clue how it would all pan out (cf. Hebrews 11:11); and
- he believed God when he could not work out why God led him the way that he did (cf. Hebrews 11:17-19).

God will test our faith to exercise it, not to destroy it, but to develop it. A faith that cannot be tested is a faith that cannot be trusted. The two are like a hand in a glove; suffering clothes faith in Christ—the two are inseparable like conjoined twins. God uses the difficulties we face to refine us and make us more like Jesus. Whatever we are called to go through, we need to remember that God keeps his eye on the clock and the temperature gauge—he knows how long and how hot is just about right for us in the steamy sauna of life.

Missing link

The glaring problem they faced was that there was something missing or *lacking* in their faith. The Greek word for *supply* is rich in meaning and varied in usage. It means 'to fit together, to join, to restore, to repair, to equip.' For example, it is used of reconciling political differences; it is a surgical term for setting bones; it describes the repairing of fishing nets; it is used of making military and naval preparations.

It would appear as though Paul is acting as a medical doctor applying healing balm to people's souls; or he could be seen as a fisherman mending the broken twine of belief; perhaps he could even be portrayed as a military commander instructing the believers to do battle with Satan. That was what Paul prayed, that they might be able to supply what was lacking in their faith.

Imagine his undiluted joy when a relatively short time later he writes them a second letter and he is able to say that God answered his prayer. 'We thank God for you because your faith is growing more and more' (2 Thessalonians 1:3). Let me give you some characteristics of true faith. It is:

- restful—the soul can be satisfied in its secure relationship with

Christ (cf. Hebrews 4:3),

- joyful—we are glad that Jesus is our Lord and Saviour (cf. 1 Peter 1:8),
- hopeful—our faith teaches us that, whilst we are blessed at present, the best is yet to come (cf. Hebrews 11:1),
- loving—Christian qualities complement and encourage each other (cf. Galatians 5:6),
- practical—even though it is inward, it will always show itself in an outward fashion (cf. James 2:20),
- patient—faith affirms that God is the perfect time keeper—he is never early or late, he is always on schedule (cf. Hebrews 6:11),
- victorious—we are walking in the train of his triumph (cf. 1 John 5:4),
- vocal—when we speak, our faith is immediately strengthened (cf. 2 Corinthians 4:13),
- ever growing—the more we exercise it the stronger it will become (cf. 2 Corinthians 10:15).

Faith is not a leap in the dark; it is not a gushy feeling we have at the end of a good meeting. Faith is something that rests on the solid promises of God, then acts on them. Acts of obedience to the word of God are acts of faith. Do we want more faith? Well, there are no shortcuts, read and then obey the word of God, and the more we do that, we can watch our faith grow!

3:11 CAN GOD? GOD CAN!

Here is a moving reminder that Paul has come to the end of himself. He has an overwhelming feeling of personal inadequacy and inability. He knows even though he cannot do it, God can. Is anything too hard for the Lord? He puts the ball back into God's court, for he is the master of the situation; he is able to solve the crisis; he can undo the tangled mess. It is a well-thought-out decision on Paul's part to say, 'Lord, it's over to you!'

Then we read of his consolation. He knew in his heart of hearts that only God could open up the way ahead. The path was littered with many obstacles and lined with many immovable hindrances. On a human level, it was impossible. However, it is in these no-go and no-win areas that God delights to prove his stunning ability; he specialises in dealing with situations just like these. He is the only God who can get us where he wants us to be.

What about his challenge? Well, Paul is resigned to the will of God. He believes that God's way is always the best way. For him there is no viable alternative—anything else is unthinkable. It may not be the easiest path to walk down but, for Paul, God's way is always the preferred option. He reckons it is much better to be alone with God than to be in the crowd without him.

God is bigger than all our problems—before a transcendent God, they are like measly grasshoppers. There is no hill too high for him and no valley too low for him. He is the God who causes Jericho's walls to tumble and, when he does not bring them crashing down, he jumps over them (cf. Psalm 18:29). He is, therefore, God of the impregnable and God of the impassable!

He is God of all our tears and fears.

3:12 LOVE, LOVE, LOVE

Operation Agape is launched in this verse. Paul's prayer shows his all-consuming desire for them is that their love may abound. This is getting our hands dirty in the service of Jesus. It is getting our feet wet in ministering to others in his name.

In this context, we need to remember that suffering is never far from his mind. Suffering is not the only problem; it is how we handle it when it comes knocking at the front door of our life. Sometimes our times of suffering can turn into times of selfishness. We can so quickly become insular, parochial, and self-centred. We become so demanding on those around us that we are hard to live with.

You see, what life does to us depends on what life finds in us. Nothing reveals the true heart of man like the furnace of affliction. Trials will bring out the best in us; they can also bring out the worst. It depends how we react and respond.

When the going gets tough, the tough get going! But where? Some people build a 20-foot wall that cannot be scaled. They shut themselves in and cut themselves off from others. Others, however, build a bridge, enabling them to reach out to others. When they do that they are brought closer to the Lord and to his people. To quote Westy Egmont: 'Conflict plus love equals growth.'

Paul prayed that *their love increase and overflow for each other and for everyone else*. And, wonder of wonders, his prayer was answered. We read all about it in 2 Thessalonians 1:3 where the apostle writes, '... the love every one of you has for each other is increasing.'

Yes, it was Paul's request that their love might be full and over-flowing—a love for one another, a love for those outside the family of God, a love for the unloved and unlovable, for none of us should feel as though people do not care. Jew and Greek, Christian and non-believer. The world is not waiting for advice about how to solve its problems. It is waiting for somebody to listen to it and love it.

It does not matter who or what they are or where they are from, we can love them through Jesus. Actually, it is a command to be obeyed. This was the badge worn on the lapel of their life. They wore their religion on their sleeve. The mark of a healthy church is when others are able to say, 'See how they love each other—and all people.'

Out on a limb

Abounding love must never be bound. It is always reaching out. It expands and is expansive. It is all-embracing. Love always looks after number two, not exclusively after number one. It goes past the call and claim of duty. It goes far beyond the suggested second or third mile. When we share love and show love to other people in an uncon-ditional, unselfish manner, we always walk away the winner. Not only are others enriched, so are we. Duty makes us do things well; but love takes us to a new level when it makes us do them beautifully.

Be realistic! Nine times out of ten, when we love this way, we become very vulnerable. But if we never step out on a limb with peo-ple and take a risk, we will never grasp the yummy fruit of nourishing relationships. In the final analysis, it is God touching men and women, boys and girls, through ordinary people like us. I like the way Charles Swindoll puts it as he uses each of the letters in an acrostic fashion:

- L is for us to listen. That shows itself when we respect and accept people enough to graciously hear what they have to say.
- O is for overlook. This says we should be quick to pass over and forgive the minor, unpleasant flaws in other people's lives.
- V is for value, which indicates a respect and honour we have for the other person. We appreciate them for who they are and we see in them someone for whom the Saviour has died.
- E reminds us to express love, for it is demonstrative. We do not just feel love or say loving things; we show it by doing what is best for the other person.

The church in Thessalonica—a place where faith was vibrant, a fellowship pulsating with life, a congregation where love was warmly felt.

3:13 THE MORNING AFTER...

Paul's final petition is that their life might be holy. Again, this request is closely linked to the soon return of our Lord. It is the second advent of Jesus Christ that is brought sharply into focus, putting everything into proper perspective. He longs that when they stand before the Lord they will be *blameless and holy*. When someone is blameless, there are no blemishes on their life. When someone is holy, there are no blots on their character.

Paul looks forward to that day when we will be called to give an account of the service we have rendered to the Lord (cf. 2 Corinthians 5:10). This is a personal interview with Jesus. Paul is reminding them that they are responsible down here for they will be held accountable up there.

He wants to present us as 'a pure virgin' to Christ (2 Corinthians 11:2). He wants his bride to be a glorious church—'a radiant church'— a church 'without stain or wrinkle or any other blemish' (Ephesians 5:27). Stains are caused by defilement on the outside, and blemishes are caused by decay on the inside. Today's church is not perfect. But then, let's not forget the words of Edward Mote (1797-1874):

When he shall come with trumpet sound,
O may I then in him be found!
Clothed in his righteousness alone,
Faultless to stand before the throne.

In other words, for us to be acceptable to God there in heaven, we must be accepted by God here on earth. There are three grounds for our acceptance. These are:

- the Beloved—Jesus—in whom we are accepted (cf. Ephesians 1:6);
- the belief—the gospel—through which we are accepted (cf. 1 Timothy 1:15); and
- the behaviour—pleasing the Lord—by which we are accepted (cf. 2 Corinthians 5:9).

One day, one glorious morning, Paul's prayer will be finally answered, for we know that 'when he shall appear, we shall be like him, for we shall see him as he is' (1 John 3:2). We shall be Jesus look-a-like's in eternity!

A Trinitarian feel

Paul's aspiration is quite unique—the Trinity is involved in it. He addressed the Father and the Son in verse 11. In verse 12 it is highly probable that '*the* Lord' refers to the Holy Spirit, since '*our* Lord' at the end of verse 13 specifically refers to Jesus Christ. If this is so, then this is the only prayer in the New Testament that is directed to the Holy Spirit!

The normal pattern for prayer is to the Father, through the Son, and in the Holy Spirit. Since the Spirit is the sanctifier of the believer, and this is a prayer for sanctified holy living, the address to the Spirit is proper and certainly not out of place.

Marks of a healthy church

The essence of a good church is:

- knowing answered prayer,
- getting on with the job in hand,
- standing up and being counted for the Lord,

- resolutely facing a myriad of troubles when they arise,
- winning the battle against the enemy,
- showing strength of character,
- having stability in our personal commitment to Jesus,
- keeping an eye on a future eternity, and

- believing the countdown to Christ's coming is getting lower every day.

The outcome is inevitable—our faith will mature, our love will abound, and our life will be holy. That means we will be geared to the times and anchored to the word of God. We are up to speed with current affairs, and we look at events unfolding all around us through the lens of eternity. We are relevant! Says Paul in three punchy statements:

- Grow wiser.
- Grow stronger.
- Grow purer.

CHAPTER FOUR
THE SKY'S NOT THE LIMIT

While on a hazardous South Pole expedition British explorer Sir Ernest Shackleton left a few men on Elephant Island, promising that he would return. Later, when he tried to go back, huge icebergs blocked the way. But suddenly, as if by a miracle, an avenue opened in the ice and Shackleton was able to get through.

His men, ready and waiting, quickly scrambled aboard. No sooner had the ship cleared the island than the ice crashed together behind them with an ear-splitting din. Contemplating their narrow escape, the ruddy explorer said to his men: 'It was fortunate you were all packed and ready to go!'

With one voice, they replied: 'Whenever the sea was clear of ice, we rolled up our sleeping bags and reminded each other: "He may come today."'

4:1-2 IN FIFTH GEAR

Have you heard the latest definition of an optimist? It is someone who believes the preacher is almost finished when he says 'finally.' From a purely statistical point of view, it is interesting to note that in chapters 1-3 there is a total of forty-three verses, and in chapters 4-5 there are another forty-six to add to the total. So the big question is, what does Paul really mean when he says, *finally*?

It is almost like a change of gear as he moves into overdrive. He ups the ante. He raises the stakes. The word could be better translated 'and now.' It is the punchline. A watershed. A transition. In a deft touch, Paul turns from narrative to exhortation, diverting attention from himself to them. Or as John Stott says, he 'moves from his apologia to his appeal.'

Having said that, Paul's sudden shift of theme does not mean that there are no tangible links between chapters 3 and 4. For one thing, his prayer that the Lord would cause them to grow in love and holiness (3:12-13) is what paves the way for his teaching about both issues in verses 3 and 9.

Paul has given the young Thessalonian believers a crash course in Bible doctrine in chapters 1-3; in the following two chapters he encourages them to let the rubber hit the road. They have learned all about it in terms of theory, and now they need to go and live it out in the real world and prove to themselves that it does work.

Doctrine is gripping stuff—the Michelin syndrome!

Hitting the parade

The bottom line in our life is that we should be walking in step with the Lord. To quote William Cowper (1731-1800), 'O for a closer walk with God.' In fact, that is a picture often painted in the word of God. We are to 'walk worthy of the vocation wherewith we have been called…we are to walk in love…we are to walk as the children of light.' Those three references are all culled from Paul's letter to the Ephesians.

Why a walk? The Christian faith at that time was often called 'the Way.' What is more appropriate than 'a walk along the Way?' Paul's use of this particular term incorporates the idea that believers must not remain static.

- It demands life—for a dead sinner cannot walk.
- It entails growth—for a little baby cannot walk.
- It requires liberty—for someone who is bound cannot walk.
- It cries out for light—for very few of us want to go for a stroll in the dark.
- It cannot be hidden—for it is witnessed by all.
- It suggests progress—towards a goal.

The Christian life begins with a step of faith and that single step should lead to a life of consistently walking by faith. There is no room for immobility. Paul says elsewhere that 'we live by faith, not by sight' (2 Corinthians 5:7). Such childlike faith is not a step into the dark; it is a leap forward into the light. How should we then walk? Paul leaves us in no doubt that we are to walk in…

- holiness (verses 1-8),

- harmony (verses 9-10),
- honesty (verses 11-12), and
- hope (verses 13-18).
  Walk on with your head held high. Walk tall!

A man under God's thumb

Paul tells the church in these opening verses what God expects from them. His language is forthright, to say the least. Plain-spoken. He pulls no punches. Paul's use of the word *instructions* is indicative of how seriously he feels about this entire matter. It is a word that was often used either for a military command or a civil order; it is a term more in keeping with a judicial setting, for it was frequently employed by magistrates at the bench in a court of law.

His impassioned concern and burden is that his friends in Thessalonica should strive for excellence in their Christian experience. So he reminds them of the will of God for their life—a no turning back mindset that he wishes them to embrace. He desperately wants them to live a life that is pleasing to the Lord Jesus—a path of implicit obedience to the word of God. We adopt that outlook when we jubilantly walk in the ways of the Lord and are totally abandoned to him.

The fairly sketchy story of Enoch—the man we read about in the books of Genesis, Hebrews, and Jude—is relevant. We are not told very much about him in Scripture, but one thing we do know is that this man had a remarkably outstanding testimony in that it was said of him, 'he pleased God' (Hebrews 11:5).

Sometimes, human nature being what it is, we try to please ourselves. Maybe we fall into the trap of attempting to please other people. What really matters, more than anything else, is that we always seek to please the Lord. Paul could write, 'If I were still trying to please men, I would not be a servant of Christ' (Galatians 1:10). The inescapable fact is that he who tries to please everybody ends up pleasing nobody!

'You can please all of the people some of the time, and some of the people all of the time, but you can't please all of the people all of the time!' (Abraham Lincoln)

4:3 SHADES OF SANCTIFICATION

The six million dollar question—how do we please the Lord? There is a simple answer—by doing the will of God. According to what Paul intimates in these verses, sanctification is God's perfect will for each of us. However, the minute we mention the S-word, people are often confused. They have a potpourri of weird, wonderful, and wacky ideas as to what it is and is not.

I wonder what the word 'holy' conveys to you? What pictures does it conjure in your mind? I know it is funereally dismal to some, for they tend to associate it with no jokes, hair shirts, and freezing cold showers. It is monastic to others who link it to a solitary and celibate lifestyle. The mental picture is of stone cells, no women or kids, and no stereo or iPod.

Some perceive it to be a kind of religious sheep dip they are put through—a once-for-all experience of cleansing and commitment. Once they have been dipped or 'done,' they think everything is fine, hunky dory from then on in. Other folk see sanctification as an extraction process whereby God uses a supernatural magnet to remove all sin from their life and, from that moment on, they have no trouble pleasing the Lord. Easy-peasy. Nothing could be further from the truth!

Relationships

In the Bible, holiness is intensely practical. It is concerned with day-to-day living in the home and relationships in the church and in the wider community. We cannot be holy by ourselves. Holiness is primarily concerned with relationships, and, it seems to me, there are four areas involved:
• the relationship between an individual and our God;
• the relationship between men and women;
• the relationship between one Christian and another Christian; and
• the relationship between a Christian and his neighbour.
In other words, holiness has to be meticulously worked out in our marriage and in the context of our local evangelical church; it has to

be evidenced in our place of regular employment. Paul states quite categorically that if we cannot be holy in the every day, routine business of life, opting for seclusion in a monastery in the back of beyond will not help us.

The reality is that holiness has not had a particularly good press in recent times. It is often a non-starter with the average person. People for reasons best known to themselves are turned off by it. They see so-called holy people as those who have been soaked in embalming fluid—dour and dull with the uncanny knack of frowning on anything that smacks of hilarious fun or pleasure. But God has other ideas about holiness!

Beautiful people

Holiness of life is the gold standard.

The Old Testament speaks about the 'beauty of holiness' (cf. Psalm 96:9) in that there is an exquisite loveliness associated with it. There is something stunningly attractive about a life lived the way God intended. This means that God is designing beautiful people, not merely on the outside, but on the inside. People who are admirable, trustworthy, strong, loving, and compassionate—people who are whole. That is, people who are holy. The only explanation for their enhanced quality of life is that they are sanctified.

This is the old-time religion of the clean life and pure heart. Something incredibly positive. It means we are monopolised by the Lord; we cleave and cling to him and his precepts; we are exclusively for the Master's use. It is when we turn our back on sin and sensual pleasures; it is when we leave the world behind and burn all our bridges. To me, there is nothing more meaningful than that.

Here is the key that unlocks the door to a deeper spiritual life, leading us to a new dimension of Christian living. It enables us to scale new heights with the Lord. Here is life beyond the higher plane—on the highest plateau—a sanctified life. Basically, it means we are set apart by him, for him, and unto him. Even after God has declared us righteous, his next step is to make us righteous. Such is sanctification.

131

This is the heart of Old Testament theology. There we read that the Sabbath was sanctified as a special, one-in-seven day of rest; the tabernacle and temple were both sanctified as they were set apart by God's immanent presence; God sanctified the nation of Israel as his own treasured possession; he sanctified the sons of Levi to serve in his courts in a priestly ministry.

The triple P

Sanctification is strangely similar to our salvation in that it is in three distinct tenses. We can say, we have been saved, we are being saved, and one day we will be saved. We also declare that we have been sanctified — in the past; we are being sanctified — in the present; and we will be sanctified — in the future, it is prospective.

Yesterday, we were set apart from the penalty of sin. That is positional in nature. It is what happened at the moment of our conversion to Jesus Christ. Today, we are being set apart from the power of sin. This is progressive in that it is an ongoing, daily experience. In that sense, it is gradual. Tomorrow, in God's timing, we will be set apart from the presence of sin. This is perpetual, for we read, 'How great is the love the Father has lavished on us, that we should be called children of God. Dear friends, now we are children of God…we know that when he appears, we shall be like him, for we shall see him as he is' (1 John 3:1-2).

Sanctification is an ongoing process, not a hit or miss goal. It is the process of growing closer to Christ! It begins for us in a new nature with our conversion to faith in Christ on earth, and it ends for us in a new body, face to face with Christ in heaven.

- We look back and say, Christ for me.
- We reflect on the present and say, Christ in me.
- We look forward with anticipation into the future and say, Christ with me.

All for one, one for all

The word *sanctified* is almost the same as the word 'holiness' in that they both come from the same root. The ethos and heartbeat of sanctification is that the Lord has set apart him that is godly for himself. With that thought in mind, it is fascinating to discover that the Trinity plays a major part in our sanctification. Jude 1 reminds us that the Father decrees it—it is his sovereign purpose and plan. Hebrews 13:12 tells us that the Son determines it because this is one of the benefits of the atonement. Romans 15:16 indicates that the Holy Spirit directs it through the application of the word of God to our life.

A similar note is struck in John 17:17-19 where the Saviour prayed in his high priestly prayer in the upper room, 'Sanctify them by the truth, your word is truth.' The word of God is the agent of sanctification. As we read the word and hear it ministered, it has a profound cleansing effect on our life. It meets our need; it shows up the spots and stains; it reveals all the blemishes—we see ourselves as God sees us.

Then as we allow the water of the word to wash and purify us, we will become more holy and more like Jesus. This great ministry of sanctification, therefore, implies cleansing. The Lord is looking for clean vessels, and the only way to do that is for us to mortify the old nature and feed the new man, that is the gist of Paul's teaching in Romans 6-7.

It suggests commissioning, for in Christ we are vessels designed for higher service. We are sanctified so that he might send us out into a lost world with the message of eternal, redeeming love. We should also be practising our position in Christ—it contemplates a Christ-likeness. In other words, we should be holy within and without, just like the Lord Jesus.

Holy or holey

Sanctified...to live like saints.

Contrary to church law, saints are not those who have been canonised, but those who have been called by God and cleansed by his Son's precious blood. They are not those set in stained glass on

133

a Gothic cathedral window, but those living in today's world in a pagan culture. A little girl who attended worship in a place with a lot of stained glass windows was asked what a saint was. 'A saint is a person the light shines through,' she replied. Every Christian is a saint and every saint is a Christian.

All of this is a matter for the heart and the heart of the matter is our personal holiness. That was ever the supreme concern of Robert Murray McCheyne, the nineteenth-century pastor from Dundee in Scotland, who often said: 'My people's greatest need is my personal holiness.' He went on to say that 'we are as holy as we choose to be.'

I do not know what impact that has on your heart, but I find it enormously challenging. In moments like these, George Jackson's (1866-93) hymn says it so eloquently:

I want, dear Lord,
A heart that's true and clean;
A sunlit heart, with not a cloud between;
A heart like thine, a heart divine,
A heart as white as snow;
On me, dear Lord,
A heart like this bestow.

Reality check

God is much more interested in our character than in the career we pursue—in who we are than in what we do. One of the telltale signs of a deteriorating society is a loss of moral integrity. When this foundation stone begins to crack and erode, the effect is nothing short of disastrous.

That is where Christianity has been outstandingly different from day one. God's people have vigorously campaigned against moral decline by upholding personal holiness. Down through the years of church history, Christians have been committed to purity of heart and life in spite of prevailing winds and many siren voices clamouring for their attention. They have dug in their heels and obstinately stood their ground.

Why have so many of God's people remained resolute and defiant? The only explanation is found in these verses. It would be so easy for us to look around and wring our clammy hands and bemoan our lot. Sometimes we say, it has never been so bad before! The fact of the matter is, there is nothing new under the sun, and what is happening across the world today is certainly not a last-days phenomenon.

A blast from the past

When we scan the writings of many Old Testament prophets we discover they were grappling with exactly the same problem. There is incident after incident that in one way or another has influenced the rise and fall of many cultures and that in its wake has left a dark shadow on the tarnished lives of many individuals.

A couple of prophets are fairly obvious examples—both having served in this capacity prior to the fall of Judah under the Babylonian invasion of 586 BC—Habakkuk and Jeremiah.

When Habakkuk surveyed the landscape of his era, he saw a people who deserved the righteous judgment of God but, at the same time, they were desperately in need of his mercy and salvation. This ancient preacher described his land as a country riddled with unimaginable violence. He said it was renowned for its rampant iniquity and had become a byword for inherent wickedness.

It was a culture where truth was denigrated to such an extent that lying was the norm; there was vanity and idolatry as people were immersed in themselves—a spirit of narcissism prevailed; there was horrific oppression and widespread abuse of those who were less fortunate and not able to defend themselves; robbery and assault was pretty much the norm—it was rife and commonplace. There was little or no love lost between the warring factions; strife and contention constantly arose among the people. They defiantly ignored the law, perverting the course of justice; basically, they did what they wanted to do and left other people to pick up the tab.

I assure you I am not exaggerating for all these despicably heinous sins are listed in 1:2-4. Sound familiar? You bet it does! It is no wonder that Habakkuk reacted and responded the way he did—he pleaded with God to intervene; he passionately bargained with God to do something about it before it was too late and before the people had gone beyond the point of no return. He sought the Lord to put a halt to the moral pollution that had covered the land like a thick blanket of acrid smoke.

The other prophetic stalwart is Jeremiah. Like Habakkuk, we find that Jeremiah lived in Judah during its final stage of political, moral, and religious collapse. He was there in the months leading up to the pivotal moment when the curtain fell for the very last time. He saw it for himself and he did not like what he saw; it broke his sensitive heart.

It is amazing how two men react so differently to the same kind of situation—Habakkuk screamed and shouted at the Lord, but dear old Jeremiah sobbed his heart out. He wept gallons of tears; all his pent-up emotion was released through his shedding of much holy water. He just could not believe he was seeing what he was seeing; quite frankly, he could not take it in. It was all too much for him.

Jeremiah 6 catalogues one sin after another and it appears, at the end of the day, that the people had come to such a point where sin no longer shocked them. They were de-sensitised. They had grown so accustomed to moral pollution that their face failed to turn crimson red when they encountered grimy impurity. They got used to living in a murky environment. They had put up with so much voyeurism and villainous behaviour over the years, that now they did not even blush with embarrassment at sin—an unmistakable giveaway that holiness is conspicuous by its absence.

That was then. Times have not changed—today is no better. If anything, it is marginally worse, if that were possible. All the more reason why we need to be the kind of people Paul is talking about in this chapter. In a grim and dirty world, we should be sold out to Jesus Christ. We should be men and women who, like the men of Isaachar, know what is happening, fully aware of all that is taking place on our front doorstep. Allied to that, we must be a generation for God whose life is not tainted and whose perception is not coloured or influenced by it.

This is the emphatic challenge we face as believers in the third millennium—there is a patent need for us to be different and stand out in the crowd. We must be! We dare to be! We should be men and women who, unashamedly, quick march under the unfurled banner of holiness. Lelia N. Norris (1862-1929) rallies each of us—as squaddies in God's army—with these stirring words:

Called unto holiness, children of light,
Walking with Jesus in garments of white;
Raiment unsullied, nor tarnished with sin,
God's Holy Spirit abiding within.
'Holiness to the Lord,' is our watchword and song,
'Holiness to the Lord,' as we're marching along:
Sing it, shout it, loud and long,
'Holiness to the Lord,' now and for ever.

4:3B-5 STRAIGHT TALK ABOUT SEX

When unbelievers look at us they should see a life that is attractive and beautiful, for we are numbered among those who know and love the Lord. It is in that context that Paul moves on to talk about something of mega importance to all people in every generation. He addresses the prickly subject of our relationship with members of the opposite sex. Vintage Paul, he handles it tenderly and tactfully. He deals sensitively with the subject of sex.

At the same time, however, there is a toughness to his approach when he reminds them of the serious consequences of disobeying the word of God. It is straight talk about moral purity.

'Here we have grass-stained advice from someone following Christ in the grassroots of life.' (Charles Swindoll)

It is a fair assumption to make that these words are rarely, if ever, preached upon. They are not very high on the popularity ratings for selecting as our favourite Bible portion—definitely not in the top three, never mind the top ten. And yet they are exceedingly relevant in a post-Christian, postmodern era.

We live in a grossly immoral society where anything, and I mean, anything, goes. The standards of acceptable behaviour have plummeted to an all-time low. We are on a downward spiral; we are teetering on the brink of disaster. We have gone full circle. We are living dangerously as we have returned to the days of Noah and Lot.

It is indubitably obvious that we live in a sex-mad culture. John MacArthur writes: 'We live in a culture that is indulging itself in every conceivable and inconceivable sexual activity.' Not only is sexual sin tolerated in any form by any one with anyone else at any time, in any place, in any way; more than that, it is advocated, promoted, encouraged, and aggressively marketed through every media we can possibly think of on the basis of freedom of speech…whose freedom?

There is so much innuendo in the 60-second advertising campaigns shown in the frequent commercial breaks on our television screen. What do scantily clad, blonde beauties have to do with selling fast cars, fast food, or fast computers? It does not matter which way we turn; we are constantly bombarded and blitzed by it. Because of that, many vital issues are blurred in the almost impenetrable moral fog so prevalent at this moment.

Ann Widdecombe MP, speaking in a House of Commons debate in 2000, said, 'Let's face it, we are not a happier society as a result of the liberalisation of the seventies. We have record rates of divorce, record rates of suicide, record rates of teenage pregnancy, record rates of youth crime, record rates of underage sex. We should invite people to recognise that the Great Experiment has failed. You cannot have happiness without restraint.'

Power of purity

This is an hour of enormous need and the great need of the hour is for believers to maintain moral purity. Paul here is gutsy, but he is honest and sincere to the core as he probes into the nerve centre of our life. He is right on target as he pinpoints the very things that cry out for immediate attention.

The practice of purity causes us to stand out from the world like a glistening diamond versus coal.

We are saints; we are sanctified; we are called to live a separated life unto the Lord; we are told to be different from the world; we are exhorted to be a holy people. All this can only mean that God is looking for folk who are sanctified through and through (cf. 5:23).

- Purity of life.
- Purity of heart.
- Purity of mind.

Fundamentally, a thrice-holy Lord is looking for the younger set to flee youthful lusts. He is looking for middle-aged folk to show by their lifestyle and behaviour that God's way is the best way. He is looking for seniors to set a superb example of godliness and real contentment.

Sex and sanctification

In one inspirational breath, Paul declares, *It is God's will that you should be sanctified* and, in the very next breath, he says, *that you should avoid sexual immorality*. Whether we realise it or not, sanctification radically affects every department of our life. It is like an anti-virus program operating in the background for each of us protecting internal vulnerabilities against external threats.

'The plain things are the main things, and the main things are the plain things.' (Alistair Begg)

Paul's teaching here is plain, clear, and distinct. He tells it like it is. There is no shilly-shallying with him. The Christian should have nothing to do with that which is labelled immoral—neither in our mind or heart, with our eyes or body. There is no escape hatch; there is no bolthole that we can squeeze through. He calls for a clean cut with everything that smacks of immorality. He makes an earnest plea for us to be at odds with society.

The problem in Thessalonica is not dissimilar to that which faced the believers in Corinth—a sexually oriented and sexually explicit community—a culture riddled and renowned for hard porn and sexual vice. But, Paul says, in spite of your cultural habits, old patterns, and former lifestyle, the Lord does not tolerate sexual sin. He never has! He never will! The baseline is that the church of Jesus Christ cannot live like the devil's promiscuous world.

So far as Scripture is concerned, this is not a relative morality; it is an absolute standard. A blue-ribbon, biblical standard. No matter how much the world may try to squeeze us into its mould, this standard does not change; it does not fluctuate; it is not raised or lowered depending on the direction of the prevailing wind.

We need to be clear in our own mind that it is not just the act that Paul is thinking about; it is the attitude as well. The old adage holds true, if we play with fire, we will get badly burned. We should avoid it like we avoid the plague. It is doing what Joseph did when Potiphar's wife tried to lure him into bed—the minute he saw her coming down Petticoat Lane, he ran a mile as fast as his legs would carry him in the opposite direction (cf. Genesis 39:7-12).

Saying 'no' to intimacy

Let me spell it out clearly so that we are left in absolutely no doubt as to what Paul is teaching. It means absolutely NO:

- sexual wrongdoing whatsoever;
- fooling around on the back seat of a car;
- premarital sex even though we may be committed to a long-term, loving relationship with that person;
- messing around with someone else's partner because we are fed up and bored with our own;
- same-sex relationships;
- hard or soft porn from salacious books or glossy magazines that we find on the top shelf of the newspaper stand or when surfing the Net;
- visiting highly dubious chat rooms or telling smutty stories;
- entrance to strip clubs or entertaining even the thought of using a prostitute;
- sitting up late to watch risqué movies on television.

Paul's directive is calculatingly blunt and without apology; he says, 'Have none of these things going on in your life.' It is a blanket ban! I appreciate the way J. B. Phillips translates verse 3 when he says, 'God's plan is to make you holy, and that entails first of all, a clean break with sexual immorality.'

Self-control

Allied to that is an overwhelming sense of privilege. We should be in charge of our own body, and when we are, God is glorified. That is what Paul says in verse 4, *each of you should learn to control his own body in a way that is holy and honourable.*

This is a skill we have to learn, as it does not come naturally or easily. It is not something that someone else can do for you; you have to do it yourself! I cannot pass the buck and blame the other person. The underlying thought is that I am responsible for my own actions.

It is a lesson we must learn if we are to grow spiritually and if our life is to count for the Lord. We need to gain the mastery over our body, so that we will not be slaves to our lusts. We need to know victory over the flesh and see the enemy running when he would seek to seduce and tempt us.

We are in a battle. The conflict is internal. The world is against us. The flesh is easy meat for the devil. As John MacArthur says: 'It is your unredeemed human flesh that is the beachhead to sin' — hence the Pauline injunction to control it.

There is a link here to Paul's comment in 1 Corinthians 6 where he is on a similar wavelength, and also to his insights in Galatians 5. The key to controlling our body is the Holy Spirit. If we walk in the Spirit, we will not fulfil the lusts of the flesh! Ah, that is what Paul says in verse 4!

So the key to controlling our body is walking in the Spirit. The key to walking in the Spirit is being filled with the Spirit (cf. Ephesians 5:18). And the key to being filled with the Spirit is letting God's word dwell in us richly (cf. Colossians 3:16). As always, the focus is on our relationship with Jesus Christ.

Staying away from the edge

Paul is talking here about self-discipline for purity is a conscious choice; it does not just happen. At the end of the verse, Paul reminds us of the degree to which this control is to be exercised. It is to be in a way that is *holy and honourable.*

To be 'holy' means to be separated unto God from sin, to be separated unto purity. And 'honourable' means to be worthy of respect. In other words, our body is to be so separated from sin that it is worthy of respect toward the God who owns it, who dwells in it, and whom it represents, and toward the church of which it is a part.

To me, that sends a clear signal which says: we are to live our life not asking how far can we go and not go over the line, but how far can we stay away and be utterly set apart from sin and bring honour to our body which is God's and which should be used for the glory of Christ.

A wrong kind of passion

Paul focuses on the peril when he writes, *not in passionate lust like the heathen, who do not know God.* What a strong indictment that is! *Passionate lust* is an incredibly strong term; either word is strong enough, but when we put them both together, it reinforces all that Paul is saying.

The word 'passion' means excited emotion, uncontrollable desire, compelling feelings, overpowering urges. It is used here in a bad sense; we find the same phrase employed in Romans 1:26 and Colossians 3:5. The word for 'lust' is an out-of-control craving. It is, according to Frederick Buechner, 'the craving for salt of a man who is dying of thirst.' This is what happens when people sink to abject depths of crass immorality.

We are encouraged to look at the activities of the pagan population milling around us and see how they operate. Paul leaves no stone unturned when he says that their life is governed by lust; they are controlled by their passions; they are ruled by sensual desire; they live according to the dictates and demands of the flesh. In the final analysis, they do not know the Lord Jesus Christ; they have never entered into a personal, dynamic relationship with the living God.

Again, Paul reckons we should be different for we know the Lord. God is a reality in our life. Therefore, in terms of moral behaviour, we should be an example. We should be setting the tone of every conversation; we should be seen to be above and beyond reproach in the wider community; we should exercise utmost care and caution in the programs we watch on television or at the theatre; we need to be highly selective in what we allow our eyes to focus and feast upon. That inevitably means some stuff will be classed 'out of bounds' for one who is sensitive to the person of the Holy Spirit.

The fact is, if we fantasise and tantalise ourselves with sin, we end up morally and spiritually weakened, massively so. The omens are not good—remember the fateful, one-night stand of David and Bathsheba! That means from Paul's incisive teaching in verse 5 that we must not ignore the flashing warning lights. We must be ultra-careful, for it is the glory of Christ that is at stake. Because of who we are in Christ, we need to set a good and godly example to all those around us.

The man is an idiot who drives through a red light! So is the man who speeds up when he sees an amber caution!

4:6 WHEN 'NO' MEANS 'NO'

Ethics are important and core values are essential—we cannot live or do without them. What we believe determines the way we behave! One impacts the other. It is apparent that such a principle undergirds every aspect of life. It holds equally true when it comes to dealing with the often-tangled emotional web of interpersonal relationships, especially those we enjoy with the opposite sex.

It is a thorny patch we are walking on in this section but we cannot avoid it as Paul talks about a divine prohibition. He really lays it on the line as to what weighs heavily on the mind and heart of God. We are left in no doubt as to what the Lord thinks about the entire scenario—*no one should wrong his brother or take advantage of him.*

When a man commits fornication and/or engages in adultery, the ramifications are huge—it affects so many innocent lives to a greater or lesser extent. The upshot is often immeasurable and the damage incalculable. Adultery is where inclination meets opportunity. It takes two to tango outside of God's will. Sexual immorality hurts both parties in one way or another. Both the one doing the lusting, and the one being lusted after.

Having said that, we can narrow the issue down and say it has primarily a twofold effect. One, the offender does wrong in that he seriously oversteps the mark. He goes beyond the boundary; he goes too far; he exceeds the limits; he goes over the line and, in so doing, violates another person's body. Consequently, he transgresses.

Two, when the person commits such a blatant sin, he takes advantage of the other person. He is only thinking about himself and his personal gratification—a momentary thrill. To all intents and purposes, such a person is guilty of fraud. He wants something that does not belong to him and he goes for something that is not his. An individual who rides recklessly down this path is covetous and falls foul to the avarice and selfish greed of his heart. He has ruthlessly asserted himself on another individual and is, therefore, guilty of cheating.

He leaves behind him a trail of broken hearts, a long line of broken lives, and a string of broken promises and vows.

This is unbelievably strong language that Paul employs. And yet, when we sit down and hear what God says, we know it is true to life, and we also know it makes an awful lot of good sense.

Man...he's my brother

Paul uses the word *brother* that, in itself, is most illuminating. This is the only time the inspired apostle uses this particular word. It means not only a brother in the Christian family; it goes far beyond the confines of that, for it also includes our fellow man. In other words, it is not exclusive to the people of God. It is all-inclusive, for no person made in the image of God is omitted; it is all-embracing, for no one person in the world is excluded.

The implication is that this kind of behaviour is not acceptable, it never has been acceptable and, no matter how we dress it up, it never can be acceptable. It is never viewed as the norm in the eyes of the Lord. And, because of that, we can never justify it.

What are the consequences of such grossly outrageous and immoral behaviour? Paul says that *the Lord will punish men for all such sins.* People are inclined to forget that God sees what goes on in the intimacy of the nation's bedrooms. When the soft light is switched off, by no stretch of the imagination is the Lord left in the dark. Biblically, sin is always associated with the dark, and holiness is always associated with light. It is much better to see where we are going!

John MacArthur writes: 'Sexual sin disregards God; it ignores his holiness; it spurns his will; it defies his commands; it rejects his love; it flaunts his grace; it abuses his mercy. It is disobedient; it is selfish; it is ingratitude; and God will avenge it.'

Sooner or later it will catch us up; it will come back to terrorise and haunt us. We cannot hide from God in time and we certainly cannot run away from him in eternity. Let's get this straight, whether we like it or not, there is definitely coming a day of accountability—a day of reckoning when all will be revealed. God sees all things, he knows all that happens, and all impurity he will judge.

Cause and effect

If any one of us happens to fall in this way, the good news is there is for-giveness with the Lord if we genuinely seek him in repentance. Although failure is never final, our repentance had better be genuine. Constantly going back to the well for forgiveness without meaning it is libertine.

Sure, the Lord will forgive our sin, which says a lot about his mar-vellous mercy and generous grace; but, understand this, we will have to live with the serious repercussions of such a disastrous step for the rest of our life. Given time, there may be a measure of healing; the odds are, however, that the scars will always remain with us.

That is one of the prime reasons why, in matters of leadership in the local church, Paul writes to young Timothy in the manner he does; he makes no bones about it when he declares that such men, i.e. elders and deacons, should be 'the husband of one wife' (1 Timothy 3:2).

I believe the same high standard is still appropriate today for all those involved in any kind of Christian leadership in church and mis-sion. It is an interesting turn of phrase, for it does not only mean that he is married to one woman at a given point in time; it essentially means that he is a one-woman man.

Some folk prefer to give it a different name, but at the end of the day, sin is sin. Someone severely criticised their pastor on one occasion for preaching against sin in the life of the Christian. They felt that sin in the life of a believer was different from sin in the life of an unconverted person. The godly pastor thought for a few minutes, then said, 'Yes, you're right, it's worse!'

God will never condemn sin in a sinner and, at the same time, condone it in the life of any one of his children, though he will still forgive us if we genuinely repent. We are, after all, only human. To err is human, to forgive is divine. Bishop J. C. Ryle of Liverpool said: 'We must not expect sin, excite sin, or excuse sin.'

4:7 SUNSHINE IN THE SOUL

Paul challenges us to keep the whole issue in perspective by looking at it from an eternal vantage point—*For God did not call us to be impure, but to live a holy life.* This is the rationale behind Paul's sweeping instruction in the previous verse. It puts the spotlight back on the exalted Lord. God has called each of us to a life of holiness, or what could be termed, a life of wholeness. He wants us to move out of the fog of our impurity into the bright light of his holiness.

That is why he saved us, redeemed us, chose us, and cleansed us; his ultimate goal is that we might be a holy people. His aspiration for us is that we might be like Jesus; his dream for us is that we might reflect his Son through our life, a life washed in his precious blood. He longs that we might be vessels unto honour that will glorify him.

4:8 FLOUTING GOD'S LAW

This immensely challenging section concludes with Paul speaking about our profession—*Therefore, he who rejects this instruction does not reject man but God, who gives you his Holy Spirit.* This phrase is a sign saying, Trespassers Will Be Prosecuted. Paul says, if you do not listen to what I am telling you, it is not me you are rejecting; it is not the elders you are ignoring; it is not your friends and family you are opposing; it is the Lord that you are standing against.

The fornicator and adulterer is someone who flatly rejects God, not man. The individual who does that is in a sad and sorry state; he is backing a loser all the way. Richard Mayhue crystallises Paul's thinking when he writes: 'The one who continues to live immorally rejects God's Spirit, rejects God's will, rejects God's call, rejects God's word, and rejects God's pleasure. To put it simply, they reject God.'

There is a lot more to this verse than initially meets the eye. A closer reading indicates that there are three basic steps to a life of holiness. We need to:

- recognise his presence in that we have been given the Spirit of God and he abides within us;
- respect his person in that he is the Holy Spirit; and
- receive his power for he alone can make us holy.

The stark choice, the simple choice, is ours. We can look at it like this: do we live our life on a horizontal plane in the weakness of the flesh, or do we live our life vertically in the dynamic and power of the Holy Spirit? As the Puritans used to say, 'A holy man is an awesome weapon in the hand of God.'

Paul is making an impassioned plea for purity in these verses so that we might be enabled and energised by him to live for Jesus in a world that is rotten to the core. What a tremendous challenge—a rousing challenge—for us to live for God in a sex-mad society.

'Purity involves more than a passing glance to see how much dirt we have under our fingernails. It requires a good, soaped up, scrubbed down Saturday night bath.' (Charles Swindoll)

4:9-10 PHILADELPHIA—NOT CHEESE, BUT LOVE

Now about brotherly love we do not need to write to you, for you yourselves have been taught by God to love each other. And in fact, you do love all the brothers throughout Macedonia. Yet we urge you, brothers, to do so more and more.

We feel the change of atmosphere when Paul moves from chastity to charity; there is a distinctly different tone in these verses. Paul says,

'I want to talk to you guys about brotherly love.' This should be the hallmark—trademark—of the Christian. He wants us to abound in affection.

General William Westmoreland was once reviewing a platoon of paratroopers in Vietnam. As he went down the line, he asked each of them a question: 'How do you like jumping, son?'

'Love it, sir!' was the first answer.

'How do you like jumping?' he asked the next.

'The greatest experience in my life, sir!' exclaimed the ebullient paratrooper.

'How do you like jumping?' he asked the third.

'I hate it, sir,' he replied.

'Then why do you do it?' asked the bemused Westmoreland.

'Because I want to be around guys who love to jump!'

The brand of love that Paul refers to is 'philadelphia' love—the love that binds our hearts together. We are the children of God, brothers and sisters in the global family of God; he is our Father, and he is love. In other words, the more we live like God in a life of purity, the more we will love one another. It is a love of deep affection that brings us out of our ivory theological towers to get involved in helping others who are struggling in the trenches of life.

It is a family love for we have a kindred heart and mind; we share something in common. Like the paratrooper, we enjoy being around those who love to jump! The ground was level at Calvary. It was said of those in the first century church, 'See how they love each other.'

It is a fragrant love for when there is love shared among us, there will be a pervasive richness and a sense of wonder in the atmosphere. We can tell a mile away if people love one another; we can also tell if people are getting on one another's nerves.

It is a fruitful love for we will want nothing but the best for each other; we will not rest until we see Christ shining from one another's lives; we will seek to discern the glory of God in all that we do together in his name.

Love one another

Paul says they were *taught by God*, which seems quite remarkable. That is how they were able to do it. It was the work of God in their heart. It was an operation of the Holy Spirit deep down within.

- God the Father taught us by example when he gave the Lord Jesus to die for us.
- God the Son taught us when he said, 'A new commandment I give unto you, that you love one another.'
- God the Holy Spirit taught us when he poured the love of God into our heart when we trusted Christ.

We are to show love to all the brethren—without exception. None are to be left out; none are to feel excluded in any way. Not easy, sometimes. It goes against the grain at other times. The ditty is right when it says:

> *To dwell above with saints in love,*
> *That will indeed be glory,*
> *To dwell below with saints we know,*
> *Well, that's another story.*

Sometimes we hurt each other by the comments that we make and by the things that we do—or, perhaps, do not say or do. There are just some people who are easy to get along with—people with whom we have an instant rapport; there are others who rub us up the wrong way and tramp on our toes. There are some folk with whom we hit it off, and others whom we feel like hitting! We have an easy relationship with some, but it is more strained with others. Some of God's wonderful people are touchy-feely; others are tetchy and keep us at arm's length.

We all have our own ideas; we will always have our differences of opinion; we have our peculiarities—it is just that some are more eccentric than others. We are as different as chalk and cheese. But, says Paul, it does not matter what we are like, we can still love each other.

Love ultimately wins the day, no matter how long it takes. Love overcomes the whole gamut of problems. Love goes beyond the jarring clash of personality and culture. Love gladly accepts the other person for who and what they are. Love always finds a way through the maze of complex issues.

149

Touching people's lives

What does Paul have to say about the expression of such love? We discover that their love was well known throughout the whole of Macedonia. How did they do it? It appears that one of the most obvious ways was through the engaging ministry of hospitality. Open heart. Open home.

Love is the hinge on which hospitality turns to open its unlocked door.

From Hebrews 13:1-3 we are exhorted to show hospitality to three kinds of people—saints, strangers, and those who are suffering. Paul was all too aware that they were loving many different types of people, but he urged them to keep it up. They were not to pause and mark time or even maintain the status quo. He wants them to go out and break new ground for the Lord; he wants them to expand their love, to reach out more and more. We can never get too much love and we can never give too much love.

4:11-12 TO BE HONEST WITH YOU...

Having given them a lecture on love, Paul moves on to give them some instructions on integrity—walking in honesty. The opening phrase—*make it your ambition*—is an encouragement and an incentive to them to be ambitious. There is nothing wrong with healthy ambition; it all depends what it is focused on. Is it popularity, power, position, or prestige? If it is, we are barking up the wrong tree.

Paul uses the same word three times in the New Testament. In Romans 15:20 it was his all-consuming passion to reach the unreached with the message of Jesus and his love—he wanted to tell the gospel to the untold millions. Again, we come across it in 2 Corinthians 5:9 where his sincerely held desire is that in everything he might please the Lord Jesus. And, here, it is a threefold ambition, for we are *to lead a quiet life, to mind our own business and to work with our own hands*. What does he mean by each of these?

• Do not irritate!

To lead a quiet life is to be tranquil on the inside. It is not what we see advertised in the tabloid press when they encourage us to pay a visit to the local health shop to buy a bottle of tablets designed to give us perfect peace. It is not the hermit mentality either.

It is living on the ragged edge with a peace in our heart and mind. Contentment. It is when we feel relaxed in God's love as we rest in his care. It is all about learning to lean on the Lord. This rich quality is found as we wait upon the Lord. Others will see the Lord through our actions.

• Do not interfere!

Paul bluntly tells them not to meddle in other people's affairs. They are to keep their nose clean and not barge into situations unless first invited. They must not gatecrash another man's privacy. One translation says, 'Do not be a busybody.' This applies to every aspect of life—in the church, in the local community, in business, and certainly in the family. We would save ourselves a lot of peeved aggravation if we took this to heart.

• Do not idle!

There is no virtue in living like a parasite or a moocher. If we have a job to do, we thank God for it, and get on with it. Do not be a time waster. We should use every moment God has allocated to us and invest it wisely for him. Antonio Stradivari, the great maker of violins, said, 'If my hand slacked, I should rob God.'

'Why bother working?' is the all-important question. As the old saying goes, the devil finds work for idle hands to do. It was Mark Twain who said, 'I do not like work, even when someone else does it.' Honesty is not the best policy for the Christian—it is the only one. That is supremely the reason why we need to be men and women of ambition.

Impacting our world

There is another angle to view it from—the world is watching. The unconverted are looking at our life, and they miss nothing! They see us; they know us. If we are the kind of people that God wants us to be then the man next door will respect us for who we are, and what we are. In other words, we will bear a good testimony.

Remember Enoch, for that is how he operated. If ever there was one, here was a man who walked with God, who pleased God, and who, when he was gone to glory, was really missed. People in the neighbourhood were genuinely sorry to see him go, such was his positive influence.

What a stimulating challenge for us to live so as to be missed and to live so that Christ will be magnified. Sure, we may be out of step with the world, but we will be in tune with the Lord, and in touch with the Lord. Will Rogers encourages us to 'so live that we wouldn't be ashamed to sell the family parrot to the town gossip!' To me, that is what being a real Christian is all about; it is immensely exciting!

4:13 RAPTURE READY!

I love the *Peanuts* cartoons. One of my favourites is the one that involves a fairly intense conversation between Lucy and Linus. Looking out a window, Lucy wonders: 'Boy, look at it rain…what if it floods the whole world?' 'It will never do that,' says Linus, with real conviction in his voice. 'You see, in Genesis 9 God promised Noah that would never happen again, and the sign of the promise is the rainbow.' 'You've taken a great load off my mind,' replies Lucy, to whom Linus responds: 'Sound theology has a way of doing that!' That is precisely what Paul offers in these verses—sound theology!

• The practical results of Christianity (verses 1-12).
• The personal return of Christ (verses 13-18).

What we have here is a twofold picture: a church energised in the Spirit—the people of God radiating holiness—and a church expectant in the world—the people of God reflecting hope and living in keen anticipation of the second advent of Jesus.

The next major world event is the return of Jesus Christ.

Statisticians tell us there are 1,845 Old Testament references to the Second Coming of Christ—a total of 17 books out of a possible 39 give it eminence. When we move across to the New Testament, the figures are no less impressive. For example, of the 260 chapters in the New Testament, there is a minimum of 318 references to the Second Advent. That averages 1:30 verses dedicated to this truth. By any stretch of the imagination that is quite staggering. When we probe further, we discover that 23 of the 27 New Testament books refer to the subject of the Lord's return.

It is interesting to note that three of these books are one chapter letters that were written to specific persons on a single subject. Another piece of info worth knowing is that for every prophecy on the first coming of Christ when he was born as a babe in Bethlehem, there are eight prophecies on the Second Coming of Christ. That tells me this truth is central to the word of God. It is, therefore, a biblical message!

Living well, dying well

This is a chapter of truly remarkable contrasts, such as:
* life—death;
* here and now—there and then;
* thoughts on time—exploring eternity;
* those wide awake—those fallen asleep.

Basically, Paul is talking about living well and dying well. To die well—dying with dignity—means we embrace a wonderful hope that looks forward to a better day when we shall see the King in all his unerring beauty. Charles Wesley's (1707-88) splendid words reflect this princely attitude:

> *Happy, if with my latest breath*
> *I may but gasp his name;*
> *Preach him to all, and cry in death,*
> *'Behold, behold the Lamb!'*

Hope in a no hope world

Hope. Just what postmodern man is searching for—the trouble is, unlike Job, he often looks in the wrong place. He asked the double-barrelled question, 'Where then is my hope? Who can see any hope for me?' (Job 17:15).

When we see what is happening all around us in today's world we could easily be driven to the precarious edge of despair. Man's cherished dreams have not been fulfilled; his ideals have not been realised; his best-laid plans have been shattered. There are times when our back is pinned to the wall; when we have that awful sinking feeling in the pit of our stomach; when we feel like giving up and giving in; in frenetic moments like that, we urgently need hope.

I love the way the author talks about a better hope in Hebrews 6:19 and likens it to an anchor for the soul. That means when the sands of time are shifting and sinking, we have a hope that is sure ('firm') and steadfast ('secure').

- A sure hope—it cannot break.
- A steadfast hope—it cannot slip its moorings.

Hope with a capital H gives us the encouragement we need to go on with the Lord; it enables us to fire on every cylinder for Jesus; it keeps us plodding on through deep furrows when the burdens of ministry are heavy; it helps us hang in when life's battles are unbelievably hard. Hope is not a sedative. It is not a soporific pill that we swallow with a glass of water. It is more like a surging rush of adrenalin in the vein of the Christian. Where there is Christ, there is hope. When focused on Jesus, hope springs eternal in the human breast.

The passing of time destroys many of our fondest hopes as they slowly fade and die. As the years roll by—and the older we are, the faster they seem to go—the Christian's hope becomes much more glorious. Solomon in his wisdom said in Proverbs 4:18 that 'the path of the righteous is like the first gleams of dawn, shining ever brighter till the full light of day.' The closer we are to the Lord's appearing, the brighter that hope shines in our heart. A new day is dawning!

A similar chord is struck in Jeremiah 29:11 where God came to the aid of his beleaguered servant, one for whom hope appeared to have all but evaporated. He said, 'I know the plans I have for you, plans to give you hope and a future.'

That brand of hope will put a twinkle in our eye; it will put the sparkle back into our life; it will add a metre to our every footstep. Why? Because we have something to live for today, and so much to look forward to in all our tomorrows.

The world hopes for the best—the Christian has the best hope.

The hymnwriter, Jim Hill, captures this inspiring theme:

There is coming a day
When no heartaches shall come,
No more clouds in the sky,

No more tears to dim the eye;
All is peace for evermore
On that happy golden shore,
What a day, glorious day, that will be.

Running scared

Paul starts the ball rolling by talking about their fear, *Brothers, we do not want you to be ignorant about those who fall asleep, or to grieve like the rest of men, who have no hope.*

The folk in the church in Thessalonica were extremely worried. Puzzled. Perplexed. They were going through real agony of mind. Barely a day slipped by when they did not experience deep anguish of heart. They were antsy. Restless. Fidgety. By the minute, they were getting themselves into a state of muddled anxiety. Like the proverbial string on a bow, they were uptight and riddled with doubts. It has been well said that 'doubts are the ants in the pants of faith.'

The big problem was that some of their close friends and loved ones had died and they were concerned lest those who had died would miss out at the Second Coming of Jesus Christ. All sorts of gargantuan questions were going through their mind: Would they be left behind? What has actually happened to them? Are they all right? Shall we see them again? Where are they now?

John Stott hits the nail on the head when he writes, 'Such questions arise partly from a natural curiosity, partly from Christian concern for the dead, and partly because their death reminds us of our own mortality and undermines our security.' That is the reason why they were so incredibly upset and I reckon, if we had been in their shoes, we would probably have felt much the same. Perfectly understandable.

'The fear of death troubles our lives like a hurricane sweeping over a serene harbour,' notes Charles Swindoll. 'And, anchored in the shallows, our little boats of faith are easily dashed against the rocks by fear's fury.'

Ignorance is not bliss

Before we get too deeply into this section, it is helpful to realise that these verses are more pastoral than theological. Paul is not writing to teach the nuances of eschatology. He is, however, going out of his way to alleviate their acute grief and give these sad folk some informed answers to their hard questions.

The foremost difficulty they wrestled with was that their fear was based on ignorance. They knew a lot but they did not know all they needed to know. They knew that Jesus was coming back, but there were a lot of things that did not seem to make sense. In their state of mind, two and two did not make four. Had they mistaken what Paul taught them, or were they just no more than a little confused about the whole event.

The fact is they eagerly wanted the Lord to come. They knew it was the climax, the culmination, the great event that signalled the pinnacle of redemptive history, and they did not want to miss it! That explains why Paul says what he does in the opening phrase, *we do not want you to be ignorant.*

Actually, this is one of four key areas about which Paul clearly indicates that ignorance is definitely not bliss. The other references are in 1 Corinthians 10:1 with regard to events in the Old Testament era; Romans 11:25 in relation to the ultimate restoration of Israel; and 1 Corinthians 12:1 where he talks at considerable length about the manifestation of spiritual gifts. Here, in verse 13, the preacher talks about death.

Death is usually the last thing we want to talk about; it makes us squirm, feel uncomfortable, and a little awkward. We naturally recoil into a protective shell when someone brings the subject up; we much prefer to blank it out. And yet, life being what it is, we cannot walk away from it.

Death tends to be an unwelcome intruder into our life; generally speaking, it is an uninvited guest into our home. Death has been variously described as the king of terrors and, at the same time, it is the terror of kings. It was the apostle himself who described it in 1 Corinthians 15:26 as man's 'last enemy.'

Word pictures

I read of a unique funeral custom conducted by a certain group of African Muslims—close family and friends circle the casket and quietly gaze at the corpse. No singing. No flowers. No tears. A peppermint candy is passed to everyone. At a signal, each one puts the candy in his or her mouth. When the candy is gone, each participant is reminded that life for this person is over. They believe that life simply dissolves.

It is intriguing to discover that the Bible uses a wide range of metaphors for death; in a remarkable way, each one shows what it is, for it demonstrates the true character of death. For example, in Proverbs 14:27 death is set before us as a snare, 'The fear of the Lord is a fountain of life turning a man from the snares of death.' Another is found in Psalm 18:4 where David admitted that death is like sorrow. The shepherd king says, 'The sorrows of death have entangled me.'

A third illustration is taken from Isaiah 9:2 where the great evangelical prophet sees death as a shadow. He reminds us of those who are 'living in the land of the shadow of death.' The last one is in the New Testament where we see death as a sting. Paul challenged death in 1 Corinthians 15:55 when he asked the question, 'Where, O death, is your sting?' And then, right here in verse 13, death is described as sleep.

It is not surprising that many cultures, from day one, have referred to death as a euphemism for sleep. It is worth noting that the word 'cemetery' is a derivation from an ancient Greek word that means 'the place of sleep.' That was how the early believers viewed it; from that perspective, it was an optimistic stance to take. In that sense, it really was a synonym for a dormitory, a place where people sleep. The stillness of a corpse bears a certain resemblance to a person in slumber.

Actually, it is a phrase that occurs from time to time in the Old Testament where we read that this king or that patriarch 'rested (slept) with his fathers' (cf. Asa in 2 Chronicles 16:13 and Hezekiah in 2 Chronicles 32:33). The main idea in such cases is that these figures were now at rest following a lifetime of strenuous activity.

Sleeping saints

Most of us appreciate that sleep is a word that promises a great deal—it reminds us that physical death is not the end. Let's face it, those of us who go to bed at night expect to get up in the morning! We all know from many years of personal experience that sleep is temporary and transient. Fleeting and passing. It does not last!

When a Christian dies, it is like going to bed—they have fallen asleep in Jesus. When they place their head on the pillow, they are waiting for the dawning of a new day, longing for the resurrection morning. After the evening of rest, there comes the morning of rejoicing.

On the tomb in South Africa of Lord Baden Powell, founder of Boy Scouts, are the words: 'I am not here, only my body is.'

When our friends and family pass away and are taken from us, we say to them two simple, meaningful words, 'Good night!' But—and here is the source of our great hope—when we meet again, we will greet each other with the immortal words, 'Good morning!'

Paul gave them a brilliant illustration when he used the example of sleep to convey what happens to a Christian at the point of death. It has been said that 'Christ made sleep the name for death in the dialect of the church.' He is certainly not talking here about soul sleep, as some folk have suggested. That would be a travesty of truth for the Christian is never more alive than when he is in the near presence of Jesus.

Coping with life after death

Paul, realist as always, now follows up his illustration with a simple word of instruction. He knows that when we lose a loved one we will sorrow; we miss them. We are crestfallen; at times, inconsolable. We feel it deeply. Sure we do. Don Carson observes: 'The Bible everywhere assumes that those who are bereaved will grieve, and their grief is never belittled.'

There is a vacant chair in the corner of the room or around the family table; there is an empty feeling in the life and the old heart throbs. Memories are precious but, at times, they can be painful, and they certainly linger. We find ourselves in the doldrums. But, says the apostle, it is only for a short time. A wee while.

Bereavement is a most poignant human experience and there is a fair measure of emotional shock to cope with. To lose a loved one is to lose a part of oneself. It is hard to explain; it is difficult to put into words. Having lost our only son, Timothy, my wife and I can readily identify with the comment made by Leighton Ford, noted evangelist and mission leader, whose oldest son died at age twenty-one: 'The struggle is to bring our faith and emotions together.'

When we look at the unsaved person—the man or woman who dies without knowing the spine-tingling joy of sins forgiven and a right relationship with God—they live and die without God and without hope. There is a terrible sense of finality to those words. When the curtain drops for them, that is it. Unbelievably sad. Tragic. Devastating. Mind you, it did not have to be that way, and it is so unnecessary. But when a Christian dies, they immediately go to be with Christ, which is immeasurably better.

Staring death in the face, the pagan world stood in despair. A typical inscription on a grave reveals this fact: 'I was not. I became. I am not. I care not.' How miserable the world is about death. A poster caption read: *The first two minutes of a man's life are the most critical.* Graffiti underneath exclaimed: *The last two are pretty dicey as well!*

What a marked contrast! There is just no comparison for when the Christian dies, he is absent from the body and present with the Lord (cf. 2 Corinthians 5:6). In a sense, we do not lose a loved one, for we know where they have gone. Our grief is not a dead-end grief for we never say a final goodbye to a fellow believer. Partings here are brief. Short-lived. There will always be another time.

I often think of the words in the high priestly prayer of the Lord Jesus that are answered at the homecall of every believer. There in the upper room, he interceded to his Father and said, 'Father, I want those you have given me to be with me where I am, and to see my glory' (John 17:24). That adds a new dimension to death; it puts it all in perspective for now we see it from a slightly different angle.

4:14 HOW FIRM A FOUNDATION

Paul declares emphatically, *we believe*. It is always good to meet a man who has his feet on the ground and who knows what he believes. What does he believe? Two fundamental truths, Jesus died and the Lord is risen! This is the irreducible core of the gospel; it is what the apostles preached and what the church believes.

Here are facts that can never be altered or amended, moved or shaken. Data that is sure, stable, and solid. A glorious certainty that cannot be trashed. Cardinal truths—they are the central tenets of our faith. We say a hearty 'amen' to them. An empty cross and an empty tomb say all that needs to be said! Death has died; love has won; Christ has conquered! Hallelujah!

So what? Paul goes on to say, *because of this, we believe*. In other words, since that is what happened to Jesus Christ, the same will happen to those of us who know him and love him. Down here in this world, we are meant to walk in his footsteps. Jesus died on the cross, but that was not the end of the story. He rose again on the third day, on that first Easter Sunday morning. For us, we will die, but thank God, we shall rise also.

That means the Rapture is built not on a theological whimsy, but on the substitutionary death of Christ that was a perfect satisfaction to God for sin. Since Jesus fulfilled all the conditions that God laid down for the forgiveness of sin, he transformed death into sleep for us. To borrow the now famous words of Paul, at one fell swoop the Lord effectively took the sting out of death.

Paul reminds us in 1 Corinthians 15:20 that Christ is 'the firstfruits of those who have fallen asleep'—he is the token that one day the harvest will be gathered home. What a memorable day that will be! Bodies will rise from the earth to be reunited with the soul and we shall meet the Lord. According to 1 Peter 1:3 and Romans 8:23 we are waiting for 'the redemption of the body.' Herein lies our blessed assurance, the solid ground of our certitude. That, in a nutshell, is our hope. Bill and Gloria Gaither focus our confidence in the Lord Jesus Christ with these words:

Because he lives I can face tomorrow;
Because he lives all fear is gone;
Because I know he holds the future,
And life is worth the living
Just because he lives.

4:15 GOD SAID IT, I BELIEVE IT

Paul is at pains to remind them that this promise is not a figment of his fertile imagination. There is nothing illusory or dreamlike about it. He wants to reinforce his teaching to them that he is definitely not leading them up the proverbial garden path or down some blind alley. He is not pulling the wool over their eyes in order to lull them into a feeling of false security. He says, *this is the word of the Lord*—a divine utterance; a direct, unabridged revelation from the living God.

John MacArthur notes, 'This is not a philosophical speculation, it is not religious mythology, and it is not some kind of fable fabricated by well-meaning people who want to make folk feel good because of their sorrow.' It is none of that. This is God's pure word, period.

We take the phrase at face value; it means what it says, and it says what it means! The real implication is that we can believe it for it carries authority. One hundred percent authentic. Totally reliable. Utterly credible.

Alive or asleep

Paul then develops the argument by drawing attention to the two types of people who will be most affected with the return of Christ. These are the participants of the Rapture. First, those who are alive and, second, those who are asleep.

The whole emphasis in Scripture is on the sudden, soon return of Jesus Christ. In fact, there is nothing to stop us thinking it may even be today. His advent is imminent and impending. The Lord is at hand as he could come back at any moment. Our redemption is nearer today than it was when we first placed our trust in him as Lord and Saviour. Jesus is standing at the threshold waiting for the final signal from the Father. It has never been so late before; the countdown to zero hour is getting lower every day. Yes, I really do believe in my heart that it is as close as that.

We could be the generation alive when Jesus breaks through the clouds.

If we are, we will not experience death. It has happened before. Yes, it has! Remember Enoch (cf. Genesis 5:24). When his walk with the Lord ended, he left this world not by the dark tunnel of death but by the golden bridge of translation. Remember Elijah (cf. 2 Kings 2:11). He is another fine example, for when his work for the Lord was done, it was instant glory—the now you see him, now you don't syndrome!

And when we put them both together, we can say with the old gospel song: 'When labour's ended (Elijah) and the journey's done (Enoch), then he will lead me safely to my home.' Or another one expressed it like this, 'O joy, O delight, should we go without dying.' Someone said, tongue in cheek, that we are not looking for the under-taker, we are looking for the up-taker! The line in the hymn sums it up beautifully when it says: 'the sky, not the grave, is our goal!'

Facing the facts

There is no point in us burying our head in the sand—we have to face reality. And the watertight fact is this: there are countless millions of God's dear people who are now absent from the body and present with the Lord. There is a vast innumerable company of choice saints who have gone on before us, and right now they are with Christ. They have died; they have been laid to rest; they are those, according to verse 14, who have fallen asleep in Jesus. The nagging questions are, would they:

- miss out at the Second Coming of Jesus?
- be downgraded to a category of lesser saints?
- be no more than eternally disembodied spirits?
- be seen as tag-ons simply coming along for the journey?

That was the real burning issue—the major question they were wrestling with in the early church.

First things first

Look another time; see the rare privilege that is theirs. Deservedly so! Yes, they will rise, says Paul, there is no question about that. But they will rise <u>first</u>. That is the life-changing word, *first*. That is, these folk do not miss out. How could they? Why should they? They will not be left behind when Jesus comes for his own; they will not be excluded or disadvantaged in any way. There is no remote possibility of that.

John Stott makes the comment: 'The apostle's emphasis is on the unbreakable solidarity which the people of Christ enjoy with him and with each other, and which death is utterly unable to destroy.' The Lord never short-changes his people.

They are going to get the front seats. They will have the place of honour when the roll is called up yonder.

I like to think of it like this: those who have died trusting Jesus have caught an earlier train to their final destination of glory. Today we are standing on the station platform, and who knows, we may be on the next one! That is what happens when our number is up, and our time is up.

This is what dying well—dying with dignity—is all about. It is being ready to go when the special moment arrives. As David reminds us in Psalm 23:4, we go through the valley of the shadow of death with our hand in his. He takes us right through into the full light of his glorious presence, into a land of fadeless day. He leads us into a place where there is fulness of joy and eternal pleasures to be enjoyed. It is maybe a touch surreal when we think about it today, but it is really exciting—it is something to get enthused about.

Paul was absolutely right when he said in Romans 14:8 that whether we live or die, we belong to the Lord. No matter what way we look at it, if we know the Lord, we are winners every time! In light of all that Paul has been saying, let me remind you of the words of a great hymn penned by Avis M Christiansen:

> *Darkness is gathering, but hope shines within,*
> *I know I'll see Jesus some day!*
> *What joy when he comes to wipe out every sin,*
> *I know I'll see Jesus some day.*
> *Yes, I'll gladly say it again:*
> *Sweet is the hope that is thrilling my soul,*
> *I know I'll see Jesus some day.*

I read a story the other day which touched my heart—the story of a little five-year-old girl who was watching her big brother die of an incredibly painful disease. He was much older than she, and she loved him a lot. After he died and the funeral was over, she said to her mother: 'Mommy, where...where did my brother go?' Her mum took her up in her arms and said to her: 'He went to heaven to be with Jesus!' The little girl said: 'O!' That was all, her mum's answer satisfied her mind; it answered her curiosity.

Not long after that incident, she heard her mother having a conversation with a friend and her mum was weeping and saying: 'I've lost my son...I've lost my son...I've lost my son!' Later in the day the five-year-old went to her heartbroken mother and said: 'Mommy, is somebody lost when we know where they are?'

Now, we know the answer to that question; the answer is no one is lost when we know where they are! That sums up what Paul has been saying in a handful of words; it crystallises his eschatology: they do not lose out in any way and they will not miss the great event of the gathering together of the church when Jesus comes. That is the immutable promise of Scripture; it is the unswerving commitment of the risen Lord to his people!

4:16-17 SIGNS OF THE TIMES

'Maranatha' was the customary greeting in the early church. Down the street, in the market, across the fence, when God's people met one another this was what they invariably said—Maranatha! The word actually means 'the Lord is coming.'

Two thousand years have come and gone since the Lord first made that glowing promise to his bewildered disciples in the upper room (cf. John 14:3). So much has happened across the world since then. A lot of water has gone under the bridge when we think of some key events, within the last 100 years, of cosmic significance—two great world wars, the establishment of the modern state of Israel, the emergence of Europe as a major player in global politics, the political clout and economic influence of China, the dollar-effect in world markets

(America sneezes and the rest of the world catches a cold), the fall of communism, the rise of Islam, the threat of a nuclear holocaust, globalisation, international terrorism, etc.

Today we are well past the eleventh hour, and with the darkness deepening, time is fast running out. When we read the signs of the times, they tell us it cannot be long until Jesus returns.

The prophetic clock is synchronised with God's time.

It ticks steadily forward at its own pace, with its own schedules to keep.

Standing on the promises

The truth that Paul emphasises in these verses could be described as the next great event on God's prophetic calendar. Lift off for glory is number one on God's agenda for the church—the moment when millions are missing. This is the believer's ultimate trip—something to really look forward to with a purring feeling of heightened expectancy in our heart. It is what the gospel song calls that 'great gettin' up morning.'

Is it any wonder Paul finishes the chapter by saying that this wonderful truth should be a means of mutual encouragement to us within the global family of God. It means that when:

• the going gets tough, hang in there—Christ is coming;
• we feel beaten in the fight, one day we shall overcome —Christ is coming;
• we feel rejected and of no use to the Lord, we should not lose heart—Christ is coming;
• we say farewell to a loved one and life does not seem worth living, look, it will not be long until we meet up—Christ is coming.

This is not a cop-out attitude. It is not an opt out clause in our contract of salvation either. It is not adopting the ostrich mentality and burying our head in the sand. It is not saying, 'Stop the world, I wanna get off!'

It is looking forward with a flame of hope burning in our heart; it is an electrifying excitement combined with a fair bit of fervour and bated breath when we contemplate what awaits us. It is the sitting on the edge of our seat mindset; we are so intoxicated and inspired with this truth that we are standing on our tiptoes. Jesus Christ is coming—there is better on before. The best is yet to be. The grave is not the goal, for we are born and bound for glory.

According to schedule

Paul drafts out a program; he draws up a kind of schedule. There are no fewer than six 'P' characteristics surrounding this wonderfully exciting event in God's unfolding purpose and plan.

- It is personal.
- It is powerful.
- It is purposeful.
- It is practical.
- It is precious.
- It is permanent.

The one returning from heaven is the Lord himself—it is *personal.* An angel will not be sent in his place as a last minute substitute. There will be no other representative from the Godhead despatched. No emissary will be sent from above to escort us home to heaven—Jesus is coming! The Greek in the text is emphatic. There is no messing around here: Jesus is the bridegroom coming to take his bride home to heaven.

The message Jesus shared with his disciples prior to going to Calvary underlines this unassailable fact. There he told them, 'I will come again' (John 14:3). A similar message was echoed by the angels on Ascension Day as he took off from the Mount of Olives to the east of the golden city of Jerusalem. They said, 'This same Jesus, who has been taken from you into heaven, will come back in the same way you have seen him go into heaven' (Acts 1:11). Nothing could be clearer. He said it himself and his word is his bond. Jesus Christ is a man of unimpeachable integrity and there is no reason to doubt what he says.

He came and died as the Lord of glory; today, at the Father's right hand, he is the Lord in the glory; when he comes in power at the end of the age, he will be the Lord with glory; but here, at his coming to the air for his pilgrim people, he is the Lord from glory.

Sounds from heaven

The coming of Christ is *powerful*. J. B. Phillips captures the drama: 'One word of command, one shout from the archangel, one blast from the trumpet of God and the Lord himself will come down from heaven!'

When we stop and think about it, that means there are three welcome sounds intimately associated with the advent of Jesus. The first is the sound of the shout. Really, this is a military expression and it indicates a command or an order that is given. It is as if the troops are standing at ease and the command issued is 'Come to Attention!'

He will speak with the voice that wakes the dead. In fact, three times in the New Testament do we read of our Lord raising his voice to the level of a shout, and each time it is followed by a resurrection.

The first recorded instance is at the grave of his close friend Lazarus in John 11 when, after he spoke a few words, Lazarus emerged as large as life. There he was, standing at the doorway of the tomb. It is probably fair comment to say that if Jesus had not singled Lazarus out for special attention, he would have emptied the entire cemetery.

'The Lord Jesus is the world's worst funeral director for he broke up every funeral he ever attended, including his own.' (Dennis Bennett)

Says something, doesn't it! A track record to be proud of!

The second recorded incident was on the cross at Calvary when Jesus shouted in glorious victory and triumph, 'It is finished' (John 19:30). Matthew's account of this event indicates that some graves were opened and many of the saints of God arose (cf. Matthew 27:50).

The final occasion is here in verse 16. Again he will shout and an innumerable company from the four corners of the earth will rise to enter into his immediate presence.

I was interested to read that at the time of the millennial kingdom which is later, it says in Psalm 47:5 that 'God has ascended amid shouts of joy, the Lord amid the sounding of trumpets.' There, he goes up with a shout; but here, at phase one of his coming, he comes down with a shout!

Michael-angel

The second great mover and shaker in this 'out of this world' drama is the unexpectedly high level of involvement by the archangel Michael.

He can safely be described as the chief prince of the hosts of heaven. He is number one in the angelic pecking order and it appears from reading between the lines that he has a varying range of responsibilities.

In Jude 9 he is involved in the realm of controversy in relation to the precise whereabouts of the body of Moses. In Daniel 12 and Revelation 12 he is hailed as the defender of the nation of Israel during the dark days of the period of Tribulation; there we see him in a primary role of conquest. In Daniel 10 he is very much to the fore in the realm of conflict, especially as it is linked to the challenging problem of unanswered prayer.

Michael's participation is a clear signal to a watching world that three things will have happened: one, all the nefarious hordes of hell will have been roundly defeated; two, death will have lost her sting; and three, the grave will not have gained the victory.

This is the singular moment in time when heaven breaks off diplomatic relations with planet Earth; it is that one favourable moment when the blood-washed nationals of heaven are summoned home to glory.

When the trumpet of the Lord...

The last notable sound in the sequence of the advent adventure is the triumph of the trump of God—the 'last trump' mentioned by Paul in 1 Corinthians 15:52. When silver trumpets were sounded in the Old Testament era, it was a rallying call for the people to engage in worship, or to strike camp and walk on to some new locale, or even to go to war. The trumpets were used for all different kinds of events. Primarily, though, they were used for festivals and celebrations, convocations and judgments. They were used any time anybody wanted to assemble a crowd together to say anything to them by way of public announcements and proclamations.

I was intrigued to read in Exodus 19:16-19 that the trumpet was used to call the people out of the camp in order to meet God—a trumpet of assembly. I believe that occasion was a foreshadowing of this great event outlined here by the apostle Paul.

In Zephaniah 1:16 and Zechariah 9:14 a trumpet was used as a signal of the Lord's coming to rescue his people from wicked oppression—a deliverance trumpet. On a similar note, I believe this is a mere echo of what will happen when the Lord returns to snatch us out of this present evil world. James M. Black (1856-1938) penned the familiar words:

> *When the trumpet of the Lord shall sound,*
> *And time shall be no more,*
> *And the morning breaks, eternal, bright, and fair;*
> *When the saved of earth shall gather*
> *Over on the other shore,*
> *And the roll is called up yonder,*
> *I'll be there.*

When the trumpet sounds in that great day, 'unto him will the gathering of the people be' (Genesis 49:10). Then will be held what the writer to the Hebrews refers to as 'the assembly of the firstborn in the air' (12:22-23) as many sons and daughters are brought from afar and taken home to glory. This is the principal role of the one who is the captain of our salvation.

When we look at this happy occasion through the lens of Scripture, we find that Jesus is frequently seen as the one who gathers his people...

- historically (cf. Mark 4:1),
- congregationally (cf. Matthew 18:20),
- universally (cf. Ephesians 1:9-10),
- adventually (cf. verse 16).

Fanny Crosby (1820-1915) expressed it well:

> *What a gathering, what a gathering,*
> *What a gathering of the ransomed*
> *In the summer land of love,*
> *What a gathering, what a gathering,*
> *Of the ransomed in that happy home above.*

Take heart, when we think of the noise associated with this rather auspicious and grand occasion, there is no way we will ever sleep through it!

Raison d'être

Sometimes we ask the fairly obvious question, why is Jesus coming back? It is *purposeful*, for here is the reason behind it—he is coming for you and me. First, the dead—then, the living.

This is a capital truth that oozes words of bright encouragement. It reiterates the judicious belief that those who have gone on before us are not treated as second-class citizens in the kingdom of God. In no sense will they lag behind the rest of us who are alive and kicking when the Lord returns.

It also affirms our eternal position in Christ, for Paul refers to the *dead in Christ*. A lovely phrase. The bottom line is, if we are in Christ, we are always in Christ, whether alive or dead! 'And,' as John MacArthur says, 'when you die and that body goes into the grave, that body reposes in Christ. That belongs exclusively to him. That is his personal and eternal possession and he will reclaim it from its decomposed dust.' This is the heartbeat of Paul's teaching at the end of Romans 8 where he reminds us that nothing and no one can separate us from the love of God in Christ Jesus. We are glued to him with an unbreakable bond. Because of grace, we are hermetically sealed and we routinely find our focus in him.

- We live in Christ,
- we die in Christ,
- we are dead in Christ,
- we stay in Christ,
- we will live again in Christ!

Caught up!

What is the Lord coming back to do? At the risk of sounding simplistic, we will be transported supernaturally into a new world; he is returning to snatch the saints away and he will do it with an awesome use of irresistible force.

Saints are snatched from the clutches of Satan, snatched from the fallen world, snatched from the serious limitations of the flesh, snatched from the jaws of death, snatched from the confines of the grave, snatched away from the coming wrath of God.

The one who, in a moment of time, plucked us as brands from the burning will, in that final day, pluck us out of this present evil world. When he returns, he will claim us for himself, and as if that is not enough, he will relocate us by moving us into a new place for our eternal habitation—a place he is preparing for us right now, the city of the living God.

This is all entailed in the phrase employed by John in Revelation 20:5 when he speaks of the first resurrection. It is interesting to note that there are three phases to this particular activity, each of which corresponds to the Jewish harvest. They spoke of the time when the firstfruits were reaped and presented to the Lord Jehovah; a while later the harvest was gathered home; that was followed by the picking up of the gleanings. A fuller account is detailed in God's calendar of redemption in Leviticus 23.

In relation to our Lord's program, this would remind us of the first-fruits being gathered in at his resurrection on that first Easter Sunday morning; the harvest will ultimately take place as and when the trumpet sounds; the gleanings will be collected at various times during the period of seven years Tribulation.

In the twinkling of an eye

His coming is *practical* for in that day 'we will be changed' (1 Corinthians 15:51). It probably appeals to my warped sense of humour, but I cannot help but think that this is an excellent verse for a church crèche—'we will not all sleep, but we will all be changed!'

It will happen in a moment, in the twinkling of an eye. It will be just as fast as that, quicker than the batting of an eyelid. Talk about split-second speed—Jesus does not drag his heels. And when it occurs, see what he is going to do. He will give us all a brand new body. He will kit us out for heaven; we will be fitted for glory in clothing that will have God's designer label attached to it. The decay, disease, and weaknesses that plague and ravage our body now will be stripped away. The things that tear and wear us down will no longer have a grip on us.

This body of humiliation will become a body of glorification; this mortal frame will put on immortality; and this body which is presently corruptible will put on incorruption. In other words, in a flash, we will be like the Lord Jesus himself.

This is where the words of John the beloved apostle come into sharp focus for he says in his first epistle, 'We know that, when he appears, we shall be like him for we shall see him as he is.' When Jesus returns, he will upgrade all his people to the status of Christ likeness, even in their own body. An irreversible act. Great news!

The extraordinary work of sanctification that commenced at the point of our conversion will then be complete. The astoundingly good work he begun within our heart when we handed over our life to him will then be finished (cf. Philippians 1:6).

We'll understand it better

The coming of the Lord Jesus is exceedingly *precious* — we will not only be like him, but we will be with him — and that for all eternity. The meeting in the air will be the best, biggest, and brightest meeting we will ever be in. No wonder it is in the air for there is not a stadium on planet Earth that could contain the goodly crowd.

Satan is labelled 'the prince of the power of the air' but on that day the air will not be his domain, it will belong to the believer. We will be on cloud nine — a seventh heaven experience. As pleased as punch and totally enamoured with Jesus as the centre of attraction.

Death is the great separator, but Jesus Christ at his advent is the great reconciler.

It holds the mouth-watering prospect of a happy and joyful reunion as we link up with those who have preceded us. I have no doubts at all that we will recognise our loved ones in heaven and together we shall worship the King in his impeccable beauty. The Bible does not reveal all the details of this reunion; for whatever reason, it is strangely silent on the subject. We are left to read between the lines, as it were.

When Jesus raised the widow's son from the dead, we read in Luke 7:15 that he tenderly 'gave him back to his mother.' This seems to suggest that our Lord will have the felicitous role of reuniting broken

families and friendships. On the snow-capped Mount of Transfigura-
tion the three disciples knew and recognised Moses and Elijah (cf.
Matthew 17:1-5). They did not have to be introduced and this appears
to indicate that we will know our loved ones in glory.

There are many things down here that we do not fully understand,
but then we will know and it will all make sense. Many questions today
go unanswered, but over there all will be made plain. Our dilemma is
that so long as we are down here on earth, we see through tinted glass,
but then it will be face to face. In this life we only see the underside
of the tapestry—the threads hanging all over the place, and at times it
does not look particularly good. It is difficult to recognise the pattern
when lying face down on the carpet! Too close for comfort on this
earth. On the other side, however, we will fully appreciate the words
of Anne Rose Cousin (1824-1906):

I'll bless the hand that guided,
I'll bless the heart that planned,
When throned where glory dwelleth
In Immanuel's land.

Over there Romans 8:28 will become a wonderful reality.

Not till the loom is silent
And the shuttles cease to fly,
Will God unroll the canvas
And explain the reason why,
The dark threads are as needful
In the weaver's skilful hand,
As the threads of gold and silver
In the pattern he has planned.

It is worth noting that the word *meet* carries the idea of meeting a
royal person or an important person. That says it all, for we could not
encounter anyone more important than our Lord Jesus Christ. And we
certainly could not ever hope to rendezvous with anyone of such regal
splendour than the one who is acknowledged as King of kings, Prince
of princes, and Lord of lords. Moments with majesty.

On and on, and on

How long will it last? A day, a week, a month, a year? No! Thank God, it is *permanent*. Forever with the Lord. Eternal. Perpetual. Bliss unending. Pleasure for evermore. For us, it may have an entry point, but there is no exit—we are there to stay!

The great goal of redemption is not just to rescue us from sin and judgment, but to relate us to Christ. We shall enjoy face to face contact with the Lover of our soul, and that for ever. What an exciting prospect which sets the pulse racing and the heart beating faster. The years that must pass before it all breaks in upon us will seem like seconds once the joy of it has burst upon us.

- What a consummation!
- What communion!
- What a Christ!

Each day is one day nearer. Each step is one step closer.

4:18 CHEER UP...JESUS IS COMING!

Paul said, *Encourage each other with these words*. If this great truth does not encourage us, I do not know what else will. Paul does not say that these wonderful truths should prompt us to set dates, or sell our possessions, or watch for Christ's return from the highest mountain. Nor does he suggest that we should go our merry way without paying any further regard to these future events.

Rather, God wants us to take this knowledge and use it to cheer and comfort each other. When we grieve, we need to be encouraged with these truths so that our sorrow will be permeated with hope, not despair.

When it comes to the Lord's return, we are not on the organising committee—we are on the welcoming committee!

We find enormous strength in the fact that one day our Lord will call us home to be with himself, strength even when we cannot understand why bad things happen to good people, strength when we wonder if our evangelistic efforts are worthwhile, strength when we become tired and weary of struggling against temptation.

When we think of the Second Coming of Jesus, there is:

- a sound to hear,
- a sight to see,
- a miracle to feel,
- a meeting to enjoy, and
- a comfort to experience.

Perhaps today

We know the Lord is coming, but we do not know when. Let's pull out all the stops and live a life of walking close with the Lord. Will Christ's return be an embarrassing intrusion or a glorious climax to life for me? When we think seriously about the Second Coming of Jesus, does that thought bring peace and excitement to our heart, or does it foster frustration and uneasiness?

The challenge is unmistakably clear—we are ready for heaven, but are we really ready to meet the Lord? Will you join me in saying, 'perhaps today!' I first came across those words when I visited the grave of the late Dr. M. R. DeHaan in Grand Rapids, Michigan. Among other comments on his headstone were those two unforgettable words, *'Perhaps Today.'*

Recall the passion in John's prayer when he found himself exiled on the craggy Isle of Patmos; he cried from the depths of his heart, 'Amen. Come, Lord Jesus' (Revelation 22:20).

CHAPTER FIVE
LIGHTING THE DARKNESS

What is the difference between ignorance and apathy? I don't know and I don't care!

That is the way a lot of people feel about the Second Coming of Jesus Christ—they do not know and they do not really care. Yet the Bible keeps repeating the theme over and over again. Sadly, some folk have switched off. They have grown used to it in the same way that people become accustomed to the familiar Westminster chimes of a grandfather clock in the lounge.

Making the connection

Every time Jesus and Paul talked about the future, they connected it to the present. Bible prophecy was never meant to be an end in itself. The whole purpose of prophetic truth is not to tickle our ears as we engage in hours of mindless speculation; it is more like a catalyst to spur us on. It is the great motivator. The end times should cause us to reshuffle our priorities in the present times, helping us set our personal agenda so that we live a radical gospel before needy men and women.

The Lord's soon return should compel us to share the gospel more urgently; it should drive us to serve him more faithfully; it should be the incentive we need to give ourselves to others more freely. This high-powered truth is specifically designed to light a fire under our life, to fan the flame of godly living in our heart.

Left behind

The return of Jesus will have a profound effect upon those who are left behind. For the Christian, as we saw in the previous chapter, it is great—a new day is dawning. That noble truth is what prompted Horatius Bonar (1808-89) to sing:

> *I see the last dark bloody sunset,*
> *I see the dread Avenger's form,*
> *I see the Armageddon's onset,*
> *But I shall be above the storm.*

For the sinner, it is not quite so good for the night is falling and the darkness is deepening. To one, the future is sheeny bright and inspiring; to the other, the future is bleak and eerily ominous. The long night-time of Satan's dominion will soon give way to the sun-up of Christ's coming for his own.

It may help if we looked at it like this: phase one of the advent program of Jesus is when he comes to the air for his people (cf. 4:16); phase two is when the Lord comes to the earth with his people (cf. Revelation 19:11-16). Stage one is the 'parousia'; stage two is the 'epiphania' from which we get our English word, *epiphany*. Primarily, it speaks of the revelation—the unveiling—of Christ.

In these verses, Paul draws back the curtain and shows us what happens in between the two stages of the Lord's return. Paul envisages an event taking place that he calls *the day of the Lord*—a day of devastation, destruction, doom, and damnation. Paul informs us in this earth-moving section of this climactic, cataclysmic day soon to come in human history. The bottom line is, there is a woefully serious crisis facing the sinner.

5:1 HISTORY IS HIS STORY

Paul begins by saying, *Now, brothers*. That in itself is a giveaway phrase; it is a clear indication that he is about to introduce a brand new subject—a classic telltale sign that he is moving on to new ground which he has not covered before. He is turning a corner as he wants to look at coming events from a fresh perspective; he wants to view things from a different direction.

It is fair to say that while he is talking about the general scenario of the end time, he moves from one key event—the Rapture of the church—to another major happening that is labelled the day of the Lord.

In his next breath, Paul refers to *times and dates*—an interesting little phrase that only appears three times in Scripture—Daniel 2:21, Acts 1:7, and here.

When our Lord used the term in Acts 1, it was in reference to Israel, not to the church of Jesus Christ. It speaks about the coming kingdom. That is why Paul says, *concerning times and dates we do not need to write to you.* It is worth pointing out that two different Greek words are used, *chronos (times)* and *kairos (dates)*—two kinds of time. It is true to say that they could be used interchangeably, and they could be overlapping.

John Stott reminds us that 'usually *chronos* means a period of time and *kairos* a point of time, a crisis or opportunity.' If we take a moment and separate the two words, *chronos* is the word from which we derive our English word *chronology*, meaning clock time or calendar time. The other word, *kairos*, means seasons, epochs, events. It looks at time, not from the specific viewpoint of a day and an hour; it views time from the perspective of an event, an epoch—something significant that has happened.

We talk about the times of the Gentiles, or modern times; we mean by that that this period of history is characterised by certain events. In this context, the folk in the church in Thessalonica are curious about events that relate to the end of the world; they are fascinated and want to know more about the epochs that shape and mark the end of time.

The fact is, some things they definitely need to know; some of the finer details in the small print they do not need to know; and some things they know already!

The Second Coming of Christ 'is not a toy to play with, but a tool to build with.' (Warren Wiersbe)

5:2-3 BLIND DATE

Paul goes on the offensive when he says, *for you know very well.* It is fascinating to discover that the phrase *very well* comes from the Greek word *akribos* meaning, you know exactly. It is a word that emerges out of painstaking research whereby someone is able to arrive at a logical conclusion.

Paul says, 'Look, you guys know precisely what I am talking about; you know perfectly well what I mean when I say what I do; you know with a high degree of accuracy that this great event is something which is totally unexpected—I have told you that already!' It sounds as though Paul is getting fairly hot under the collar with those individuals who had nothing better to do with their time than speculate about the future.

It seems to me that he lectured them like this: 'You know that nobody knows the date; therefore, you cannot know it either!' God has chosen in his sovereign wisdom to leave us in the dark about the date. Even his Son, the Lord Jesus, does not know when it is! Why? So that every generation would live in light of the reality that it could happen in their lifetime. Therefore, it is not what we say we do not know that should concern us; it is what we do know already that should really bother us!

All things apocalyptic

Having cleared the air, the veteran Paul goes on to talk about the *day of the Lord* and its special significance to the end time sequence of events. This is a most intriguing phrase as it pops up all over the place, especially in the prophetic section of the Old Testament. We read about it in half a dozen minor prophets—Joel, Amos, Obadiah, Zephaniah, Zechariah, and Malachi; and in the trio of major prophets—Isaiah, Jeremiah, and Ezekiel.

In virtually every instance it is an incredibly negative picture that is painted. The focus is on judgment and anger, desolation and havoc being mercilessly wreaked on this earth. It is a vigorous attempt to bring the average citizen low—it is all about driving people to their knees.

Six times it is referred to as a day of doom and four times it is spoken of as a day of vengeance. On the day of Pentecost, Peter made more than a passing reference to it in his sermon and later on he wrote about it in his second epistle. It is also mentioned in the gospels of Matthew and Luke and, again, John in Revelation covers a lot of ground.

Whatever the New Testament writers understood about the day of the Lord, they gleaned their info from the Old Testament prophets. It is, therefore, a biblical term—a solidly Scriptural expression.

There are many 'days' mentioned in the Bible:

- 'the days of Jesus' life on earth'—the time lapse from Bethlehem to Calvary (Hebrews 5:7);
- 'the day of salvation'—this present age when God's grace is drawing people to himself (2 Corinthians 6:2);
- 'the day of Christ'—the coming millennium when Jesus will rule and reign on planet Earth (Philippians 1:6);
- 'the day of God'—a future eternity (2 Peter 3:12).

Satan's reign of terror

When we speak about the Day of the Lord, we are talking about a period of severe trial on earth which falls in-between the two stages of the Second Coming of Jesus Christ. This is often referred to as 'the Tribulation, the great one!' It is designed to last approximately seven years, and it should never be seen as a period only spanning twenty-four hours. It is much too intense and far-reaching for it to be crammed into a single day! And that is the issue that Paul is addressing here in a thumbnail sketch.

Jeremiah 30:7 describes it as 'the time of Jacob's trouble.' The evangelical prophet Isaiah sees it as 'the day of vengeance of our God' (61:2). John later refers to it in Revelation as 'the day of wrath of the Lamb' (6:16-17). Joel portrays it as a 'great' and 'dreadful' day (2:11). Reading between the lines, this will be a time slot of frightening, spine-chilling, blood-curdling events.

It is a day of unprecedented happenings—many of them outlined in the Olivet Discourse of Matthew 24. Much of what will happen is also detailed in the centre section of Revelation, chapters 6 through 19. Scary stuff. Enough to make the hair stand on the back of your neck. Here is the fate of planet Earth in the day when Jesus Christ rises to shake the nations.

Predicting the unpredictable

The out of the blue suddenness of such a moment is presented with vivid clarity, for it will come *like a thief in the night*. We need to show a touch of realism at this point; the triple truth of the matter is:

- no one knows when a thief is coming;
- no one really expects a thief to come; and
- no one sits up and waits for a thief to come.

He just comes! Unannounced. Unscheduled. Unexpected. And as far as the ungodly are concerned, he will take everything from them.

It is not the norm for a burglar to send a you-have-been-warned postcard to his potential victim. Even an Irish thief does not leave a calling card!

A Texan called into Sam's Club one afternoon. In his keenness to pick up his latest piece of gadgetry, he suffered a senior moment and left his car keys in the ignition. Ten minutes later when he came out of the store, the car was gone. He contacted the police department, and they whisked him home. On the journey he did nothing but berate human nature, saying how bad people really were.

Next morning when he opened the curtains he could hardly believe his eyes. His pride-and-joy Cadillac was sitting outside — gleamingly immaculate, valeted inside and out. When he opened the door, he found a note which read: 'Dear Sir, I'm sorry for taking your car. It was a dire emergency, please accept my apology. I have filled your tank with gas and have enclosed two complimentary tickets for the Dallas Cowboys.'

The Texan could not believe his luck; he was overwhelmed with the apparent kindness and thoughtfulness of the person who had temporarily borrowed his vehicle. That evening he and his wife went to the ballgame. Wonderful!

However, upon returning home, when they walked in through their front door they very quickly realised the place had been ransacked. All their stuff was gone — they had been cleaned out. You see, the thief also had their house key!

People are unprepared; in all honesty, they never really expect it to take place in the first instance. It happens to the man three doors down the road, not them! They feel safe living in a cotton wool cocoon in cloud-cuckoo land. When it happens, as it will, they are caught on the hop, with omelette on their face.

The schedule is unmistakably clear: when the trumpet sounds, the Lord comes to the air, and the Christians are immediately translated to glory. At that point the Holy Spirit is removed and the 'man of lawlessness' or the antichrist, as he is better known, is revealed (cf. 2 Thessalonians 2:3). The whole world is taken by surprise as a cynical populace is caught napping. Sound asleep! Basically, man falls down on two counts:

- he failed to hear the word of God; and
- he failed to heed decisive warnings from God.

This is not unlike an event in Boston in 1919.... In 2004 the Boston Public Library opened a new exhibit to commemorate the 85th anniversary of a strange event—the Great Molasses Flood—that killed 21 people and injured 150. On 15 January 1919, an enormous steel vat, containing 2.3 million gallons of molten molasses, burst.

Hot sticky waves of syrup thirty feet tall destroyed buildings, crushed freight cars, wagons, automobiles, and drowned people. One author called it the 'Dark Tide.' The enormous tank had been poorly designed. Company officials reacted to the constant leaks by repainting the tank to match the leaking molasses. Out of sight, out of mind!

These people knew the molasses vat was dangerous, but did not do anything about it. Their only contribution was to give the vat the appearance of normalcy. The lesson is, what we ignore today may drown someone tomorrow. When it comes to the end times and tomorrow's world, the man is a fool who pretends nothing is wrong by painting over the seeping cracks!

Spiritual hallucination

The unbelievable seriousness of the Day of the Lord is intimated when the apostle describes it as a time of delusion, for they will be saying *peace and safety* when, in reality, there is none. It is conspicuous by its absence. Anything there is will be transitory in nature and will not last for long.

It is also hailed as a time of menacing darkness. Morally and spiritually, it is an era when the heart of man is as black as coal. In the natural world there will be certain phenomena as hinted in Joel 2 that will cause a measure of darkness—the sun, moon, and stars will withdraw their shining. The Lord himself said, 'For then there will be great distress, unequalled from the beginning of the world until now, and never to be equalled again' (Matthew 24:21). So this day is unexpected and unmitigated.

It is a time of turbulent chaos and intercontinental destruction. Like a surfer being forced under by too large a wave, this is wipe-out, a repeat of the Holocaust. Only this time it will be so much worse that it does not bear thinking about. As the pace of events unfolds at fever pitch, all will reach a climax at Armageddon, often referred to as World War 3. The conflict of the ages will zoom in on the devastating consequences of man's pugnacious decision to ignore the pleadings of God's Spirit to trust his Son.

In the labour ward

The primary signs of the Lord's coming, Paul tells us, are like *labour pains on a pregnant woman*. An interesting metaphor and one that is fairly common in Jewish apocalyptic literature. At first, the pains are not intense at all. My female sources tell me they are more uncomfortable than painful. They are bearable. A woman may feel one, and then not feel another for fifteen or twenty minutes or more. But as the moment of birth approaches, the pain gets a little more acute—and the pains get closer together. There comes a point where the woman has to make a dash for the maternity wing of the local hospital! The birth of a child cannot be delayed.

- The pain grows.
- The intensity grows.
- The frequency grows.
- And then…a child is born.

Times will be frightfully bad but—to add fuel to the raging fire— they will escalate out of hand so rapidly. The world and global affairs will appear to be recklessly out of control, but God's finger remains on the button. It is a time of tumultuous judgment from an angry God on the nations of the world.

However, after this, and after the purging of the nation of Israel, there will be born the age of the kingdom. Yes, there will be weeping and pain for a handful of years. Then Christ will come in phase two of his advent program, and after a long troublesome night of seven years, cock-a-hoop joy will come in the morning. There are drearily dark days ahead for planet Earth, but for the sinner, the worst is yet to come.

5:4-5 SHEEP AND GOATS

The difference between the groups of people Paul is talking about is crystal clear from the terms that he employs. It is true in every sense to say that there are only two kinds of people in the world—those who know the Lord and those who do not. Saints and sinners, and there is no one else!

It is a classic them and us situation. Paul speaks of them as *you*; he refers to the others as *those*. The contrast is patently obvious when Paul says, we are *sons of the light* and they *belong to the darkness*. On a similar vein, he says, we are *sons of the day* and they *belong to the night*.

A catchy title over these few verses might read something like this: night people versus day people! See what Paul says about each of them. Night people are associated with darkness, sleep, and drunkenness; day people are associated with light, alertness, and soberness. There is a world of difference in the here and now, but there is also a huge difference in the there and then. In the grand scheme of things, we are world's apart!

This idea comes out very powerfully in verse 9 where Paul says, *For God did not appoint us to suffer wrath but to receive salvation through our Lord Jesus Christ.* In other words, the Christian will never experience wrath as we have been chosen by grace to receive the free gift of salvation.

The Christian will never know wrath as we have been appointed to know Jesus.

That takes us right back to 1:4 and the durable doctrine of election—the only way to escape the coming judgment. In that sense, the people of God are unique!

Old and new

We can look at this truth from a slightly different perspective when we recognise the fact that the Bible divides history into two ages or aeons. John Stott in his commentary makes this distinction: 'From the Old Testament perspective they were called "the present age" which was evil and "the age to come" which would be the time of the Messiah.'

As well as that, the two ages were sometimes represented in terms of night and day. The present age was like a long dark night, but when the Messiah came, the sun would rise, the day would break, and the world would be flooded with light. We find glowing hints of that in Luke 1:78-79.

Scripture also instructs us that the Lord Jesus is that long-awaited Messiah and that, therefore, the new age began with his arrival on the scene. One writer makes the welcome comment: 'Jesus was the dawn of the new era; he ushered in the day; he proclaimed the break-in of the kingdom of God.'

At the same time, we all know that the old age has not yet come to an end. John writes in his first epistle that 'the darkness is passing and the true light is already shining' (2:8). That can only mean one thing, for the time being the two ages overlap!

Unbelievers belong to the old age, and are still wallowing in opaque darkness. But those who belong to Jesus Christ have been transferred into the new age, into the kingdom of effulgent light. In Christ we have amply 'tasted...the powers of the coming age' (Hebrews 6:5). Already, because of amazing grace, God has brought us 'out of darkness into his wonderful light' (1 Peter 2:9).

I believe John Stott is absolutely right when he argues, 'Only when Christ comes in glory will the present overlap the end. The transition period will be over. The old age will finally vanish, and those who belong to it will be destroyed. The new age will be consummated, and those who belong to it will be fully and finally redeemed.'

Darkness and light

That is the point which Paul is making in verses 4 and 5: whether we are ready for Christ's coming or not depends on which age we belong to, on whether we are still in the darkness or already belong to the light. It is only if we are in the light that we will not be taken by surprise!

So far as the apostle is concerned, there is no hazy blur in his mind when it comes to the ultimate destiny of those who know the Lord; by the same token, there is no confusion in his thinking as to the eventual destiny of those who do not know the Lord. For one, it will be eternal light—a place where God is present; for the other, it spells everlasting darkness—a place where God is absent.

It follows, therefore, because of who we are and what we are, we are meant to be different! Here is a resoundingly stirring challenge to the people of God. Paul pulls no punches as he tells it like it is. He is straight to the point; he goes for the jugular every time when he says, 'Get a wiggle on!' Up and doing!

The question is, how can we reach such a state of preparedness? We do not want to be caught trafficking in sin when our Saviour breaks through the clouds and comes to deliver us. We need to keep our house in order in anticipation of his imminent return. We also need to get the word out to the world that no one need experience the dreadfully awful horrors of the Day of the Lord.

Paul puts his head on the block when he says to the believer: do not be indifferent today because tomorrow is secure. To the non-Christian, there is an equally forthright, no-holds-barred message: do not be fooled because today seems calm; there is a gathering storm on the horizon.

5:6 SLEEP WALKERS

Be awake! The Carolinian preacher, Vance Havner, said: 'This is a day of anarchy in the world, apostasy in the professing church, and apathy in the true church.' We are not meant to be spiritual Rip van Winkles—sleeping saints. There is no room for apathy, laziness, or complacency in God's kingdom of light. We need to snap out of our comatose lethargy and be liberated from a couldn't-care-less attitude. This is not the time for us to be resting on our laurels.

In today's speak, Paul is saying, do not begin to dream like the world around you is dreaming; do not fall into the trap of living in a fantasy world of make-believe. Our purpose for living in the third millennium is not to accumulate massive wealth or make a big name for ourselves—our real reason for living is to use our abilities to the full in the centre of the will of God.

We need to get serious and stay in the orbit of God's plan for our life. And be real. And be relevant. To put it simply, if we belong to the day, our behaviour must be daytime behaviour. Let's not sleep or even yawn our way through this life.

Stop living in silk pajamas. Stay awake!

On the *qui vive*

Be alert. Actually, we should be living our life in a constant state of red alert. Hawk-eyed. Eagle-eyed. Vigilant. On the lookout. Our eyes should be open wide so that we may be able to lead a life that is balanced.

The thought here is of someone who is not easily ruffled—they have a calm outlook on life. This is the kind of person who hears tragic news, but he does not lose heart; someone who experiences difficulties but does not give up, for he knows his future is secure in God's hands. Unflappable. Nonchalant.

The world can be roughly divided into three groups of people: the few who make things happen, the many who watch things happen, and the vast majority who have no idea what in the world is happening. Paul warns us in this verse not to be categorised by the ignorance of the masses, but to always be on our toes.

5:7 THE BEER FACTOR

The contrast is glaringly obvious when we look at unconverted people as Paul describes them—they are said to be like drunken men whiling the hours away in a stupor—*For those who sleep, sleep at night, and those who get drunk, get drunk at night.* Such folk are enmeshed in a fool's false paradise, oblivious to the harsh realities of what lies before them. They keep their life on track by using the drugs that the world provides.

Their lack of sobriety is self-inflicted. Self-induced. They have no one else to blame but themselves. If they slouch around with a befuddled mind that cannot think clearly—that is their problem. Intoxication and inebriation with the devil's demon of alcohol will do all sorts of wild and weird things to the system.

Not convinced? Take a walk downtown any weekend and look at the poor souls coming out of the pubs, bars, and clubs—the worse for wear! These folk batten down the hatches; they put a lid on life, because their problems are blanked out. Sure they do; the trouble is, it does not last! They are not looking for, nor are they alert to the things of God. Basically, they are so wrapped up in themselves, that they are garishly overdressed. Their hedonistic pursuit of pleasure is such that they flatly reject anything that even remotely smacks of God.

5:8 BATTLE READY

Be armoured! Paul writes, *But since we belong to the day, let us be self-controlled, putting on faith and love as a breastplate, and the hope of salvation as a helmet.*

• Wake up!
• Get up!
• Clean up!
• Dress up!

The picture is of a soldier on duty. The coat of armour provided is designed to protect and preserve us. It covers our most vital organs and it means we are not needlessly exposed to the enemy. With a single stroke of his pen, Paul effectively eliminates the vulnerability of the sentry on guard duty. He will be all right; he will be fine so long as he is wearing the armour! George Duffield (1818-88) wrote the familiar hymn in which he encourages us to:

> *Stand up, stand up for Jesus!*
> *Stand in his strength alone:*
> *The arm of flesh will fail you;*
> *Ye dare not trust your own.*
> *Put on the gospel armour,*
> *Each piece put on with prayer;*
> *Where duty calls, or danger,*
> *Be never wanting there.*

The breastplate could be made from a variety of metals or materials—such as chain mail, or gold, or heavy cloth, or iron, or leather. At the end of the day, the material did not really matter; what counted more than anything else was the high level of protection it offered to the soldier. In our day, it is comparable to a bullet-proof vest.

The parallel to the helmet in today's world is a motorcycle helmet, something that protects the head from potentially fatal blows designed to crush the skull. It is interesting that many motorcyclists in America today still reject the idea of wearing a helmet, wanting to feel the wind in their hair, and to be better attuned to their environment (by their way of it). However exhilarating that may be, it is still high-risk when it comes to head injuries.

Paul was not the first to employ such excellent imagery; he borrowed this absorbing concept from Isaiah 59:17. Ironically, Paul describes this armour in Romans 13:12 as 'the armour of light.'

Faith and love are like a breastplate to cover the heart—faith toward God and a love for the people of God. Hope is a helmet that protects the mind. In two lines of text, we have faith and love and hope—a triad of supreme Christian qualities; three lofty virtues we expect to find in anyone who is walking in the light.

Facing down the enemy

They can be effectively used as three great defences when we meet temptation. Faith is a bulwark against the devious tactics of the enemy. In what sense is that true in our life? Put it like this: sin is a result of distrusting God. To be honest, I cannot spell it out any clearer than that! The Lord is someone who is eminently worthy and deserving of our trust.

For example, we can trust the Lord's person—for he will be consistent with his attributes; he will never deviate from his character; he has perfect integrity. We can trust his power—for nothing is too difficult for him; nothing is too hard for him; nothing overwhelms him; no one gets the better of him! We can trust his promise—for his word is his bond; if he says something, he will do it; if he promises something, he will keep it. We can trust his plan—for the Lord reigns; he is sovereign; he is in total control of all that happens in our life.

God does what he does because he is who he is!

The ramifications of this are incredible, if we believe it! When temptation strikes at our weakest point, we have nothing to fear; there is no need for us to fall into the trap set by the enemy, for if we do, we are casting a dark cloud of aspersion on the credibility of God.

To nail it down, it means when we buckle and cave in under pressure and start to worry about the future, then we are really saying, 'Lord, we know you said you are in charge, and we know you said this problem was no big deal to you, and we know you said you could handle it, and we know you are working to a plan, but we just do not believe it at this moment in time!'

No doubt about it, we are the losers if we end up going down that dead-end road; however, we are on the winning side if we accept that God knows what is best for every one of us.

A soft side, not a soft touch

Faith acts as a breastplate. That is the hard side! Any military history student will tell us that a Roman shield also had a soft side! Underneath that hard armour was soft cloth to warm the body. And that, says Paul, is love! This is the other side of the plate, as it were. 'The outer surface shines with faith and the inner surface is lined with love,' writes John MacArthur.

All sin in our life reflects a failure to love the Lord in a way that we should. When we think about love, we are thinking about that which is the prime object of our affection and adoration. Whoever is the supreme focus of our love is going to control what we do, what we say, and what we think. In effect, they are going to become our god! The Lord Jesus is the only one who deserves to occupy that unique place in our heart.

So when we sin and when we succumb to temptation, we are really saying that the Lord is not number one in our thinking; he has been sidelined to just another figure in our life. He has been elbowed out to make room for another!

See what Paul is driving at? The hard side of our breastplate—that resilient, resistant strength—is that we believe God; the soft side is that we love the Lord. And when the two of them are interwoven and fully operational, we become impregnable!

Helmet of hope

'Hope is hearing the melody of the future. Faith is to dance to it.' (Anonymous)

Paul moves on to talk about the helmet of hope! In Ephesians 6:17 it was 'the helmet of salvation.' Here it is the *hope of salvation as a helmet*. The subtle difference between the two renderings is the inclusion of the word 'hope.'

That begs the question, what is our hope? It is the inescapable fact that one day Jesus Christ is returning for his people. Paul refers here to the future aspect of our salvation; it is the final dimension that is uppermost in his mind. We will protect ourselves against the cruel ravages of temptation when we realise what we are going to become in the glory!

I came across a comment that encapsulates all that Paul is sharing with us in this verse: 'When faith is weak, love is cold; when love is cold, hope is lost. When faith is strong, love is zealous; when love is zealous, hope is firm.' That to me is what marks out a real, card-carrying Christian from the cynical Joe Blow strolling around the shopping mall.

The genuine believer with an authentic lifestyle is someone characterised by faith, love, and hope; this is his battledress and, at the same time, it is his defence against the inexorable onslaught of the deeds of darkness. True then, no less true today, light and darkness are at opposite ends of the spectrum. Poles apart. If we know Jesus as Lord and Saviour, we are sons of the light and sons of the day; we are different from other people, we are meant to be, and that is the way God intended it should be.

5:9-10 THE GENIUS OF GRACE

So far Paul has linked how we should behave on who we are—children of the day, and sons of the light; now he goes on to base who we are on who God is and on what he has done for us—*For God did not appoint us to suffer wrath but to receive salvation through our Lord Jesus Christ. He died for us so that, whether we are awake or asleep, we may live together with him.*

Paul makes two defining statements in this duo of verses. In verse 9 he tells us quite specifically what God did not do; and in verse 10 he spells out the implications of what Jesus Christ has done!

It is enormously helpful to join the two declarations together. First, from a more positive angle, God appointed us to receive the gift of salvation; second, the Lord Jesus died for us so that we might live eternally in him. Our ultimate salvation, therefore, depends on the ripening of God's purpose, and our future life rests solely on the death of Jesus. That implies our hope of salvation (which Paul referred to in verse 8) is well-founded, for it stands firmly on the solid rock of God's sovereign will and Christ's atoning death. It is not resting on the shifting sands of our own performance or roller-coaster feelings.

Sometimes we are like a yoyo—up and down! Other times, we are like the Grand Old Duke of York in the children's nursery rhyme—neither up nor down!

We can face the future with a high level of confidence because our long-term destiny is not focused exclusively on who we are, but on who God is—as revealed in the cross of the Lord Jesus Christ. That really takes the pressure off us; by the same token, it ensures all the glory goes to him.

The fact is, when God spills out his wrath like a dam bursting its banks on the Day of the Lord, it will not be coming in our direction—we are safe and secure in Christ. And when he empties out his final wrath in eternal hell, it will not have our name written on it either. It is not our portion. It is not our lot. It is not what we have been chosen to receive. It is not our divine allocation. Christ has already taken all of this for us! We will miss it because we are not there; we are with Christ having trusted in the Lord as our Redeemer and Saviour.

Our salvation is wonderfully assured; it is a gilt-edged guarantee and nothing and no one can stop it coming to us (read Romans 8:31-39). We are as sure of heaven today as if we were already there! We were once the children of wrath, but no more, now we are the sons of God!

The full-blown fury of the anger of God will never land in our lap! We may have an appointment with death as is intimated in Hebrews 9:27, but we certainly do not have a date with the wrath of God. That is one attribute of God that we will never have to face or contemplate; we are destined for the throne, born and bound for glory!

194

Life and death

It is thrilling to realise that our future prospects are all dependent on what Christ accomplished at Calvary. He died for us. It is personal, for he died with my best interests at heart. Similarly, he died in your behalf. To quote the hymnwriter, Phillip P. Bliss (1838-76), 'in my place condemned he stood, [he] sealed my pardon with his blood.' He gave his life as our substitute when he went to the cross as our representative. He did for us what we could never in a month of Sundays possibly do for ourselves. He died that we might live.

As John Stott says: 'Thus his death and our life are deliberately contrasted and inseparably connected.' Our life is due entirely to his death, and the kind of life he has won for us is a life lived 'together with him.' It can be explained like this: he died our death so that we might live his life! This is tremendous, for through his death we have been not only reprieved, but also reconciled!

He not only let us off the hook, but he also let us in to his family!

And all the manifold blessings of this life with him will be ours whether, at his advent, we are awake or asleep. Christ wants us dead or alive—we do not miss out either way! That is Paul's inimitable way of getting back to the nitty-gritty of what was really bothering the believers in first-century Thessalonica. In life and in death we participate fully in the abundant life we have in Jesus Christ. In a word, Paul says, be alive, because Jesus died for us at Calvary. Whether we live or die we enjoy the presence of the Lord. Life with a capital L.

Paul encourages us to live with eternity in view. This is what living expectantly is all about; it is living in the future tense. When we live this way, we will be mentally active, spiritually alert, and prophetically aware.

5:11 GETTING ALONGSIDE PEOPLE

In a final attempt to rally the troops, Paul says, *encourage one another and build each other up*. It is so easy to lose sight of God's perspective—not unlike Winnie the Pooh whose favourite pastime is to put his head in the honey jar. A beautiful analogy. Most of us enjoy deliciously sweet things. Solomon writes that 'pleasant words are a honeycomb, sweet to the soul and healing to the bones' (Proverbs 16:24). To what extent are we using words to build one another up? Keep your head—including your mouth—in a honey jar...

Think about it—try to visualise someone in your mind's eye who is discouraged or anxious, someone who is physically ill at home or in hospital, someone who is always giving out, someone who is lonely or spiritually drifting. What can we say to encourage such a person? And how will we say it to them when God gives us that golden opportunity?

Most of us realise that this world is no friend to the people of God; it can be a tough, unforgiving place, as many of us know to our cost. It is so easy to get hurt and chivvied by it. That is where the local fellowship is different—it should be a lush oasis in the middle of a sandy desert, a rest stop in the marathon of life, a honey jar in the dark forest, a community of mutual support. We are in it together and we owe it to each other to share one another's burdens and joys. The reality is there are broken hearts in every pew.

Paul's careful use of the word *other* is designed to emphasise the reciprocal nature of Christian care. It is a two-way thing! We are not to leave it to an elite of professional counsellors. Sure, they have an important job to do, and sometimes they are essential; but caring and encouraging one another are ministries that belong to all members of the body of Christ. The ministry of encouragement is like oxygen to the followers of Jesus. We need to realise that no one is useless in this world that lightens the burden of it to anyone else.

In one *Peanuts* storyline, Linus has just written a comic strip of his own and he craves Lucy's opinion. Frame 1: Linus tentatively hands Lucy his comic strip and says, 'Lucy, would you read this and tell me if you think it's funny?'

Frame 2: Lucy pats her foot, and a little bit of a grin comes across her face. She looks at Linus and says, 'Well, Linus, who wrote this?' Linus with his chest heaved out and a great big smile says, 'Lucy, I wrote that.'

Frame 3: Lucy crumples it up, throws it to the side, and says, 'Well, then, I don't think it's very funny.'

Frame 4: Linus picks up his comic strip, throws his blanket over his shoulder, looks at Lucy and says, 'Big sisters are the crab grass in the lawn of life.'

Such is life sometimes, even in the local church. We can easily be the crab grass in the manicured lawn of somebody else's life. No wonder Paul encourages us to be positive in our relationships.

5:12 LEADERSHIP IN THE LOCAL CHURCH

'Coming together is a beginning. Keeping together is progress. Working together is success.' (John C. Maxwell)

This theme is immensely important to them. In fact, it is not only apposite to them, it is right up-to-date for your church and mine, two thousand years down the road. It is just so practical and down to earth that it takes the wind out of our sails.

Paul gives us a set of crisp, clear guidelines to follow which will enable us to maintain purity in our fellowship. It is not just a matter of believing sound doctrine, or crossing our theological T's, or preaching the whole counsel of God. It is more! Much more!

Our life should be a reflection of the beauty and loveliness of Jesus. God could have used mirrors to reflect his person, but he did not. He could have sent angels to reveal his character, but he did not. He gave that indescribable privilege to his children, to us in fact. Therefore, says the apostle, we should be examples of godliness to those all around us.

Paul indicates to us how fellowship can be deepened and, at times, damaged. He shows us that we have a solemn responsibility to each other in the Lord because we are members of the same family. So when we opt out of our responsibilities to each other, and neglect to care for each other with a heartfelt compassion, and ignore the principles God has set down, how terribly sad it all is! Each of us is like a wheelbarrow full of loose bricks, we are dependent on the skilful hands of others to build us up and help us see the mortar of the clearcut truth of God's love.

We are meant to be brothers and sisters, bonded together in Christ. After all, Paul has said it before and he says it again, we are family! We need to face up to the fact that no earthly family is perfect. And, dare I say it, no church family is perfect either. There are problems in every company of the Lord's people. It is just that some are much more serious than others. Some appear to be trivial and insignificant. Others look as though they are insurmountable and Everest-like. However, at the end of every day, whatever the nettlesome issue at stake is, we are still part of a family.

Happy families

A happy family is a priceless blessing. Not just a game…

What are the essentials for a happy church family? What are the ingredients for a warm, vibrant church? It seems to me that where there is love and care and understanding, where there is a sense of mutual help and healthy respect, where there is a tough but tender form of discipline, all these combine to bring immense joy and stability to the family of God.

How will this be seen? It will be evident in our attitude to one another in private and in public. It will be seen in the various activities — inside and outside church — in which we are involved. It will be highlighted in our affinity with the Lord Jesus.

That explains why Paul moves slowly but surely in this mini section, dealing tactfully with two main areas of truth, which are both hypersensitive matters. When he feels the need to give them a piece of his mind, he does so; when he reckons they need a chunk of his heart, he does that as well. Either way, he handles the obvious difficulties and potential fallout with an extremely delicate touch. Not like a bull in a china shop!

The preacher is talking about our conduct and composure in the local church. We have no idea what prompted Paul to write in the manner in which he did. We do know that the Thessalonian church had responsible leaders, since Luke singles out Aristarchus and Secundus for special mention in Acts 20:4.

The likelihood is that some church members were feeling a little peeved and had been disrespectful towards their leaders; the chances are they had directed towards them some stinging criticism. On the other hand, some of the leadership team may have provoked this reaction by their heavy-handed or autocratic behaviour.

Quite frankly, we are whistling in the wind—for we do not know the prime reason for the backlash. I can only imagine that a lot of it can be attributed to sore feelings of hurt pride because someone tramped on someone else's toes. And they picked the feet with the big juicy corns! The common denominator is that Paul rejected both attitudes as totally unacceptable behaviour.

Leaders lead…

Paul makes it very clear that churches should enjoy the rich benefit of pastoral oversight but, as John Stott suggests, 'they are not meant to monopolise ministries, but rather to multiply them!' We must never forget that God has ordained leadership for every local assembly of his people. That is why we have elders and deacons—Spirit-filled individuals who lead the flock of God in a way that is God glorifying.

Those involved in such leadership roles should be men of vision as well as being those who can sell that vision to others. They need to be flexible and able to adapt to the changing needs in a given situation. They are not those who dig their heels in, nor do they drag their heels either. Spiritual discernment is an absolute must as is the ability to make and take decisions. We are talking here about people who will act, not always react. It is all about leaders who lead from the front and, at the same time, still retain the spirit of a servant. Servant leadership—the Jesus model.

They should be men of prayer whose life is in touch and in tune with the Lord. Men who have a heart for God and a big heart for his people; men who can see the big picture in relation to the purpose of God for the world and for his people in the world. In the final analysis, we are looking for men of God, men of the word of God. When we have good, godly, gifted people in positions of leadership, we should respond to them in a threefold manner.

Leaders...where the action is

We should *respect* them! Two vitally important phrases provide the basis for such a healthy respect—*among you* and *over you*. The underlying concept is this:

- as a leader they are over us, but
- as a brother they are among us.

In other words, our respect for them should be based on the fact that even though they are our leaders, they are still our brothers. It is apparent that there is a minimum of three areas in which they are deserving of our loyal support. The first is in relation to their activity. All those in positions of leadership are meant to be workers, not passengers; team players, not spectators. They are supposed to be down on the field of play, not standing on the terraces cheering or complaining.

According to Paul, they should be those who *work hard*. I can tell you from experience, this is not a Sunday only, one-day-a-week job! This is a service that at times can be so wearisome, tiring, and demanding that we fall into bed at night exhausted.

The word that Paul used conjures up a picture of rippling muscles and pouring sweat. Paul applied it to farm labourers and to the physical exertions of his own tent making (cf. 2 Timothy 2:6). He also used it in relation to his apostolic labours as in 1 Timothy 4:10 and to the sheer hard work of his dedicated colleagues as in Romans 16:12. He linked it in with those who labour in preaching and teaching as in 1 Timothy 5:17.

Shepherding is no easy task; it is an arduous role. There are buckets of tears to shed as well as sackfuls of joys to share. There are many ups and downs. There is that which is conducted up-front, but often there is so much more carried out behind the scenes. The average person in the pew has little or no idea of what goes on beyond the glare of the public eye, which is probably a good thing.

Leaders...carry the can

We respect them because of their authority—it is President Truman's 'the buck stops here' syndrome. A similar argument is advanced by the anonymous writer when he says, 'Remember your leaders, who spoke the word of God to you. Consider the outcome of their way of life and imitate their faith...Obey your leaders and submit to their authority. They keep watch over you as men who must give an account. Obey them so that their work will be a joy, not a burden, for that would be of no advantage to you' (Hebrews 13:7, 17).

Those men privileged to exercise godly leadership of a pastoral nature have a solemn responsibility as they invest their life in caring for others. They have the superintending role of an overseer in that they watch over people. Among other duties, they are to:
- feed the flock with the truth of God's word,
- lead the flock by example and testimony, and
- plead for the flock before the throne of grace.

Such an anointed individual is in touch with the living God, in touch with reality, and in touch with the people to whom the Lord has called him to minister. He will have both eyes wide open as he constantly scans the congregation to see how folk in the pew are getting along in their relationship with the Lord. Inevitably, as an under-shepherd, it means going after those sheep that have strayed because the grass looked greener on the wrong side of the fence and picking up those that have been wounded along the journey.

Why bother? Because one day, at the judgment seat of Christ, leaders will give a full and factual account of their time spent in that local church. And when they do, they want to be able to do it with a big smile rather than a doleful grunt. The verdict of the Lord Jesus on this God-driven style of ministry is best summed up in the one-liner, 'I am among you as one who serves!'

In short, the elders who oversee local congregations have no justification for behaving like Protestant mini-popes, or adopting the Rambo style of much secular management that insists on the right to manage, often to the detriment of its workforce! 'Do as I say, not as I do!' What Jesus advocates, and Paul stands shoulder to shoulder with him on this issue, is a servant leadership where humility and gentleness are the dominant features. The Jesus-style of leadership is best seen when we take a basin of water and a towel and wash other people's smelly feet!

Leaders...talk the talk

An elder or a leader will always be able and willing to sit down with the people of God and open up the word of God to them—Paul speaks at the end of verse 12 of those *who admonish you*. It portrays an ongoing ministry where a motley group of believers are consistently reminded—personally and corporately—of biblical truth. It is all about teaching and applying Scripture in a collective sense and that is supremely important, but it should also incorporate those times when individuals are discipled on a one-to-one basis.

The Greek word for *admonish* that Paul uses is more often than not used in an ethical context and it generally means to warn against bad behaviour and its tragic consequences. Yes, there are times when leaders need to crack the whip. It is the kind of necessary instruction that might be given to someone who is in serious danger of going off the rails. Being a negative word, it is often coupled with teaching as in Colossians 1:28 and 3:16.

Both these vital roles belong to the brief of those in pastoral leadership, implying that good elders are not spineless or toothless individuals. I hasten to add that such a word does not denote a harsh Draconian-type ministry.

'While its tone is brotherly, it is big-brotherly.' (Leon Morris)

'Big-brotherly' not in the Orwellian sense of the phrase, but the idea that there is someone in the church leadership who is genuinely looking after our spiritual interests. There is no need for us to smell a rat, for this is not an old-style, red flag, totalitarian regime; rather, it is total care within the family of believers.

What attitude should the members of a local church adopt towards those in leadership? 'They are neither to despise them, as if they were dispensable, nor to flatter or fawn on them as if they were popes or princes, but rather to respect them, and to hold them in the highest regard in love because of their work,' notes John Stott. This unique combination of appreciation and affection will enable pastors and the people they lead and serve to live in peace with each other.

5:13 ROAST PASTOR FOR SUNDAY LUNCH

In saying what he does, Paul takes the whole matter a logical step forward. We should appreciate these people for what they do for us and, at the same time, we should also show our affection for them in the Lord—*Hold them in the highest regard in love because of their work.*

Ever wondered why there should be such a refreshingly positive response to them? Why should we back them and bless them? The answer is found in Paul's teaching in Ephesians 4:11-13. There we are reminded that their gift of leadership is from the Lord, and from God's perspective, a pastor is also his gift to his church. Therefore, all those in Christian leadership should never be taken for granted.

Sadly, it does not always happen that way. I certainly know and you probably know as well of situations where pastor and people are constantly on a war footing; to put it simply, they are at logger-heads with one another. An unhappy experience like that does little or nothing for the glory of God. It is incredibly painful for all those unfortunate enough to be caught in the crossfire between the rival factions. It massively inhibits the church's life and growth as well as seriously damaging the church's public image.

When church fellowships pass through traumatic times of upheaval and disunity it often has long-term repercussions that we fail to realise. You see, bi-polar unity is not unity at all, but warring factions—similar to what was experienced at the Men's Basketball Championships. Nine times out of ten, such public fallout's are detrimental to the local church both in the short term and in the longer term as well. That reiterates what Paul is saying: we should always endeavour to see the goodness and grace of God in the life of those holding down leadership positions. By the same token, we should do all in our power to stand by them and encourage them in the work they are doing.

John Stott sums it up so well when he acknowledges: 'Happy is the local church family in which pastors and people recognise that God calls different believers to different ministries, exercise their own ministries with diligence and humility, and give to others the respect and love which their God-appointed labour demands!'

LIP...Live In Peace

The third facet of Paul's thinking in relation to our attitude to leaders is that we should genuinely thank God for them. This is the fundamental thought behind Paul's comment, *live in peace with each other*. A most unusual kind of phrase to use in this context! It appears strangely out of place.

Well, nothing could be further from the truth, for our good friend Paul is no fool! As they say, he was not born yesterday; this guy is grounded to reality. He has been around long enough to know what goes on in churches; he knows what happens behind closed doors; he knows what takes place in the rough and tumble of everyday life in the average congregation.

Sure, it is a fact of life that we will not and do not always agree with those in leadership roles; we will not and do not always see eye to eye with them. There will be things they do and things they do not do that, to be honest, we just do not like. But, says Paul, in light of eternity, those differences do not matter. In spite of how we feel at a given point in time, we still owe it to them, to the wider inclusive church family, and to the Lord, to sincerely thank God for them. Why? Because of what they are and because of who they are. We have gone full circle!

5:14 DEALING WITH PROBLEM CHILDREN

It is a fair comment to make that we get all sorts of sheep in a flock. Sheep are generally noisy, dirty, stupid animals which follow each other's lead and react to danger with confusion. Without pushing the comparison too far, we get all kinds of people in a church fellowship. There is the infamous trio of yelpers, helpers, and skelpers! They have often been described as the so-wise, the unwise, and the otherwise!

It was A. J. Gordon (1836-95) who classified church members as figureheads, soreheads, and deadheads. I think I would add another to his list, hotheads!

In the previous section, the focus was on the leaders, and that is hugely important because it has to be right at the top; now, in these verses, Paul widens the net and talks about the rest of us lesser mortals as he reminds us that we all have a unique ministry to one another. This is how the body of Christ is really meant to function.

As Philip Arthur says with keen insight to the problem, 'As far as Paul is concerned, these vital pastoral tasks were not the sole province of the top tier of church leadership. One certain way of ensuring that the job is done badly is to leave it to those in oversight positions. There is simply too much to be done!'

Without doubt, such a key ministry is the responsibility of the church membership at large. It is the members of the body of Christ having a mutual care and concern for each other. In this instance, there is much more than nice thoughts, pious platitudes, and weasel words that are needed; care and concern require robust action. Paul does not mince his words when he lays down the law with four commands to take on board.

• *Warn those who are idle*...the 'won't do's' whatever!

This refers to those believers who are blithe when it comes to ful-filling their church responsibilities. They are careless, stubborn, out of step with the leadership, and out of line with the word of God. It is not unreasonable to assume that they are the same lackadaisical, what-right-have-you-got-to-tell-me-what-to-do people, breaking rank with the rest of the church fellowship as well as the leadership.

Our initial response is relatively straightforward; they are to be reprimanded in love. It is hard to say it, and even more difficult to do it, but there are times when it is necessary to confront others with the truth so that their rebellious behaviour might be corrected. Bearing in mind Galatians 6:1, there is a place to do it, a time to do it, and a proper way to do it. These are the hard-hearted people in the congregation.

• *Encourage the timid...*the 'want to's' however!

We are to come alongside and draw near to those saints who get down in the dumps rather easily. There is a time for getting close to people. We are to encourage those who are prone to give up and those who are tempted to give in; we are to try and lift them up.

This may involve us giving them a few words of comfort, or offering to them a pair of listening ears. It may even mean that we just show them in some other concrete way that someone genuinely cares for them and about them. By its very nature, this is a hands-on approach that Paul is advocating.

There are always quitters in every church family; a sad fact of life but, unfortunately, all too true to life. The baseline is that it is always too soon to quit. For whatever reason, there are those who perpetually look on the dark side—Paul wants us to show them the sunny side up. These are the faint-hearted people in the church.

• *Help the weak...*the 'can't do's' whenever!

The verb for *help* presents a graphic picture of the undergirding that those who are weak need. It is as if Paul wrote to the stronger Christians and said to them, 'Hold on to them, cling to them, even put your arm around them!'

Ours is a support ministry in the best sense of that word as the reference here is to those who are weak in the faith. They have not grown up in their relationship with the Lord. They are still on the milk when they should really be eating and enjoying the meat of the word of God. To all such, Paul says, we should hold on to them; bear them up; care for them; stand by them; and stand with them for as long as it takes to see them through. I suppose we could say that these dear friends are numbered among the broken-hearted.

'No one is useless in this world who lightens the burden of it to anyone else.' (Charles Dickens)

These three categories of people could be easily described as the problem children of the church family, and take it from me, every church has them. Some more than others!

Part of the problem is their spiritual diet—they were feeding their soul on trivialities, titbits, and takeaways. Nothing substantial. Plenty to lick their lips about—but nothing to sink their teeth into. None of us will grow big in God if we seek to exist on spiritual junk food—what I call, the McDonaldisation of the church.

Patience is a virtue

That is why the final arrow in Paul's quiver is mega important. He challenges us to *be patient with everyone*. We have seen it so often before and here we see it again: Paul is a realist.

- An optimist sees only opportunities.
- A pessimist sees only problems.
- A realist sees the opportunities presented by problems!

The travelling preacher does not run around with his head in the clouds; he is a down-to-earth bloke. He knows this will not be easy, for there will be many times when we are pushed beyond our limit; when we have just about had enough, and we feel as though we can take no more; when we have that sinking sensation in the pit of our stomach. In such moments when we are pulling out our hair, Paul suggests that we need to think outside the box—we should be patient and give these folk who are driving us round the bend some quality time, and show them Jesus.

It appears that the apostle is exhorting us to be long-tempered (as opposed to short-tempered) for that is the accepted meaning of the Greek term for 'patience.' Such a wonderful virtue is an attribute of God as in Exodus 34:6 and Psalm 103:8; it is also spoken of as a fruit of the Spirit and a top characteristic of love as in Galatians 5:22 and 1 Corinthians 13:4. The bottom line is, since God has been infinitely patient with us, we too must be patient with others.

It conveys the idea of being tough and durable in the face of stiff, unrelenting, intense pressure; it is manifesting a quiet, steady strength that can handle the stress and the strain; it is being able to cope with very real feelings of disappointment, hardship, and pain.

When push comes to shove, it is all about self-control, for God does not want us to operate with a short fuse. He does not expect us to sit on a time bomb! People can be so discouraging; they promise so much, only to disappoint and, in situations like that, it would be so easy to throw in the towel. That is the last thing we want to do for the church must never be the kind of army that shoots its wounded!

It is helpful to realise that woven into the fabric of this brief section is the thought that we should always watch our motives. Sure, this is what happens in a family and this is what happens in a local church. Human nature, we say. By the same token, it is an equally valid point to make, it may be human, but it is also sinful. Such behaviour can never be condoned!

5:15 GETTING EVEN

'I will never permit any man to narrow and degrade my soul by making me hate him.' (Booker T. Washington)

That is why Paul says, *Make sure that nobody pays back wrong for wrong, but always try to be kind to each other and to everyone else.* Here is an allusion both to the teaching of Jesus in the Sermon on the Mount and to his own refusal to hit back that we read of in 1 Peter 2:20. Paul is simply saying that we should never retaliate and try to get even with a brother or sister. There is no loophole, no get-out clause, in the wording of Paul's injunction.

We should be ultra-careful what we return to them, no matter what missile they have fired our way. The temptation is for us to want to get our own back; we want to stand up for our own rights; we want to take everything into our own hands and settle old scores. The local church ought to be a place where kindness and generosity flourishes—not a battleground for getting even! In divine math, two wrongs never make one right! It was Confucius who said that 'many hands make right work.'

A mother ran into the bedroom when she heard her seven-year-old son scream. She found his two-year-old sister pulling his hair. She gently released the little girl's grip and said comfortingly to the boy: 'There, there. She didn't mean it. She doesn't know that hurts.' He nodded his acknowledgement, and she left the room. As she started down the hall the little girl yelled at the top of her voice. Rushing back in, she asked: 'What happened?' The little boy replied: 'She knows now!'

We should endeavour to be genial and considerate and only do what is good, as ultimately, this is the only way to overcome evil. So I am suggesting we adopt a radical approach that is not out of this world, but it is straight out of the word of God! Maybe we need to ask ourselves the question, WWJD? What would Jesus do? His way may not be the easy way, but it is always the best way.

We should be an integral part of the solution rather than exacerbating the problem. Better to be effective extinguishers rather than putting more fuel on the fire. In today's litigious society, we in the church are here to build bridges not set up barricades. It is the mindset that turns the other cheek and says, I want to help you; not one that reacts with hostility and declares, I am going to sue you!

When we find ourselves in explosive situations like those mentioned above, we should show the love of Jesus to those people who get under our skin and cause us enormous frustration. It is good to remember that God always has the last word. In the book of their life, he alone writes the last chapter. We should be happy and content, therefore, to leave it all with him.

'Good for good, evil for evil: that is natural.

Evil for good: that is devilish.

Good for evil: that is divine.' (Saint Augustine)

Smoothing the ragged edge

All that Paul has been saying in this section is appropriate for every church and, in many ways, what we have here is a beautiful vision of the local church as a community, not only of mutual comfort and encouragement, but of mutual forbearance and service as well.

'Lord, you have searched me, you know me; Lord, help me be the kind of person you want me to be! Lord, let the beauty of Jesus be seen in me...Lord, let there be love shared among us...Lord, bind us together with cords that cannot be broken.'

We know what happens when God answers that prayer in our life, there is a minimum of two results—we will respect our rulers and our behaviour among the brethren will bring glory and praise to the peerless name of Jesus.

5:16 STACCATO SAYINGS

No matter what angle we view it from, the emphasis from here on in is on practical Christianity; it is geared to living for God in the here and now. Candid comments. Paul is not sitting like some bespectacled professor in an ivory tower—he is on the level. Here is distilled wisdom at its finest and best. We are meant to enjoy life, not endure it!

In this paragraph there are seven sayings that give us a life permeated with rapturous joy and zest. The most magnetic people on planet Earth should be those in the family of God, for their experience of the grace of God is invigorating, astounding, and contagious. It knocks us sideways, such is its amazing power. It sweeps us along on a tidal wave of blessing. In Christ alone, we have something to sing and shout about. We have every reason to be infectious in our unbridled enthusiasm for the Lord.

Sadly, for so many of God's people, life appears to be one big long bore. Their most exciting encounter is found on the nightly soap opera beamed into their home from some television company only interested in winning the ratings war with the other channels. The network's only motivation is financial—to get the viewer to watch the commercials. But what a horrible way to go about it—sometimes tacky and salacious, often times vulgar and suggestive, it is the highlight of such folk's day. Feeding their soul on a diet of sleaze, they are really missing out, big time!

This closing section reminds us that we can experience life to the full if we embrace and personalise these seven pertinent, pithy sayings. Richard Mayhue writes: 'These short statements strike at the very heart of the Christian life; each is a command that expects obedience; these imperatives could be viewed as the ABCs of Christian living.'

Joy 24/7

The first, *be joyful always*, extols the delights of a life in tune with the Lord. This is the shortest verse in the Greek New Testament. It means we have something in our spirit that the world does not have. We have a joy, deep down in our heart.

I heard a brother make a shrewd, tongue-in-cheek observation on one occasion that some of God's people have a joy that is so deep, it never rises to the surface! Happiness depends on what happens to us and what is taking place around us, but this joy is centred in Christ. Our circumstances change; the tide of events ebbs and flows; our fortunes fluctuate, they rise and fall; our emotions can be like the proverbial yoyo; yet, even when life goes flip-flop, we still have a joy in our heart, 24 hours a day, 7 days a week = 24/7. Not just some of the time, or most of the time, but all of the time.

Christ gives us his peace and his grace; here it is his joy that is imparted to us. This exquisite blessing is ours when we abide in him (cf. John 15:1-11). When our life is lived in the fulness of the Holy Spirit then joy is a fruit much in evidence (cf. Galatians 5:22).

Paul taps in to what the Psalmist invited God's people to do years earlier, for we read, 'Come, let us sing for joy to the Lord; let us shout aloud to the Rock of our salvation' (Psalm 95:1). In another Psalm, the Old Hundredth, he says, 'Shout for joy to the Lord, all the earth.' We shout for joy for there is exuberance in knowing and worshipping the risen Lord Jesus!

In the context of the local church meeting, Paul is issuing not an order to be happy, but an invitation to worship, and to joyful, vibrant, lively worship at that. So many of our church services tend to be unforgivably gloomy and boring; when we walk through the glass doors, it seems as though we are walking into a morgue, for people are so doleful and apathetic. We start at 11.00 sharp and end at 12.15 dull!

Our penance is over! There is no need to be like that; our times of worship should be a celebration of felicity and faith — a joyful rehearsal of what God has done and given us through the Lord Jesus Christ.

At the same time, there is no need to go over the top and swing from the crystal chandeliers in the sanctuary or dance up and down the plush carpeted aisles, for we need to recognise that, as we engage our heart and voice in worship, we do so with a sense of reverence, awe, and humility.

'The most wasted of all our days are those in which we have not laughed.' (Sebastien Chamfort)

5:17 STAYING IN TOUCH

The baseball game was tied with two outs in the bottom of the ninth inning. The batter stepped into the batting box and made the sign of the cross on home plate with his bat. Yogi Berra, Hall-of-Fame catcher for the New York Yankees, was behind the plate. A deeply religious man as well, Berra wiped off the plate with his glove and said to the pious batter, 'Why don't we let God just watch this game?'

Letting God just watch! Whatever the theology when applied to the outcome of a baseball game, it is terrible theology when applied to the way we live our lives and carry out the work of the church. A bit like British Prime Minister Tony Blair, when asked whether he and President George Bush prayed together when they met at Camp David, his response was, 'We don't do God!'

The apostle highlights the desirability of a life lived in touch with the Lord and the futility of leaving God out. *Pray continually* underlines the necessity of keeping short accounts with the Lord. The idea is not round-the-clock praying where we are never off our knees, for that is impossible, unrealistic, and unworkable. The idea includes praying in our bathtub, at mealtimes, while working, in the car.... Heaven knows we need it in the car sometimes!

Staying in close touch with God is what Paul has in mind. It is a broadband prayer experience where we are never offline. We are always-on messaging, to use today's communication parlance. It is essential that we keep the lines open and ensure the proper channels are always clear—it does not work if there is a blockage between our heart and heaven. It is being able to converse and chat with the Lord at any time of day or night. To all intents and purposes, we have a hotline to heaven. 'Prayer is a shield to the soul, a sacrifice to God, and a scourge to Satan,' is the observation of John Bunyan.

A prayerful attitude like this means we consciously live in the atmosphere of Christ and breathe in the rarefied air of heaven. It is experiencing the reality of Psalm 91:1, for we 'rest in the shadow of the Almighty.' Nehemiah knew all about it—at the same time as he was thinking on his feet he was sending a quick prayer up to heaven (cf. 2:4). Nehemiah could identify with George Failing when he said: 'He who does not pray when the sun shines will not know how to pray when the clouds roll in.'

Such moments are times when we sense his nearness, and live in the place where God answers prayer. The Lord is only a prayer away—he sees our every sigh; he hears our every sob; he is familiar with every sentence we utter—that is what fellowship with the Father is all about. We get rid of the burdens as we hand them over to him. And when we do that, we find release in our heart and, as a consequence, joy abounds. Because prayer frees us from the anchors of life that drag us down and drain our joy. He is El Shaddai, the God who is just what we need, the God who is enough. Exciting!

'Is prayer your steering wheel or spare tyre?' (Corrie ten Boom)

Can't pray, won't pray

It needs to be emphasised that Paul is not only speaking about our personal prayer life. The general context would lend a fair amount of weight to it being corporate prayer. The depressing experience of many evangelical churches is that the prayer meeting is either a relic of the distant past, or else it is the worst attended meeting in the course of an average week. For reasons best known to themselves, people refuse to turn up for a Wednesday night prayer meeting!

If praise and worship is so important that we push it to the top of our agenda, surely prayer is compellingly indispensable! It is crucial to the church's ongoing impact in the community that we make time to pray with one another. Serious intercession should be the hallmark of an evangelical ministry, the life and soul of a spiritually healthy congregation. A biblical ministry that is signally blessed is usually one underpinned with prayer.

John Stott reminds us that 'we should be praying for our own church members, far and near; we should be praying for the church throughout the world, its leaders, its adherence to the truth of God's revelation, its holiness, its unity, and its mission; we should be praying for our nation, our parliament, and our government, and for a just, free, compassionate, and participatory society; we should be praying for world mission, especially for places and peoples resistant to the gospel; we should be praying for peace, justice, and environmental stewardship; and we should be praying for the poor, the oppressed, the hungry, the homeless, and the sick.'

Stott offers this challenging comment by way of conclusion when he genuinely wonders '... if the comparatively slow progress towards world peace, world equity, and world evangelisation is not due, more than anything else, to the prayerlessness of the people of God.' I imagine, in fact I know that there is more than a grain of truth in his analysis of the situation as it stands at present.

5:18 AN ATTITUDE OF GRATITUDE

'Some people are always grumbling because roses have thorns; I am thankful that thorns have roses.' (Alphonse Karr)

The third of Paul's sayings is where he proposes that we express our bowled over sense of gratitude to the Lord—*give thanks in all circumstances, for this is God's will for you in Christ Jesus.*

Thankfulness should always characterise the Christian as he says to himself, 'Praise the Lord, O my soul, and forget not all his benefits' (Psalm 103:2). Even a grumpy old man like Jeremiah recognised the truth that 'the Lord's compassions never fail, they are new every morning' (Lamentations 3:22-23). When we give thanks in all circumstances—the good, the very good, and the not so good—we are manifesting the gift and grace of contentment. In other words, we are happy with our portion in life. OK, maybe it could be better, but it could also be an awful lot worse!

I read of an interview with a balloonist who was grounded by appalling weather at an international ballooning festival. When asked if he was disappointed, he said, 'I would rather be on the ground wishing I was in the air than be in the air wishing I was on the ground.'

- Thanks *for* everything. No!
- Thanks *in* everything. Yes!

A superb example that springs to mind is the story of Paul when he found himself in a rat-infested Philippian prison. He did not sit around bemoaning his lot; he was not complaining about all that had happened to him; he did not whinge about human rights or carp on because he was denied access to his attorney; he did not get all worked up into a feeling sorry for himself kind of frenzy; instead, he praised the Lord in his dank, underground cell—an eloquent tribute to the grace and faithfulness of God.

You see, whether we find ourselves in the storm or in the calm, in deep waters or on dry land, it matters not, for his sovereign plan is designed for our good. To me, this is what living in the reality of Romans 8:28 is all about; this is what enables us to say a sincere 'thank you' for every experience he brings into our life. In the best of times and in the worst of times, we say 'thank you' to a loving heavenly Father.

The least we can do is submit willingly to his gracious providence with an overwhelming sense of gratefulness. The Christian's life is to be an unceasing eucharist. That helps crystallise what our response ought to be to all that life throws at us. The Lord appreciates and values people with thankful hearts! When all is said and done, such a mindset blends in beautifully with his perfect will for our life.

Ellen Decker tells the story of her son Ryan who, when he was a five-year-old, offered the following prayer during family devotions: 'Dear Jesus, sorry for the mess we made in the yard today.' After a slight pause, he concluded: 'Thank you for the fun we had doing it.'

5:19 ON FIRE FOR GOD

Number four of seven is a life on top for the Lord. That may seem an unusual phrase but when we see what Paul says it all fits together neatly, *Do not put out the Spirit's fire.*

We know from Ephesians 4 that the Holy Spirit is a friend—we grieve him when we hurt him. In this instance, he is likened to a fire—we quench him when we suppress him and stifle his influence in our life. Here is an impassioned plea from the heart of Paul for us to acknowledge the sovereignty and freedom of the Holy Spirit.

The danger is that we may try to extinguish him in our life and ministry. It is foolish to pour cold water on the fire of his plan for our life or even to dampen the effect of his word upon our heart. The fire burns up the dross in that it purifies us. It has incredible power so that it brings light and gives warmth.

Perhaps more than ever, we need the Isaiah experience—to be touched with a live coal from the altar and be a people ignited for the Lord. It cleansed Isaiah's mouth! We need to burn for the Lord in such a manner that men and women will be aware that we are ablaze for him. On fire for God.

'Make me thy fuel, O flame of God.' (Amy Carmichael)

5:20 WHEN FAMILIARITY BREEDS CONTEMPT

Item number five on Paul's agenda is a life being taught by the Lord—*do not treat prophecies with contempt.* When the Lord is speaking to his people through his word, we should be extra cautious about our response. We must never downgrade it; we must never devalue the word from the Lord by displaying an apparent lack of interest in it or by giving it a cool, frosty reception.

When biblical truth is proclaimed, whatever the channel, we should treat it as the word of God. It is not the voice of man. It is the living God who is speaking to us. Let's not get overly familiar with him and his word, for when we do we risk bringing contempt to our soul.

This injunction was especially relevant in the early church when they did not have the complete canon of Scripture as we have it today. That meant there were those in the congregation whom the Lord raised up with a gift of prophecy—men and women who knew and spoke God's mind and will.

In our day, we have no need for this role for we have the mind and heart of God revealed in the word of God; in the sixty-six books which make up the Bible we have a full and final revelation of God to his people.

To add to it or take from it is just not permissible and there are many serious warnings sprinkled throughout the Bible with regard to such an arrogant attitude; it is a total non-starter, for no one has the right or authority to tamper with the truth of Scripture. So, says Paul, when God is speaking into our situation and when the Lord is addressing our heart through his word, be more than just a good listener, be a good hearer!

5:21 LITMUS TEST

A radical call for spiritual discernment is Paul's sixth saying—he urges us to engage our mind in a life of testing for the Lord, hence the statement, *Test everything. Hold on to the good.*

There is especially in these critical days a need for us to examine what is before us by asking the searching question, Is this in harmony with the teaching of Scripture? We need a mix of spiritual perception and biblical insight so that we may be able to distinguish the difference between what is right and wrong. Be discriminating for all that glitters is not gold. We need to sift, evaluate, and weigh up carefully all that is said. The preacher man warmly recommends intelligent scrutiny.

The tendency in some circles is to write everything off that is branded 'new' and, not content with that, to go on and throw the baby out with the bath water. We often say 'that is not the way my father did it' meaning our earthly fathers. We need to be open-minded to new thoughts if they are scripturally sound. I believe we must be prayerful in our approach and balanced in our critique of what is presented to us. Yes, we test it for the Lord, and we hold on to what is good. That means we take on board all that is authentic; we do not fall for the counterfeit. We see through that, and we go for the genuine article! It is the Berean syndrome (cf. Acts 17:11).

There are many ways we can test what is being said, and the most obvious is the test of Scripture. Does what is being said tally with the rest of Scripture? Another way concerns the person of our Lord Jesus Christ. Is this preaching an authentic Jesus? Is it the Christ of Scripture? The fact is, no one truly inspired by the Holy Spirit would deny that Jesus Christ is the Son of God. After all, the supreme ministry of the Holy Spirit is to glorify Jesus, not to undermine him.

Another test is the gospel test. We should ask, what does the preacher say about the way of salvation? Is it by faith alone, by grace alone, by Christ alone? If it is not, we close our ears to what is being said. The last big test is the test of integrity for the lifestyle of the preacher should be in total sync with the message he is proclaiming. There should be no contradiction between what he is and what he says. He walks his talk.

The passage of two millennia of Christian study should have made the wolf in sheep's clothing an endangered species. It has not.... The wolf in sheep's clothing at times is in every man.

5:22 DON'T TOUCH IT WITH A BARGE POLE

The last principle Paul talks about is a life of triumph in the Lord—*avoid every kind of evil*. The apostle is calling God's people to a life of total abstinence. That command does not only apply to the more obvious, well-publicised sins that hit the headlines in the tabloid press, but to every form of evil.

It is not just evil in itself, but the very appearance of it. In other words, we should keep ourselves unspotted and untainted from that which is less than desirable. Do not get contaminated. Do not allow yourself to become polluted. As my mother used to say, 'If in doubt, don't do it; if there is any doubt, don't dabble in it.' If we question whether something is ethical, it almost certainly is not.

'Don't fasten your shoelaces in a strawberry field!' (Verna Wright)

Why? Well, we would not want people to think we are stealing strawberries! We should not give Joe Public a chance to talk about us, nor should we give him opportunity to point an accusing finger at us. It is sad but many a good life has been wasted and many a testimony ruined because of a moment's indiscretion. Keep yourself from temptation. At the risk of sounding simplistic, if we cannot take Jesus with us, then we should not be there!

5:23 PAUL'S WISH-LIST

When we move into the final few verses in the chapter, Paul bids them a fond farewell. He just wants to say 'goodbye' but that has not been an easy thing for him to do. He found it enormously difficult. Actually, he took six verses to close his letter. Everything he said shows his deep affection for them. He talks about:
• a faithful God,
• immensely loyal friends, and
• lasting grace, peace, and sanctification.

Paul frames a double petition in his prayer when he highlights the standard that God expects of us—*May God himself, the God of peace, sanctify you through and through. May your whole spirit, soul and body be kept blameless at the coming of our Lord Jesus Christ.*

Paul reverts to a theme near and dear to his heart—holiness of life. He dealt with it in the preceding chapter by reminding them that this lifestyle was part and parcel of God's will for them; an integral component of God's overall purpose for them. Sanctification is becoming in practice what we already are in perfection.

Without doubt, today standards are falling; when the enemy has come in like a flood; when the banner of holiness to the Lord is rarely unfurled to the breeze. Yet God's word has not changed. Living as we do in a filthy, dirty world he expects each of us to live a holy life and display godly character.

Paul indicates that this deep and thorough work in the heart of the Christian is ascribed to God our Father. It is a divine work as he makes us more like Jesus. This is what being conformed to his image is all about. It is positional in that we have been once-and-for-all set apart for God (cf. Hebrews 10:10). Then it is intensely practical as it is a daily dealing with our sin and a consequent growth in holiness (cf. 2 Corinthians 7:1). It is further described as that which is perfect for, in the bliss of eternity, we will be forever like him (cf. 1 John 3:1-3).

The expectation in our heart that one day we will see Jesus should be a spur to be the kind of people that God wants us to be. It should be enough to motivate us and set our faith on fire.

Paul prays that he might sanctify us *through and through*. This is the only time this phrase is used in the New Testament. The underlying thought is entire sanctification, for it impacts our *spirit, soul, and body*. It is when everything is under his influence and control and our life is totally yielded to him. Full surrender. One hundred percent commitment from each Christian.

It is 'God making us as holy as a saved sinner can be.' (Robert Murray McCheyne)

Shalom!

We are introduced to the living Lord as the *God of peace*. This is one of the communicable attributes of God that Paul mentions; one of those qualities that he is happy to share with those of us who are numbered among his children. He is peace personified, and because he is who he is, we can know him personally, and when we do, we can also know his peace.

You see, when he is not in control of our life, we are restless, in turmoil, and tossed hither and thither in every direction. But when he is Lord and enthroned as King, there is an inner calm, a conscious resting in him, an inward quietness, and a real sense of tranquillity. There is nothing to disturb or distract us, for we feel his peace and we know his peace.

When Paul expressed a desire for us to be blameless when we stand before the Lord Jesus Christ, it brings to mind some info that I found on the Internet. Apparently, archaeologists have discovered tombstones from Thessalonica marked with the inscription 'blameless.' That is touching, for it indicates the impact God's word had upon the early church in the first century; by the same token, I cannot think of a better way to live in the twenty-first century, nor can I think of a better way to die! We are blameless in God's eyes immediately when we accept Christ's salvation.

5:24 FAITHFUL ONE

'Faith does not operate in the realm of the possible. Faith begins where man's power ends.' (George Müller)

Paul exudes out-and-out confidence in the amazing ability of God when he writes, *The one who calls you is faithful and he will do it.* Wow! If he said it, he will do it! What a staggering comment from Paul's pen! It is branded as one of those exceeding 'great and precious promises' we read about in 2 Peter 1:4.

In essence, God upholds all those whom he calls and he fulfils all that he has promised. When people are faced with this issue of holiness of life, they tend to say, 'Me, I can't live it. It's impossible for me to keep the standard he has set. It's too much; it's too high; it's way beyond me. I've tried and failed so many times.' Paul responds, 'All right, I hear what you're saying, but look to the Lord Jesus.'

Why should we turn our eyes toward him?

• He called us.

The general call in evangelism became personalised when we bowed the knee to Jesus. It became effectual when we said 'yes' to Jesus.

• He is faithful.

The faithfulness of God is such that the Psalmist tells us it reaches even to the summit of the highest mountain. Down through the generations, the Lord has remained loyal and true and never once, not once, has he let his people down. Never has he gone back on his word. When we needed him most, was he conspicuous by his absence? No, he was always there. He has not failed us; he will not fail us; he cannot fail us.

• He is infinitely powerful.

Paul says quite emphatically that *he will do it.* Think of all that he has done for us in the past, and all that he is doing in us and through us in the present; hey, folk, if he has done it before, he can surely do it again. No problem to him! The unbelievably good news is that our ultimate security rests on the fact that God is reliable and keeps his promises.

'Having begun a good work in a person's life, there is no possibility that he will not honour his commitment and bring everything to a happy conclusion,' notes Philip Arthur.

Real worship

Why will he do it? Because he longs that we might be with him in his home forever. See the connection between this hugely positive affirmation of faith in a God who is able to do it and Paul's plea to them to be found blameless in the previous verse. Over there we will worship him with clean hands and a pure heart; we will see him in the beauty of his holiness and commune with him in spirit and in truth.

A former Archbishop of Canterbury, William Temple, says: 'Worship is to quicken the conscience by the holiness of God, it is to feed the mind with the truth of God, it is to purge the imagination by the beauty of God, it is to open up the heart to the love of God, and it is to devote the will to the purpose of God.'

Basically, that type of worship comes from the kind of person the Lord is looking for in today's world and today's church—an individual who knows that, when he gets home to glory, he will not be out of place worshipping in heaven!

5:25 BEFORE THE THRONE OF GOD ABOVE

Paul opens his heart, and with all the passion he can muster he makes a plea to the young church in Thessalonica, *Brothers, pray for us*. How unashamed the great man is of such a request; it flows naturally from his heart on to the papyrus. I wonder, how did people respond? What a direct challenge!

I imagine that many of the spiritual stalwarts would be thrilled to stand alongside him in prayer; others were perhaps a bit more cynical and may even have questioned his motive—was he simply after the sympathy vote or tying to curry favour; there were probably a few who did not take his request under their notice. At the end of the day it shows that we are all made of the same material and we cannot do without each other, especially when it comes to touching the throne—it is the power of effective kneeling.

Paul has assured them on numerous occasions of his many prayers for them down through the years; now he feels as though he needs them to intercede on his behalf. As John Stott says: 'This is a touching example of his personal humility and of the reciprocity of Christian fellowship.'

Prayer power

Think of his wonderful humility, for he is a fully-grown man; he is a seasoned campaigner when it comes to gospel ministry, and 'he is standing in the need of prayer.'

Paul is small enough to see his many shortcomings and big enough to beg for their prayerful buttress.

Think also of his open-book honesty for this is exactly the way that he feels. If he did not, he would not have asked them in the first place. It is genuine, real, and sincere. What a tremendous encouragement for them to feel that they had a vital part to play in Paul's ministry and that his success or failure was dependent, at least in part, on their faithfulness in prayer.

I fear that all too often we are inclined to forget this! Charles Haddon Spurgeon, who preached to 6,000 souls each week during Queen Victoria's heyday, was a man of remarkable gifts. He was also extremely careful to attribute the blessing that came upon his ministry to the fact that his church, the congregation that met in London's Metropolitan Tabernacle, gave itself to prayer. To Mr. Spurgeon, that was the secret to his astronomic success; so far as he was concerned, the prayer meeting was the powerhouse!

5:26 TACTFULLY TACTILE

We are encouraged to *greet all the brothers with a holy kiss.* The customary greeting in the early church was for a man to greet another man with a kiss on the cheek or forehead. It was the same principle for the ladies in the congregation. It was culturally acceptable in his day; the proper thing to do. They were demonstrating their love for each other in the family of God. Today, some cults have used this verse as a justification to introduce lust into worship. In Paul's time, it was a genuine seal of their affection and this gesture gave them an enhanced feeling of belonging to one another.

Today a big lot depends where we live and, to a greater or lesser degree, the kind of church we attend—it may be a warm hug, a pat on the back, a kiss on the cheek, a friendly shake of the hand. It could be any of those; the method is not that important, but the motive certainly is.

Surely one of the best ways to show others our love is through the acceptance we whisper to them together with a warm touch. I appreciate the way John Stott sums it up when he writes: 'The apostle's instruction is clear that when Christians meet each other they should greet each other, and that their verbal greeting should be made stronger, warmer, and more personal by a culturally appropriate sign.'

To me, the all-important truth to emerge from this Pauline suggestion is that we treat our fellow pilgrims not only with courtesy, but also with affection according to the conventions of our own culture.

5:27 FOR PUBLIC CONSUMPTION

Paul gives another one of those directives for which he is famous when he says, *I charge you before the Lord to have this letter read to all the brothers.* Paul pulls no punches when he says that he wants his letter to them to be read out in public before the whole congregation. It is not to be read only to a handful of committee folk gathered in a backroom or tucked away in a discreet corner at the back of a building. His epistle to them is addressed to the entire church family; there is something in it for each of them and there is so much in it for all of them!

5:28 GRACE FOR THE JOURNEY

Finally he writes, *The grace of our Lord Jesus Christ be with you.* What an extraordinarily great benediction! At the start of the letter, Paul said to them, 'Hello, grace to you.' Now, at the end of the letter, he writes, 'Cheerio, grace be with you.'

The life-changing grace of God saves us. It always sustains us and never fails to strengthen us. It does not matter what type of situation we find ourselves in, God's grace is sufficient in that it is immeasurable. When we think of God's amazing grace, we think of something truly undeserved. Always unearned. And always unrepayable.

Why grace? Charles Swindoll in *The Grace Awakening* says: 'What is it that frees us to be all he means us to be? Grace. What is it that permits others to be who they are, even very different from us? Grace. What allows us to disagree, yet stimulates us to press on? Grace. What adds oil to the friction points of a marriage, freeing both partners from pettiness and negativism? Grace. And what gives magnetic charm to a ministry, inviting others to become a part? Again, it is grace.'

Paul knew their surroundings; he is familiar with their situation; he is conscious of their problems and difficulties; he is all too aware of their changing circumstances. And so, the preacher man warmly commends them to the grace of God and to the one who is the God of all grace.

A concluding reference to grace was almost always his signature tune, so central was it to his whole theology. It is no empty, conventional formula, however, for grace is the heart of the gospel and the heart of God. Pass it on—grace!

The frisson of faith

Well, believe it or not, we have come to the end of the book, but the good news is, we have not come to the end of the grace of God; the grace of God is lasting, and limitless. There is always more to come, a second book, and then some! He says to each of us today, 'My grace is there for you; it is *with you,* make the most of it.'

When we do, our passion for the Lord will be contagious and, to crown it all, there will be a heady air of expectation in our relationship with the Saviour. Burning hearts. Fast-beating hearts. Nothing but hope and the grace of God can accomplish this! We will then be steady on for the off...

2 Thessalonians

CHAPTER SIX
MACRO TRUTH IN A MICRO WORLD

Second Thessalonians is a sequel to Paul's first letter to the church at Thessalonica—a church to be proud of. A quick look at the book gives us some idea as to the reason why Paul took time out to write a second epistle so quickly on the heels of the first. At the first hint of trouble, the preacher believed in nipping it in the bud.

Basically, Paul wrote to dispel the malicious rumours that were doing the rounds and clear up a misconception that resulted from his teaching on the Day of the Lord in 5:2-6. Often the message sent is not the message received. That much is obvious from his comments in 2:1-2, *Concerning the coming of our Lord Jesus Christ and our being gathered to him, we ask you, brothers, not to become easily unsettled or alarmed by some prophecy, report or letter supposed to have come from us, saying that the day of the Lord has already come.*

Maybe a dodgy revelation from a believer who got his wires crossed, or an itinerant preacher biting off more than he could chew, or a forged document purporting to come from Paul—somehow, word had begun to spread like wildfire through the congregation that the Day of the Lord had already come.

Such feverish speculation caused red-faced panic in the heart of some and cold-nosed apathy in the mind of others. The first group pressed the self-destruct button when they thought long and hard about the implications of such an earth-shattering event (cf. 2:2)—they were disturbed. Seriously so. The rest were content to hang out on street corners or lounge in their porch swing waiting for the Lord's return—as 'lazy-good-for-nothings' (cf. 3:11-12, *The Message*) they shirked all responsibility, whittled away their time 'meddling in other people's business' (NLT), and doodled.

Aerial view

Three chapters, forty-seven verses, the book is a good seven or eight minutes read! If we read the letter through at a single sitting we get a genuine feel for Paul's message. We hear his heartbeat. We catch a glimpse of his continuing desire for them to go from strength to strength in their relationship with the Lord.

In passing, it is worth noting that despite the doubts over its authenticity some of the earliest Christian writers, such as Ignatius, Polycarp, and Justin Martyr, attributed this epistle to the apostle. Paul hoped that his hand-written signature (3:17) would silence the critics casting aspersions on his integrity and those sceptical that the letter had actually come from him.

A birds-eye-view enables us to see the contours of truth in the Thessalonian terrain. The undulating hills of small print are hugely important but we must not lose sight of the big picture—a day when many people groups from around the world will say, 'Come, let us go up to the mountain of the Lord, to the house of the God of Jacob' (Isaiah 2:3).

One of the first things we notice is that the Lord Jesus Christ is mentioned three times in each chapter. Charles Swindoll says: 'Like the highest pinnacle on a mountain range, this pristine name towers above everything else and glistens with a glory all its own.' Because of him the folk in Thessalonica can ooze confidence; they can pick up the pieces and rebuild their life; they can start afresh. In spite of the hiccups they have experienced, there is no need for them to stay in the doldrums—they can emerge, stronger and better.

Chapter close-up

- A word of encouragement—chapter 1.
- A word of explanation—chapter 2.
- A word of exhortation—chapter 3.

1:1-2 SAME AGAIN!

Some things never change! There is a strong similarity between this greeting and the one Paul sent to them in his first letter. Yes, it is a standardised 'hello,' but at the same time, it is no less important and meaningful for that. He has said it before and he meant it then; why should he not say it again?

If it ain't broke, there is no need to fix it!

• An unchanged humility

In the space of a few weeks Paul has not elevated himself to any higher strata in God's society. He remains *Paul.* That implies when the blessings increased the preacher man got smaller! Even though a lot of people depended on him and a lot of churches looked to him for off-site leadership, Paul never had to visit the hat shop for a bigger size!

• An unchanged partnership

The mighty duo of *Silas and Timothy,* who shared the ministry with Paul first time around are once again included in his opening remarks. Paul does not, in fact, he cannot forget his co-labourers in the gospel of grace. There is a genuine recognition on his part of their rising value plus their immense contribution to the ongoing cause of Jesus Christ.

• An unchanged unity

Even though a few weeks or months have lapsed, the fellowship in Thessalonica is not split or torn apart. There is little mention of division or dissension among them. It seems from all reports that generally speaking they get on extremely well together. They have their tiffs and squabbles, sure they do; they are people, after all. On occasion they may have lost their head, but they never lost the plot.

• An unchanged equality

Paul again links *God* and the *Lord Jesus Christ* together in his salutation—a powerful recognition that, in a fluid situation, some things are constant. And non-negotiable. True then, it remains true to this day.

In this divine relationship, one of enduring equality, there is no weakest link.

The only difference is seen in Paul's use of the word *the* in his first letter compared to *our* in this epistle. That emphasises the solid strength of every Christian's relationship with his God—he is *the Father* but, more to the point, he is also *our Father.* It speaks of intimacy and strikes me as something that is incredibly personal. He is mine! As we plumb the depths of that relationship, we realise that the living Lord is not looking away from us in complacency but looking down on us in compassion.

- An unchanged necessity

The passing of time does not diminish God's resources of *grace and peace*. These stressed-out believers desperately needed both when Paul composed his first note to them; they were definitely not disappointed, nor did they come unstuck. In between they have sampled even more outpourings of his grace and peace—that is what enabled them to keep their head above the parapet. Tens of millions have benefited from an abundant supply down the years; the good news is that it will continue unabated right into the future—God's reservoir never runs dry.

1:3 PARAGRAPH OF PRAISE

Bless him, when Paul thinks about these folk he cannot contain his feelings, so he bursts forth into spontaneous praise. It comes from a full heart and flows naturally from a man who is on top of things. Praise from someone we respect never makes us proud, it makes us humble. It does not make us rest on our laurels. It makes us want to do better, to live up to the praise that has been heaped upon us. What an encouragement this must have been to the Thessalonians!

It is not immediately obvious in the English translation, but verses 3-10 constitute one long sentence in the Greek text. We need to bear that in mind, especially when we think of some of the tough things that Paul conveys later on. He is not writing as a detached theologian; rather, according to Philip Greenslade, 'his theological thinking is being done "on the job" and white-hot. It brims with passion and flares up with praise.' This man's faith is anchored in God and, consequently, his theology is always doxology.

Moving on with God

We ought always to thank God for you, brothers, and rightly so, because your faith is growing more and more, and the love every one of you has for each other is increasing. Well, that says all that needs to be said—what a wonderful commendation.

Actually, Paul feels as though he has no option but to say what he does. It was no more and no less than was due. If he had bitten his tongue, said nothing, and kept his counsel to himself, he would be seen as churlish or, perhaps, even jealous. Thankfully, Paul is not that kind of guy. They are up to scratch and deserve a pat on the back! These good folk were on the up and up, as we sometimes say.

They experienced remarkable progress both as individuals and as a congregation of believers. Nothing stagnant or static about them. They are making significant headway in so many areas that Paul is flabbergasted when he pays tribute to their phenomenal growth. In spite of all the ups and downs, they have taken massive strides; they are going on by leaps and bounds. They are luxuriating like a tropical plant.

When it comes to faith and love, they are not shrinking violets!

It is worth noting that there is nothing one-sided or stunted about their growth experience. Their developing faith and deepening love are both highly rated in equal measure by the shrewd apostle. Faith was flourishing and love was spreading out like floodwaters among the Thessalonians. In that sense, Paul is tickled pink; he knows in spite of all the incessant pressures they are facing that they are continuing to blossom in their relationship with the Lord and with one another. If that is what trials do for a person, maybe we need a few more of them!

Seasons of life

A man once bought a home with a tree in the back yard. It was winter and nothing marked this tree as different from any other tree. When spring came, however, the tree grew leaves and tiny pink buds. 'How wonderful,' thought the man with no green fingers. 'A flower tree! I will enjoy its beauty all summer.' But, before he had time to enjoy the flowers, the wind began to blow and soon all the petals were strewn across the lawn. 'What a mess,' he thought, 'this tree isn't any use after all.'

The blue skies of summer passed and one day the man noticed the tree was full of green fruit, the size of large nuts. He picked one and took a bite. 'Blah!' he cried, and threw it to the ground. 'What a horrible taste! This tree is worthless. Its flowers are so fragile the wind blows them away and its fruit is terrible and bitter. When winter comes I'm cutting it down.' Needless to say, the tree took no notice of the man and continued to draw water from the ground and warmth from the sun and in late autumn produced deliciously crisp red apples.

Some of us see Christians with their early blossoms and radiant happiness, and we think they should be that way forever. Or we see bitterness in their life, and we are sure they will never bear the better fruit of joy. Could it be that we forget some of the best fruit ripens late, and each type of blessing has its season?

1:4 STICKABILITY

Paul is over the moon when he reflects on the achievements of the church in Thessalonica. In fact, he is so overjoyed that he cannot keep it to himself; he seizes every God-given opportunity to convey this mind-blowing message to all the churches in the region. If bad news travels fast, Paul reckoned that he should do his part to ensure that good news travelled even faster!

Theirs was a story — a success story — well worth communicating. In today's speak, they are a hard act to follow. Regardless of the content of Paul's letters, his style was always affirming of his audience. He always began his letters by describing what he appreciated most about his readers.

We read, *Therefore, among God's churches we boast about your perseverance and faith in all the persecutions and trials you are enduring.*

There are times when persecution is overt and obvious; at other times it is more subtle and secretive. Whether it is out in the open or happening behind closed doors is really immaterial — it is our response to it that makes the headlines. Some folk cringe, curl up in a corner, and feel extremely sorry for themselves; others bite the bullet and are up for it in the strength of the Lord. Some take it to heart, others take it on the chin. When it comes into our life, as it may, we need to keep our focus on the Lord and his character. In the ebb and flow of life, the Lord's faithfulness is unchanging. What we need today is more *perseverance and faith* in our churches.

Beyond these walls

I love the story of the cockerel rolling an ostrich egg into the hen-run and saying: 'Observe, I am not trying to demoralise you, but I would like you to know the size of what is happening elsewhere.' To tell what God is doing in one place is a real boost to believers in other centres of witness and testimony. It fosters fellowship, it encourages prayerful support, and it stimulates interest. On top of that, it also breaks down barriers—we vigorously champion the cause of guarding the autonomy of the local church; we fly the flag of independence, and that is fine; but it is essential for our long-term growth and blessing that we harness a feeling of interdependence within evangelical churches.

The man who spends his time shadow boxing does not score too many points!

1:5 AN INITIATION CEREMONY

Sometimes we are on a different wavelength to the purposes of God; we fail to fully appreciate the leading of God and we question why God invades our privacy with a harsh set of circumstances. From our limited perspective, we cannot see the reason behind the divine intruder's involvement in our life.

Paul leaves us in no doubt with his inspirational assessment of their situation in verse 5—*all this is evidence that God's judgment is right*—in other words, the Lord makes no mistakes. He cannot err. He gets it right first time, every time. In God's court there is never any miscarriage of justice. As the Master Potter he knows precisely what he is doing when he allows suffering to shape our life and mould our character. He sees the income and the outcome and is never at a loss.

Paul's words ring true for many suffering saints around the world in the third millennium. There is nothing hollow about his comments. One Christian from Malaku said that recent massacres and expulsions in that region are '… according to God's plan. Christians are under purification from the Lord.' As a current Sudanese liturgy confesses: 'Death has come to reveal the faith; it has begun with us and it will end with us.'

God can grow a mushroom overnight, but it takes many years — and many storms — to grow a giant oak tree! You see, God has his own way of doing things. One of the spin-offs from us going through trials and troubles is that we are *counted worthy of the kingdom of God*. The Lord, in his sovereign wisdom, uses all the hassles and hiccups of this life to initiate us into his new-world kingdom. God's transforming grace was fitting them for their heavenly inheritance.

In the final analysis, this is all that really matters. Our rating in this world may not be overly high, but that is of little or no consequence; it is our standing in the next world that is mega-important.

The upside of today's downside is that we have everything to play for in God's game of life.

The exciting prospect of us marching through the gates of the New Jerusalem with a spring in our step gives an added incentive to us to persevere to the end of the road. The hymnwriter, Esther Rusthoi, expressed it like this:

> *It will be worth it all,*
> *When we see Jesus,*
> *Life's trials will seem so small,*
> *When we see Christ.*
> *One glimpse of his dear face,*
> *All sorrow will erase —*
> *So bravely run the race,*
> *Till we see Christ.*

1:6-7 JUST GOD

A truer word could not be spoken by Paul when he notes that *God is just*. The preacher goes on to explain the implications of the justice of God when he informs us that *he will pay back trouble to those who trouble you*. Ouch! I would not want to be standing in their shoes. These non-believers are in very hot water — big trouble, big time!

It is useful to keep in mind that when Paul asserts that God will vindicate his people, he is repeating a theme at least as old as the

Exodus. In the comprehensive Song of Moses in Deuteronomy 32:40-41, for example, the Lord himself declares, 'I lift my hand to heaven and declare: As surely as I live forever, when I sharpen my flashing sword and my hand grasps it in judgment, I will take vengeance on my adversaries and repay those who hate me.'

In the same chapter, this declaration by the Lord becomes on the lips of Moses virtually a confession of faith: 'The Lord will judge his people and have compassion on his servants when he sees their strength is gone and no one is left, slave or free.... Rejoice, O nations, with his people, for he will avenge the blood of his servants; he will take vengeance on his enemies and make atonement for his land and people' (32:36, 43).

Isaiah takes up a similar theme and finds in it a tremendous word of encouragement (cf. Isaiah 35:4); similarly, it becomes a heartfelt prayer from the lips of Jeremiah (cf. Jeremiah 11:20). So there is nothing new about this concept—it has been around for a very long time!

Lessons from the land

The story is told of two farmers, one a believer and the other an atheist. When harvest season came, the atheist taunted his believing neighbour because apparently God had not blessed him too much. The atheist's family had not been sick, his fields were rich with harvest, and he was sure to make a lot of money.

'I thought you said it paid to believe in God and be a Christian,' said the ranting atheist.

'It does pay,' replied the Christian, 'but God doesn't always pay his people in September.'

Payday is coming! If not in time, certainly in eternity, man will get his comeuppance. He will be brought to book in God's good time. No one gets off Scot-free! A just God does not settle accounts on a never-never policy. God has a long arm, a long reach, and a long memory. This is all about God's ultimate as it links in with the divine ultimatum.

A visit to Jerusalem is incomplete without a sobering jerk-back-to-reality walk around Yad Vashem, the hugely impressive Jewish memorial to the Holocaust. There, the terrible tortures to which so many innocent Jews were subjected in the concentration camps and the gas chambers are visualised and well-documented. Using modern technology, the complete record, the newspaper reports, and the frighteningly fearsome scenes that the Allies found when they liberated these camps are all displayed—a testimony that none of it will ever be forgotten.

To me, what is even more touching is the special place given to the children who perished in the Holocaust. Their memorial hall is almost totally dark, lighted only by a few flickering candles, but there are hundreds of mirrors that reflect the candles so that the impression given is of thousands of candles burning. Hidden voices, hauntingly and endlessly, call out the names of boys and girls so brutally treated and mercilessly murdered by the Nazis—Israel's way of saying that these children will never be forgotten.

Not one injustice, not one humiliation, not one act of pain or torture will ever be erased from memory. That, I believe, is a potent illustration of Paul's comments in this section. The bottom line is that God vindicates his faithful servants.

Relief beyond belief

God guarantees *relief to you who are troubled, and to us as well.* Wonderful news! In the here and now, the believer is promised all the support that God can give—in the there and then, there is the added bonus of everlasting relief. God has the uncanny ability of dispensing sufficient grace to soften the blow and lighten the load. No matter how tough and threatening the trial may be, divine relief is always sweet. It is something to savour.

A royal visit

The day when God redresses the balance is detailed by Paul when he informs us that *this will happen when the Lord Jesus is revealed from heaven in blazing fire with his powerful angels.* Wow! This is God acting tough, because he is tough. This is the firm hand of God coming down very hard on all those individuals who thought they could outwit and outmanoeuvre him. This is God getting his own back.

What an unforgettable sight; the moment when every eye will see him! This is no sideshow, but an event of cosmic splendour (like lightning flashing across the sky, Jesus said). Marvellous. Majestic. Awesome. The King of kings—the God of consuming fire—breaking through the clouds on his way back to planet Earth. When he touches down on the Mount of Olives, one of his first jobs is to deal with those who have caused God's people so much heartache and trouble. Before the Lord of glory, these guys may run but they cannot hide.

A royal entourage, the armies of heaven, accompany him on his descent from heaven to earth. He is not returning solo. Wonder of wonders, the church of God, the bride of Christ—'the wife of the Lamb' (Revelation 21:9)—will also be at his side. We who belong to the church of God will be present on this auspicious occasion when the Lord deals once and for all with those perpetrators of evil. They are ejected from his presence into the chasms of the damned. Gone forever.

1:8 SAD MAN, SADDAM

Soon after notorious dictator Saddam Hussein's capture—out of an eight-foot hole that one observer said was filled with rats and mice—he was flown to a secret location for a meeting with four members of Iraq's Governing Council. They wanted to confirm that they had indeed got their man. When the quartet were offered the chance to see Saddam through a window or by camera, they said: 'No, we want to talk to him.'

Despite his mussed-up appearance, a dishevelled Saddam was arrogantly defiant and unrepentant. Ahmad Chalabi, head of the Iraqi National Congress, said: 'He was quite lucid. He had command of his faculties. He would not apologise to the Iraqi people. He did not deny any of the crimes he was confronted with having done. He tried to justify them.'

'The world is crazy,' said Mowaffak al-Rubaie, one of the council members in the room. 'I was in the torture chamber in 1979, and now he was sitting there powerless in front of me without anybody stopping me from doing anything to him, just imagine. We were arguing and he was using very foul language.'

The four men spent about thirty minutes in the small room, confronting Saddam with his crimes. As they left, Mr. Rubaie delivered these final words to the former dictator: 'May God curse you. Tell me, when are you going to be accountable to God and the day of judgment? What are you going to tell him about Halabja and the mass graves, the Iran-Iraq war, thousands and thousands executed? What are you going to tell God?'

Typically, Saddam answered using vulgar language.

Payback time

What Paul outlines in this verse may not be politically correct, but it is an absolute certainty—God *will punish those who do not know [him] and do not obey the gospel of our Lord Jesus.* Paul makes it abundantly clear that God will have the last word in relation to sinful man. There is nothing ambiguous in this statement of intent. It says what it says and there is no room for man to wriggle or worm his way out of it. Punishment will be meted out to guilty people. As sure as night follows day, every sinner will find himself in the hands of an angry God.

Such punishment is an integral part of the divine makeup of God's character—he does it, for he is a just God and a holy God. Because of who and what God is, there is no way that man can be absolved of his sense of personal responsibility and accountability. If man chooses to stick his finger in God's eye, he will pay a heavy price for his impudence and crass stupidity. God enjoys a laugh but, when it comes to salvation and his Son, the Lord Jesus Christ, he is not to be fooled around with.

God is not seen here as a vigilante roaming the streets dispensing summary justice, but as someone who delivers the final vengeance that sinners deserve.

The believer has nothing whatsoever to fear for Paul is referring only to those who are still outside the family of God. These are people, from all walks of life and every strata of society, who know nothing of God's salvation; ordinary men and women who have no personal relationship with Jesus Christ.

To them, Jesus is nothing more than a swear word, an oath, or a word used to punctuate their sentences when they could not think of anything better to say. In fact, if the name of Jesus was removed from their vocabulary, some of them would be left almost speechless! Their conversation would dry up within minutes.

1:9 SHUT OUT

The apostle strikes a most solemn note when he writes of the ultimate fate of those who say 'no' to Jesus Christ. He spells it out with unmistakable clarity, *They will be punished with everlasting destruction and shut out from the presence of the Lord and from the majesty of his power.* Scary. Terrifying. Indeed. There is no rest for the wicked!

It is worth noting that Christian researcher George Barna has concluded from his studies that God's people are, little by little, deciding not to believe in hell. However, truth is not based on what we decide but on what God decides.

Words like banishment, exclusion, and separation all spring to our minds. But not annihilation. When a person dies, they do not cease to exist—they are not like a candle that is snuffed out and is no more. Life goes on, in another world, in a different place—it takes on a whole new format, but it is no less real.

Outlawed from the close presence of a God who is present everywhere. Erased from the knowledge of one who knows all. George MacDonald in *Leadership* writes that the one principle of hell is 'I am my own.' Those exiled to a Christless eternity will be fully aware of what is going on—read the tragic story of the rich man in Luke 16:19-31.

Repelled to an endless hole of everlasting ruin, their memory will haunt them—those opportunities to get right with God that were flatly rejected, those moments when their heart was softened by some troublesome experience or devastating trauma, those times when God spoke so clearly and they dug in their heels and spurned his offer of love and grace. Yes, eternity for them will be one long black night—a night that will never see the dawning of a new day.

John Stott describes it thus: 'The horror of this end will not be so much the pain which may accompany it as the tragedy which is inherent in it, namely that human beings made by God, like God, and for God, should spend eternity without God.'

Not for them the awesome sight of the King of kings on a regal throne. Not for them the bright worship and pure praise of the redeemed in heaven. Not for them the stunning environs of the

New Jerusalem, the city of God. Not for them the resplendent glory of a brand new world adorned with unbelievable beauty and splendour. Not for them. O, how awfully sad.

Hell's half acre

In the lone star state of Texas, there is an area of rough elevations located seventeen miles southeast of Marathon in northeastern Brewster County called Hell's Half Acre. Apparently, it is on the tourist trail. It seems that people enjoy visiting there and sending friends a postcard announcing: 'Having a lovely time here in Hell.'

That cynical attitude may boost the local economy, but it is a serious caricature of the place the Bible calls 'hell.' It is no joking matter. The man is an idiot who laughs about hell. Those who find themselves in that perilously lonely outpost, full of the debris of humanity, will have the simpering smile wiped off their face within a millisecond of arriving. They are on their own. There is a way in, but there is no way out!

'In hell, everybody will be at an infinite distance from everybody else.' (C. S. Lewis)

1:10 ON THE GLORY TRAIL

There are two sides to every coin—one side is the wrath of a holy God and divine justice, the other side is the sheer delight that he finds in his people, the church that he purchased with his own blood. God will deal with his enemies on the same day that *he comes to be glorified in his holy people and to be marvelled at among all those who have believed. This includes you, because you believed our testimony to you.*

This is the ultimate of our salvation experience in Jesus Christ—the day when the Lord will be glorified in us. We will be lit up with glory; we will glow with his radiance. C. S. Lewis lifts us to another plane when he writes: 'This God is going to take the feeblest and filthiest of us and turn us into dazzling, radiant, immortal creatures pulsating with all the energy and joy and wisdom and love that we could possibly imagine. He is going to turn us into bright stainless mirrors that reflect back his character perfectly.'

This is take-your-breath-away stuff for when we look around us on that eventful day we will be left gasping with the idyllic wonder of it all. Amidst rapturous scenes of delighted astonishment, Jesus will exceed all our expectations. What a vista! There will be no tinge of disappointment, for we will be thrilled with his awesome gorgeousness.

That is when the penny will finally drop that we are there only because of Jesus. The Lord of heaven and earth is centre stage. The spotlights are exclusively focused on him. Deservedly so.

Samuel Rutherford, the eminent Scottish minister of the seventeenth century, was once asked: 'What will Christ be like when he comes?' The answer that he gave was: 'All lovely!' One day, by God's grace, we will gaze on that lovely face of Jesus and, in the twinkling of an eye, that loveliness will become ours in such a way that we become lovely too (cf. 1 John 3:2).

1:11 THE CHRISTIAN'S VITAL BREATH

In the final scene of Tennyson's *Idylls of the King*, King Arthur, on his deathbed, voices to his friend some profound thoughts on prayer: 'More things are wrought by prayer than this world dreams of.' He was right for only eternity will reveal just how big a part our prayers have played in the ripening of the purposes of God. We will not really know till then the effect of our own words and actions on Earth.

Paul's aspiration for them is seen in this wonderful verse, *With this in mind, we constantly pray for you, that our God may count you worthy of his calling, and that by his power he may fulfil every good purpose of yours and every act prompted by your faith.*

The preacher believed in the power of prayer; he was totally committed to holding on to God for these dear folk in Thessalonica. So many of us start praying for someone or something and then give up after a few days—not Paul. He never grew weary in his faithful intercession for them, and it paid massive dividends. He kept at it! The godly Puritan John Owen (1616-83) noted that 'he who prays as he ought will endeavour to live as he prays.'

For Paul, prayer was not so much a routine exercise as a way of life. In spite of all the pressures of ministry that weighed heavily on him,

Paul's unbroken communion with God flowed naturally from a heart that knew God intimately. John MacArthur compared Paul's spiritual life to a volcano when he said: 'Beneath the thin outer crust of his life was a burning, passionate heart for God. Frequently, the volcanic heat of his heart would cause prayer to burst through the veneer of routine, surface activities.' These verses describe those internal eruptions; they reveal the red-hot heart of a man on fire for God.

His ardent longing for them is that they might know God's rich blessing and smile of approval on their life — he prayed for the right things. They have been called into his international community and Paul is enthusiastically keen for them to enjoy their heavenly Father's admiration. They have had more than their fair share of ups and downs in recent times, but all that matters is that God is with them and that God is working through them.

In fact, God has used their suffering as a fan for the embers of faith.

Father knows best

At the age of 16, in the year 371, Augustine sneaked away from his mother in Carthage. During the night he sailed away to Rome, leaving her alone to her tears and her prayers. How were these prayers answered? Not the way Monica (Augustine's mother) hoped at the time. Only later could she see that praying is the deepest path to joy.

Augustine himself wrote: 'And what did she beg of you, my God, with all those tears, if not that you would prevent me from sailing? But you did not do as she asked you. Instead, in the depth of your wisdom, you granted the wish that was closest to her heart.

'For she saw that you had granted her far more than she used to ask in her tearful prayers. You converted me to yourself, so that I no longer placed any hope in this world, but stood firmly upon the rule of faith. And you turned her sadness into rejoicing, into joy far fuller than her dearest wish, far sweeter and more chaste than any she had hoped to find.'

A people of power

In spite of their suffering and discomfort, they are plodding on and are continuing to reach out to others in the region. They are actively engaged in different forms of ministry, but the more they do the more they realise how dependent they are on the Lord for his help, and enabling, and blessing. God's power is available to them and Paul's desire is that they might know it in all its fulness.

God would equip them for the task in hand; he would enable them to be the kind of people he wanted them to be. With God's infusion of power in their life, the sky is the limit—there are no boundaries. God is in the business of multiplication—the God who took five loaves and two tiny fish and used it to feed a multitude is the same God who takes the little that we offer and makes it go a long way. A classic case of 'watch this space, see what God will do!'

Pony express

Dedication is the name of the game. When Paul's prayer for them is answered it will produce a free spirit that is willing to go to the ends of the earth for the Lord Jesus Christ. No questions asked. No demands made. No excuses offered. No problems envisaged! Such a mindset is well illustrated by one of the most fabled organisations in American history—the Pony Express—in Donald S. Whitney's book *Spiritual Disciplines for the Christian Life*.

The Pony Express was a private express company that carried mail by an organised relay of horseback riders. The eastern end was St. Joseph, Missouri, and the western terminal was in Sacramento, California. The cost of sending a letter by Pony Express was $2.50 an ounce. If the weather and horses held out and the Indians held off, that letter would complete the entire two-thousand-mile journey in a speedy ten days, as did the report of Lincoln's Inaugural Address.

It may surprise you that the Pony Express was only in operation from 3 April 1860 until 18 November 1861—just seventeen months. When the telegraph line was completed between two cities, the service was no longer needed.

Being a rider for the Pony Express was a tough job. You were expected to ride seventy-five to one hundred miles a day, changing horses every fifteen to twenty-five miles. Other than the mail, the only baggage you carried contained a few provisions, including a kit of

243

flour, cornmeal, and bacon. In case of danger, you also had a medical pack of turpentine, borax, and cream of tartar. In order to travel light and to increase speed of mobility during Indian attacks, the men always rode in shirt sleeves, even during the fierce winter weather.

How would you recruit volunteers for this hazardous job? An 1860 San Francisco newspaper printed this ad for the Pony Express: 'Wanted: Young, skinny, wiry fellows not over 18. Must be expert riders willing to risk [death] daily. Orphans preferred.'

Those were the honest facts of the service required, but the Pony Express never had a shortage of riders....

Like the Pony Express, serving God is not a job for the casually interested. It is costly service. He asks for our life. He asks for service to him to become a priority, not a pastime.

1:12 GRACE AND GLORY

The Westminster Shorter Catechism reminds us of the noble truth that 'man's chief end is to glorify God.' Paul's expressed longing for them rings true in that light...*we pray this so that the name of our Lord Jesus may be glorified in you, and you in him, according to the grace of our God and the Lord Jesus Christ.*

The supreme purpose of their relationship with God is seen in this verse — God glorified in them and them exultant in God. It is true that God does not need us for his glory to shine — his striking magnificence can stand on its own, unaided and untarnished. And it has done for millennia.

However, because of Calvary, God's dream for us — his people — is that we might see and share his sparkling glory. His aim is that we might reflect the wonders of his glory and grace, like the moon reflects the light of the sun. What a privilege is afforded us as the people of God. It has nothing whatsoever to do with us; it has everything to do with him! Robert Murray McCheyne makes the valid point that 'it is not great talents that God blesses, so much as great likeness to Jesus.'

True to form, grace and glory link arms. *According*-ly, they are inseparable. God's glory is first revealed through God's mercy to us. Glory is the finale; grace is the means to it. God shows his glory through his grace. He does not need to show his glory to us, but in his mercy and grace he chooses to do it. There can be no glory without grace!

CHAPTER SEVEN
A BLOT ON THE LANDSCAPE

Are you an optimist or a pessimist?

Two men, Jimmy and Dave, jumped off a thirty-storey building. One, an eternal optimist; the other, a doom-and-gloom pessimist. As they whizzed past the fifteenth floor, the pessimist was overheard shouting: 'Jimmy! Help! Help!' To which the optimist yelled: 'Cheer up, Dave. So far, so good!'

A pessimist thinks the world is against him—and it is. An optimist is a man who thinks the dry cleaners are shrinking the waistband of his trousers. A pessimist is somebody whose day-dreams are nightmares. An optimist thinks nothing is all wrong—even a clock that has stopped is right twice a day. A realist is what one pessimist calls another!

We are the way we are! Only the genius of grace can transform our temperament and help us see the funny side of a story and the sunny side of life. The faith challenge comes when we carry our outlook into our thinking about the future—it can either drag us down into the mud and mire or it can propel us into the fast lane for Jesus.

When it comes, therefore, to the hill and dale landscape of Bible prophecy, who is right—the optimist or the pessimist? I reckon both are right and both are wrong! (Did I hear you say: 'Only an Irishman could possibly think that!') Both, it has to be noted, are also fraught with danger:

- a Christian optimist may expect too much;
- a Christian pessimist may expect too little.

Eschatological symmetry

As we scan the horizon and seek to understand what Paul is saying in this central chapter, it is essential that we stay on track by adopting a balanced perspective on this talking-point. These truths, sadly, have caused all kinds of problems among the people of God. In some evangelical circles they have generated a lot more heat than light, and that is a pity. When that happens, it is because we have taken our eye off the ball. And the devil laughs up his sleeve at the pandemonium he has caused.

The key issue here is that Jesus Christ is coming back again. Of that there is absolutely no doubt at all. The sticking point surrounds the time frame of events associated with the Lord's coming to the air for his church (cf. 4:13-18); hence the question, if Jesus returned tomorrow, what would happen? That is what Paul seeks to answer in the next dozen or so verses as he valiantly attempts to steady the doctrinal legs of the church.

2:1-2 Think twice

Paul more or less tells these perplexed saints to treat with a pinch of salt all the baloney that is being bandied around concerning what he is supposed to have said or written. There are times when we have to stand back in order to suss out exactly what is truth and what is error. It is so easy in the midst of chaos and confusion for the truth to become blurred or frayed at the edges.

Truth is often the first casualty when men engage in a doctrinal war of words.

When doctrine becomes dogma, man's opinion becomes authoritative without sufficient grounds. It is strange—doctrine and dogma are on the same page of my dictionary—but they are worlds apart in the way that people teach them.

The reality is that we cannot believe all that we see or hear, no matter whose name is appended to it. Charlatans and scaremongers can be so convincing. We cannot always take the views of others at face value; a man lacks spiritual discernment if he swallows hook, line, and sinker all that is offered in the guise of good doctrine.

This is the nub of the matter so far as the preacher is concerned in these verses—*Concerning the coming of our Lord Jesus Christ and our being gathered to him, we ask you, brothers, not to become easily unsettled or alarmed by some prophecy, report or letter supposed to have come from us, saying that the day of the Lord has already come.*

It is not too difficult to fit all the pieces of the jigsaw together. A young child could easily do that! Some of the Thessalonian believers reckoned because the trials and troubles they were experiencing were so horrendously painful that they must be going through the time of Tribulation that Paul hinted at in chapter five of his first epistle. The fact is, nothing could be further from the truth!

That is not what Paul said and it is certainly not what Paul intended or even implied. These fidgety folk are edgy. They are on tenterhooks. Their equilibrium has been shaken. Their mind is in a twirl so they jump to all the wrong conclusions; they are barking up the wrong tree!

Predictable predictions

For centuries there have been innumerable theories as to when and how the world might end. Some well-meaning, well-intentioned people have caused all sorts of frenzied mayhem among gullible Christians with their speculation on the date of the Lord's return—so much so that people have sold up and moved to the hills; they have stocked their freezers and piled up tinned supplies in their larders. Some of them cannot explain why they acted so much out of character—their behaviour at times verges on the bizarre.

In 960 Bernard of Thuringia, a German theologian, calculated 992 as the most likely year for the world's end. Inevitably, as time approached, panic was widespread. The tenth-century Abbo of Fleury tells of a preacher in Paris who declared that at the end of the thousandth year the antichrist should come and not long after him the Judgment. Doomsayers revelled as people expected the world to end at the first millennium in the year 1000 AD. The year 999 was a boom year for monasteries. Penitents flocked in, hysterically bearing jewels, coins, and earthly possessions by the ox-cartful, hoping to cadge a little last-minute grace before Judgment Day.

Another German, the astrologer Johann Stoffler, predicted an overwhelming flood on 20 February 1524. Believers started constructing arks. A mob trampled to death one man attempting to board his specially built vessel. When nothing happened, the calculations were revised and a new date given—1588. Not surprisingly, that year also passed without any unusual rainfall.

Solomon Eccles was jailed in London's Bridewell Prison in 1665 for striding through Smithfield Market carrying a pan of blazing sulphur on his head, and proclaiming doom and destruction. Although the end of the world did not follow, the Great Fire of London did in 1666!

After studying both the Bible and the mystical messages of the Great Pyramid, in 1874 Charles Taze Russell, founder of the sect that became known as Jehovah's Witnesses, concluded that the Second Coming had already taken place. He declared that people had forty years, or until 1914, to enter his faith or be destroyed. Later he modified the date to be 'very soon after 1914.'

Herbert W. Armstrong, publisher of the magazine *Plain Truth*, declared that 7 January 1972 was undoubtedly the date to watch. The utter failure of his highly publicised prediction did not diminish his zeal or dampen his enthusiasm.

The sixteenth-century seer Nostradamus is said to have favoured 1999 as the year of a Martian invasion, while an eighteenth-century French prophetess, Jeanne Le Roger, established the year 2000 as the definitive one. Neither came to fruition!

In recent memory, for our generation, the plot thickened when hopes were raised with the onset of the year 2000—a key moment for the new millennium watchers, we were told. An unbelievable potpourri of views was advanced at that particular time; needless to say, with the benefit of hindsight, all proved false. Contrary to wild, hyped-up expectation and crazy numbers juggling, Jesus did not return.

Warren Wiersbe is right, therefore, when he counsels that 'the purpose of Bible prophecy is not for us to make a calendar, but to build character.' Date-setters are usually up-setters!

A new look at the Rapture

Paul goes over old ground in these verses when he reminds them of the coming of the Lord Jesus for his church. This is what he has spoken of at considerable length in 1 Thessalonians 4:13-18. In that passage the preacher reminded them of the impact of this event on their life in the here and now—it should encourage them and give them a sense of tremendous hope for the future. In tough times it would be a source of immense comfort and cheer to them. Such an inspirational truth would brighten any man's day.

249

The dual phrase that Paul uses in verse 1 gives us a marvellous insight into what will happen when the trumpet sounds. Yes, when the Father gives his Son the nod, the Lord will return to the air—*the coming of our Lord Jesus Christ*; and, at that same precise moment, we will be *gathered to him*. As the people of God we will be swept from the earth and assembled together with him in the sky!

Jesus comes down! The church goes up!

2:3 DEVASTATED BY DECEPTION

Winston Churchill said of Soviet Russia just prior to World War II that she was 'a riddle wrapped in a mystery inside an enigma.' It has to be said that this section (verses 3-8) ranks among the most difficult of all Paul's writings to decipher and, for that reason, has become a happy hunting ground for speculators.

Paul instructs the panic-stricken believers, *Don't let anyone deceive you in any way, for that day will not come until the rebellion occurs and the man of lawlessness is revealed, the man doomed to destruction.* He spells it out for them in such a way that they cannot help but get the message—there is no need for them to fear or get uptight over something that they will miss!

The Day of the Lord only takes place after all believers are ushered into the Lord's glorious presence at the Rapture. That is the long-awaited moment when the church militant becomes the church triumphant. Allied to that, Paul argues the point that God has fixed in the future an unmistakable event that must take place before the Day of the Lord arrives. That event still has not happened.

The argument is clinched when we realise the Day of the Lord will not come *until the rebellion occurs*—that is, the apostasy. In the original Greek text, apostasy is the basic meaning of the word 'rebellion' or 'revolt.' The same Greek word appears one other time in the New Testament in Acts 21:21 in relation to turning away from the law of Moses. It is used three times in the Septuagint to express wholesale rebellion against God (cf. Joshua 22:22; 2 Chronicles 29:19; Jeremiah 2:19).

Turncoats

The Greek word indicates a deliberate defection from a previously held religious position. It happens when man does an about-turn in relation to matters of biblical doctrine and evangelical practice. Such folk renounce the faith that they once cherished and abandon the principles that they once held dear. Sadly, the annals of history confirm the presence of many well-documented examples of those who have pursued such a reckless course of action. For the sake of clarity, it must be borne in mind that Paul is not referring in this context to apostasy in the general sense.

The ambivalent attitude that people display when running away from scriptural truth is as old as the hills; unfortunately, it happens all too often. Actually, the closer we are to the Second Coming of Christ, the more obvious and rampant such traitorous behaviour will become (cf. 2 Timothy 3:1-5; 2 Peter 3:3-4; Jude 17-18).

Since the Day of Pentecost there have always been apostate churches—like the tepid assembly in Laodicea (cf. Revelation 3:14-22), as well as a proliferation of apostate individuals, some more high-profile than others (cf. Hebrews 10:25-31; 2 Peter 2:20-22).

Men and women who ape Judas and sell their spiritual birthright are alive and well in the twenty-first century.

Rebel leader

Paul's careful use of the definite article—*the*—makes a world of difference to our understanding of what he specifically has in mind. He is certainly not referring to a ubiquitous flow or trend in the sense that apostasy is spreading on a global scale, but he highlights a precise, identifiable act of apostasy. Thus, he nails it down to a definite time and place.

As and when it happens, this singular act promises to be so big and so blasphemous that its immediate impact is colossal. Tsunami-like. Make no mistake, this is an event of immense significance and unprecedented magnitude. A tidal wave so devilishly outrageous, almost superhuman, the global repercussions are frightening.

Thankfully, Paul does not leave us in the lurch; he sticks a label on the apostasy by naming the central character connected with it—*the man of lawlessness*. That is but one of many names allocated to him in Scripture, each revealing a particular trait in his character; more often than not, however, we refer to him as the antichrist.

Satan in a human body

The antichrist is well named for a spirit of lawlessness is evident in all his actions. This endtime personage is shockingly evil and openly hostile to God and biblical truth. He has absolutely no time at all for the people of God and his hell-bent mission is to wreak havoc on anything that carries a whiff of evangelical respectability. With no sense of shame, or tinge of embarrassment, the man of sin—one more name accurately attributed to him—will live his life out in the open in wanton defiance of God's law.

When it comes to sin, he is the consummate individual. He is the personification of evil and vile behaviour. Of all the billions of godless sinners in human history, this man's depraved influence will be greater by far. Even in the Tribulation, when lawlessness spirals out of control, this Satan-energised figurehead will stand out as the one whose wicked, corrupt, and perverted leadership sweeps over the entire world—with influence never before seen. Like the Pied Piper, when he plays the tune, people will flock to him and follow along behind.

He has a charismatic personality and is adept at rallying the troops. He gathers a crowd with little or no difficulty and, within a short period of time, he has people from every strata of society eating out of his hand. He is hailed as the greatest thing to hit town since manna fell in the desert. Like any political big wheel, he promises much and delivers little. In spite of his affability, he deals ruthlessly with any who dare oppose him. Basically, he is the devil incarnate.

The antichrist is nothing more than a hotshot from hell.

Is the antichrist alive today?

That is the million dollar question.... I honestly believe that he could be alive today! The critical factor is that he has not yet been *revealed*. If the antichrist is alive today and that, as I say, is a distinct possibility, then we may know and recognise him as a leading light or an up-and-coming star on the global stage. But we cannot say that he is the antichrist for he has not yet been disclosed. In other words, his cover has not yet been blown!

Because Paul inextricably links the *man of lawlessness* with the apostasy, the implication is that it is his high-handed act of apostasy that will eventually unveil his true identity. That is what gives the game away and sensationally propels him on to the front cover of publications such as *Time* and *Newsweek*. His exploits mean that he is guaranteed massive coverage in print as well as on air—he is the top story on every major news report. A darling of the media, this is a pivotal moment in his life and a defining hour in the history of planet Earth. As John MacArthur writes: 'He will drop all pretence and the previously hidden wickedness of his character will be fully disclosed.'

Simply put, the devil breaks out of his cocoon-like shell and this anonymous Mr. Nice Guy waiting in the wings is then seen in his true colours. To me, it sounds like a monstrously evil metamorphosis. When it comes to Satan, the antichrist is a chip off the old block.

Identity parade

Prophetic pundits have been trying to identify this salacious man for generations; without success, it has to be said. Many individuals including Antiochus Epiphanes, Caligula, Nero, and in the last century, Hitler, Stalin, and others have been lauded as potential candidates. Even the brutal butcher of Iraq, Saddam Hussein, has been feted as a nominee, alongside the likes of former Palestinian hero, Yasser Arafat.

From a different stable, men like America's Henry Kissinger, Russia's Mikhail Gorbachev, and Egypt's Anwar al-Sadat have been suggested because of their shuttle diplomacy and skilful ability to engage hearts and minds in promoting world peace.

Be that as it may, in the cold light of day, we cannot escape the fact that the close association of this magnate with the Day of the Lord rules out any historical figures; otherwise, the Day of the Lord might have come centuries ago.

Certainly, many of these moguls have displayed strikingly similar quirks and tendencies to those we expect to find in this Mephistophelian person—someone who has sold their soul to the devil—a number of their character traits could easily be superimposed on that of the antichrist. Many of their features will be evident in his personality and lifestyle. A classic case of seeing yourself reflected in the mirror of someone else!

Judas the second

Paul spells out the long-term future of the antichrist when Paul says of him that he is *doomed to destruction*. Not the most promising outlook for a man to have in life! His end is sure. His eternity is the unremitting ferocity and terrors of hell. He is fixed for retribution and destined for judgment. This hauntingly evil man gets no more than he deserves—he gets his just deserts. He has it coming to him at the climax of the ages; God will inflict everlasting punishment on him and treat him like a tattered, cast-off doll.

The antichrist 'is human trash for the garbage dump of hell.' (John MacArthur)

He is in the same mould as Judas, the only other person in the Bible to be called the 'son of destruction' or 'son of perdition' (John 17:12). Putting two and two together, that tells me this title is reserved for two of the most despicable and vile people in human history. Two men, manipulated by Satan, guilty of the two most heinous acts of apostasy—their pedigree, like their prospects, is not good.

Judas who should have known better, having spent three quality years in the close company of Jesus, betrayed the Son of God—the antichrist will take repulsive infamy a few steps lower when he turns his back on his initial display of support for God, and declares himself to be God! Judas desecrated the temple with the few silver coins he received for spilling the beans on Jesus (cf. Matthew 27:5); the antichrist will desecrate the temple by committing the abomination of desolation as outlined in Matthew 24:15. This is an echo of what happened away back in 168 BC when the Syrian king, Antiochus Epiphanes IV, sacrificed a pig to Zeus on the sacred temple altar. This abominable act of arrogance caused the temple to be abandoned and left desolate.

Yes, Judas went astray, but it seems as though he did it on his own (cf. Acts 1:18-19); the antichrist, however, will lead the world astray— he will take them all the way to hell (cf. Revelation 13:5-8). Chillingly awful, but this is precisely what will happen in the imminent future.

2:4 FROM BAD TO WORSE, AND THEN SOME

Paul paints in vivid language some of the reprehensible activities of the antichrist when he writes, *He will oppose and will exalt himself over everything that is called God or is worshipped, so that he sets himself up in God's temple, proclaiming himself to be God.* This is unbelievable stuff that he is going to do, but it is true. Daringly so.

The antichrist's early moves make him look fantastically good; in fact, so good that men are enthusiastically keen to welcome him with open arms—they see him as the saviour of the world. He is the world leader they have been looking for; the one man who can sort out its huge problems.

In the first months of his globe-trotting you-can-really-trust-me campaign, he poses as a friend of religion (cf. Revelation 17:13). With bucketfuls of aplomb, he then changes tack and reveals himself in his true colours—he has his own agenda and nothing and no one will stand in his way. He dethrones God in order to enthrone himself. He puts himself on a par with God—a lot more is said about this infernal move in Revelation 13.

Energised by the devil, aided and abetted by the false prophet, the antichrist's right-hand man, the antichrist has no qualms or quibbles with what he does. He is focused. He stays focused. And so, seemingly, with not a care in the world, he rides roughshod over biblical truth and elevates himself to a position of deity in the house of God.

In AD 40 the Roman emperor Caligula attempted to set up his statue in the temple at Jerusalem as an assertion of his claim to divinity. The man of lawlessness is not only to have his statue erected at Jerusalem, but also will himself enter the temple and demand to be acknowledged as divine.

He gets what he wants — universal acclaim and worship. Men are delirious with joy for they see in him someone who can satisfy their deepest longings and provide an answer to their life problems; they happily bow down before him and gladly tow his party line.

It seems that this irreverent event will happen halfway through the Tribulation — midway through Daniel's seventieth week (cf. Daniel 9:27). If the first three-and-a-half-year period is joylessly grim (and it is), then the second half will be distressingly awful and unbearably traumatic. These are days when the antichrist will hold sway on a world-wide scale; days when planet Earth is pillaged and raped by hordes of demons; days when evil is perpetuated as the norm for mankind.

At the end of that time slot, Christ will return in glory to destroy antichrist's kingdom. On that day he will meet his Waterloo when the living Lord Jesus casts him into the lake of fire, along with the false prophet (cf. Revelation 19:11-21). A truly ignominious end, which is absolutely no less than he deserves.

2:5 A RAP ON THE KNUCKLES

Paul tries to jog their memory by giving them a nudge when he says, *Don't you remember that when I was with you I used to tell you these things?* In other words, if they had paid attention to what the apostle told them, they could have saved themselves a lot of heartache and needless anxiety. Such is life sometimes — we listen to people but we do not always hear what they say (cf. Romans 11:8)!

2:6-8A HOLDING THE REINS

And now you know what is holding him back, so that he may be revealed at the proper time. For the secret power of lawlessness is *already at work; but the one who now holds it back will continue to do so till he is taken out of the way. And then the lawless one will be revealed...*These words are a powerful reminder that the Lord God is sovereign—he rules the world; he runs the entire show; he has his finger on the button.

Nothing happens in this world without God knowing all about it; nothing takes place without his express permission—that means the antichrist will be revealed in God's perfect time. This figure of towering evil will appear only when God gives the go-ahead, only when the light turns green. Not one month before, nor one day after. On God's schedule.

God is never in a hurry, but he is always on time.

Job confessed, 'I know that [God] can do all things; no plan of [his] can be thwarted' (Job 42:2). The takeaway message is that no one—including Satan and his vast army of demonic allies—operates independently of God's sovereign timetable.

Repetition is the...

The implication from Paul's comments is that the Thessalonian believers were aware of who or what was restraining the antichrist. During the course of his brief ministry Paul had shared with them his inspirational insights on the subject. That explains his opening shot in this mini section, which runs through to verse 10b.

I just wish he had told us instead of them! To be honest with you, as a Bible teacher, I find this one-liner most reassuring—if the Thessalonian believers did not grasp the message first time around and they were listening to the prince of expositors, there is hope for the rest of us lesser mortals. It goes without saying that they were a little slow on the uptake! A bit thick in the brains department. The fabled penny did not drop.

Sometimes we preachers send ourselves on a guilt trip when the truth we proclaim does not seem to immediately sink into the heart and mind of those in the congregation. There are times when the message goes down like a lead balloon. When that happens, the devil takes us to the cleaners, we beat ourselves up, and we give everyone around us a really hard time. The fact is that many people are not as spiritually savvy as they should be or, perhaps, as we would like them to be.

A dog's life

The phrase employed by Paul has the idea of a dog on a leather leash; it can go so far and no further. It stays within the orbit that its master allows. Yes, it may strain at the leash and snarl and snap at every opportunity, but so long as the leash is in the hand of its owner, that dog is going nowhere. Its movements are limited. It is confined. Severely restricted. The dog knows it and does not like it! So it is with the antichrist, he is staying put until God says so!

Another analogy is one that some are familiar with from the days of the Wild West. The antichrist might be likened unto a wild bucking bull in the rodeo. The cowboys hold the bull tight in the chute and do not dare release it until the rider is ready. No longer restrained, the animal kicks and bucks, jumps and snorts, throws the rider, and then is corralled and taken from the ring. The crowd who paid to see it all claps, cheers, hollers, and screams. Similarly, no longer tied down, the antichrist will come out of the chute kicking and bucking, until he runs his course. And, to say the least, many who line up with his program, will pay dearly for their entertainment.

Keeping tabs on the antichrist

Over the years many gallons of ink have been spilt and miles of column inches written as commentators have sought to identify the restraining influence that Paul speaks of. Needless to say, the potpourri of suggestions has ranged from sublime to ridiculous—they embrace all that is wacky, wild, weird, and wonderful when it comes to pin-pointing this person or power.

Some folk believe that the proclamation of the gospel of grace is what keeps the antichrist at bay. Others feel it is the Chosen People—the nation of Israel that keeps him under wraps. Or even suitable legislation passed by government…. There are those who attribute his being kept in check to the proactive role of the evangelical church as salt and light in the world. I will not bore you with some of the more far-fetched notions, as they do not deserve the oxygen of free publicity.

Sensible as some of these ideas appear, they all fall short of what is essentially required. To a greater or lesser degree they revolve around human beings and, quite frankly, on his own—man is no match for the devil. It is not a recommended course of action for any man to engage in verbal fisticuffs with the dark enemy of our soul. Even Jesus said: 'Get behind me, Satan!'

If for no other reason, that fact helps convince me that the only one capable of keeping the lid on the antichrist is God himself in the person of the Holy Spirit. He is the Almighty One, El Shaddai—the omnipotent God; the God who can do it; the God for whom nothing is too difficult. Here is a God whose power is matchless and whose amazing ability is the stuff of legend—he is unrivalled and incomparable (cf. Ephesians 3:20).

Open secret

We know that Paul is operating in the real world when he says that *the secret power of lawlessness is already at work*. Of that, there is absolutely no doubt at all. There is ample evidence all around that the forces of darkness are having a field day. Satan and his minions are making hay when the sun shines. No section of society is left untouched. No street corner is left unmarked. No individual emerges unscathed after a scrap with the adversary. Nothing is sacred when it comes to the pernicious influence of the Evil One.

The devil knows a thing or two about sin—for lawlessness is spawned in hell.

And, as history confirms, he makes sin as beautifully attractive as possible. He is in the thriving business of luring men and women away from the one who can give them a genuine reason for living. With the resources available to him, he is out there in the rough and tumble of everyday life seeking to woo the masses and win their continued confidence. With an awful lot of people he is winning, as the following excerpt from an Elton John interview bears out.

The pop singer told the German magazine *Amica* in September 2001: 'I am gay and wouldn't want to be heterosexual for all the money in the world.... I've got enough money, don't have to follow any rules, don't have to be in the office from nine to five and take the kids to school in the morning. It is simply a fantastic life when you don't have any parameters. It's brilliant.' How sad....

It could be worse

Right now, times are bad. Very bad. But it could (and will) be so much worse than it is. Paul outlines the reason why it is not as bad as it could be when he refers to the influence of someone bigger than you and me in today's world. We are talking here about the same one who holds the antichrist at bay.

A person—the Holy Spirit, exerts the sovereign force that presently holds the reins on the man of sin. Only the Holy Spirit can do it. Only he has the supernatural power to keep Satan in his place. From the earliest times pre-Flood up until mid-Tribulation this is one of his unique roles. Today, like yesterday, and the day before, he successfully stems the tide of rampant wickedness; he holds back the tsunami of appalling and worsening evil in society. And he will continue so to do until halfway through the Tribulation when he will be *taken out of the way*.

That does not mean that the Holy Spirit will be entirely removed from the world, far from it. Such a scenario is impossible since he is omnipresent. It does, however, mean that the Spirit of God will take his hand off the leash and the dog—the antichrist—will be free to roam around planet Earth as he likes. That spells big trouble, big time for those who populate the planet at that point in time. Well, it all depends how they respond to his commands and leadership. (For a fuller account of the antichrist's shenanigans, see my book on Revelation, *Worthy is the Lamb*, published by Ambassador International).

2:8B THE BEAST IS BEATEN

When Robinson Crusoe's good man Friday asked him: '*Why doesn't God destroy the devil?*' Robinson Crusoe gave him the right answer, the only answer, the great answer. He said: '*God will destroy him!*'

Thumbs up! That day will come and it is not as far off as we might be tempted to think…. However, before the devil gets kicked off the field and banished to the everlasting abyss, the antichrist will be dealt a lethal blow at the Second Coming of Jesus Christ. This is the tale of two rival comings!

At the apex of his career and at the height of his power, when he seems invincible and untouchable, the antichrist will meet his end. Paul advises us that the Lord Jesus *will overthrow [him] with the breath of his mouth and destroy [him] by the splendour of his coming.*

When the returning Lord touches down on the Mount of Olives, to the east of the city of Jerusalem, he goes into search-and-destroy mode. The man of lawlessness is severely winded, his pride and reputation are seriously wounded, and he himself is worried sick that he has been brought to book in the presence of the living and holy God of the ages. Christ is the champion! Righteousness routs lawlessness. Reconciliation trumps rebellion. Nothing will prevail but sovereign love and no one will hold sway but the Son of God.

The antichrist is cornered and collared. The most hellish and powerful ruler in human history will be effortlessly crushed. One breath from the King of kings does it (cf. Isaiah 11:4). To quote Martin Luther: 'A word shall quickly slay him!' For him, the marauding Beast of planet Earth, there is no escape hatch. God has him by the scruff of the neck and he is not going to let him go!

The antichrist is lassoed with the tightening noose of divine justice.

The old warrior has a fair inkling of what lies ahead when he stands before the Lord Jesus and, without any further ado and with no standing on ceremony, he is abruptly consigned with his loyal compatriots to the 'fiery lake of burning sulphur' (cf. Revelation 19:19-21). To hell. In hell for all time. Eternal oblivion.

2:9-10A THE TAIL WAGGING THE DOG

Paul's comments are stunningly sensational for they give us a fresh perspective on the antichrist's comings and goings. They reveal him in his true colours and they also shine the main beam on his paymaster.

What we have here is a classic case of the tail wagging the dog; to change the metaphor, he who pays the piper calls the tune!

It is crystal clear that the devil is behind his every move; his fingerprint is over everything that he does. When all is said and done, the antichrist is the devil's henchman, his representative, for the duration of the period of Tribulation. His days are numbered, in more ways than one!

Paul writes, *The coming of the lawless one will be in accordance with the work of Satan displayed in all kinds of counterfeit miracles, signs and wonders, and in every sort of evil that deceives those who are perishing.*

A quick look at that statement and we are left in no doubt as to its veracity and razor-sharp honesty. Paul tells it like it is. Certain commendable features—biblical truth, reality, goodness, and spiritual life—are conspicuous by their absence; in their place is a black bag of devilish tricks and hellish events designed to curry favour with the general public. The outcome of this incredibly brief, but hugely effective 'anti-ministry' is that ordinary folk are conned and deceived. They are hoodwinked, right, left, and centre.

This endtime superman is energised and empowered by the devil himself. Every ounce of get-up-and-go that he has is given to him by the archenemy of the people of God. It is amazing what one man can do when his life is surrendered entirely to Satan—he not only fakes his own death and resurrection (cf. Revelation 13:3); he is also into performing miracles in a stupendous manner. This guy with a huge ego is in a league of his own when it comes to milking the crowd and doing the unusual.

However, whatever he does is deliberately designed to attract people to himself; each perishing Joe Public is left with mouth open wide at some of his phenomenal achievements—if the antichrist could dance on his head, he would surely have a go! A gullible audience is amazed, amused, and astonished at his outstanding ability to do the seemingly unattainable. The sad fact is that they are doomed and they do not seem to realise it. They are laughing and having so-called fun as they slide down the slippery slope into hell itself.

The antichrist is the greatest seducer of all time.

2:10B RESCUE THE PERISHING

There is a time to rescue the perishing — but, according to this verse, in that day there is no more time. Their time is up. These folk are on borrowed time. For the second time in a couple of lines Paul uses the word *perish*...such is their plight and predicament. They are going down. Down and out. Down and under for the third and last time. All because *they refused to love the truth and so be saved.*

These unbelievers failed to believe the truth of the person and work of Jesus Christ; instead, they embraced the lie that is the antichrist. They rejected out-of-hand the liberating gospel message of sovereign grace in favour of the devil's folklore and falsehoods. They signed their own death warrant when they flatly turned down God's offer of love and mercy in Christ. They could have been saved, but they were not and, therefore, ended up tragically lost.

Paul leaves us in no doubt that the only reason why men go to a Christless eternity is because they said 'no' to Jesus Christ. In that sense their ultimate fate is sealed in their own heart and mind long before it ever happens. They find themselves in a condemned cell on death row. The outcome of that split-second decision has eternal repercussions with frightening consequences.

They have no one else to blame but themselves. They brought the full fury of God's wrath crashing down on their own head. Their first night of exile, banished from God, will be repeated over and over again as time runs into eternity; for them, that means an uninterrupted season of inky-black darkness in a place where God has forgotten to be merciful.

2:11-12 SNARED BY THEIR OWN TRAP

For this reason God sends them a powerful delusion so that they will believe the lie and so that all will be condemned who have not believed the truth but have delighted in wickedness. Solemn words. They dug a hole and they fell feet-first into it.

These folk are fooled by the generosity of the antichrist and are taken in by his pontificating on all things religious. Intelligent and cultured they may be, but that does not mean they do not fall for his pretence and persuasive oratorical powers. Quite literally, for one reason or another, the antichrist has them eating out of his hand—see 666 and the philosophy behind the mark of the beast (cf. Revelation 13:17-19).

He is top dog—they are toy poodles.

Their hostile aversion to anything biblical or Christian is seen in their wholesale acceptance of the often scurrilous and defenceless untruths that the antichrist is propagating. Unashamedly they embrace a litany of lies and without embarrassment they run headlong after all shapes and sizes of gross sinfulness. When men are loosed from their moorings there is nothing that should surprise us with regard to their dissolute and deviant behaviour. Basically, they are so degenerate that they go to rack and ruin.

It has to be said that God places blinders over their eyes. He throws a screen across their mind. They are seriously deluded and God has engineered it in such a way that they accept all the nonsense that is spewed from the big mouth of the antichrist. To quote John MacArthur: 'God will sentence unbelievers to accept evil as if it were good and lies as if they were the truth. Those who continually choose falsehood will be inextricably caught by it.'

Bob Hope once said in a flippant one-liner: 'I do benefits for all religions. I'd hate to blow the hereafter on a technicality.' Impossible! We can only blow it on an essential—Jesus.

I saw a bumper sticker that said: 'If you don't believe in God, I hope for your sake you are right!' The author was not right (even if he was being ironic) because whoever we are in this world today, we are going to meet God at his throne someday!

2:13 BE SECURE!

These are wonderful words penned by Paul and especially after all the heavy stuff he has just been offloading. They are like a breath of fresh air. The preacher man says to these dear folk, be secure! We read, *But we ought always to thank God for you, brothers loved by the Lord, because from the beginning God chose you to be saved through the sanctifying work of the Spirit and through belief in the truth.*

263

Having looked at some perspectives that impact tomorrow's world in the previous few verses, Paul now looks back to eternity past and relishes the delicious relationship these dear saints have with the one who is from everlasting to everlasting. For him, this is a supremely joyous moment as he reflects on their odyssey in grace. Paul reckons he can do no better than sincerely thank God for every one of them—a people who are the apple in the eye of God.

They are deeply loved by the Lord with a love that is undying and unchanging, uninfluenced and undeserved; a love that is measureless and matchless; a love that keeps on loving in spite of…quite simply, it is a love that does not know how to do anything else but love. Irrespective of the huge pressures they faced and even though the odds were stacked against them in so many ways, they can feel secure in his love. Totally secure. They can rest and relax in the warmth of his unfailing love—a love that will not let them go.

Handpicked by God

Away back before time itself the believers in this church were personally chosen by God to be part of his international family. In mercy and grace he set his affection upon them, and when the time was right, he savingly drew them to himself. In a nutshell, that is how the doctrine of election works out in practice. It was true then, it is no less true today; if we know Jesus Christ personally we can identify with the sentiments so eloquently expressed by Paul—God loved me, and God chose me!

The end of our election, as Charles Simeon (1759-1836) pointed out, '… was to salvation itself, with all its inconceivable and lasting blessings.' We cannot explain such love, neither should we explain it away!

Joyce Daugherty, a member of Southeast Christian Church in Louisville, Kentucky, travelled to an orphanage in Donetsk, Ukraine, and it was there that she saw two-year-old Kristen. Her beautiful blue eyes framed the edges of a facial tumour, a haemangioma, but even that could not hide the baby's impish grin.

'Kristen's eyes were so alert that I just kept watching her,' said Daugherty. 'There was something special that tumour could not hide.

I could have taken any of the children I saw home with me. At the same time, I knew if I adopted Kristen, she'd have more than a new start—she'd have a new life.'

'These children are throwaways in Ukraine,' says Nancy Stanbery who has helped facilitate more than 130 adoptions in that land. 'Most Ukrainian families are afraid of a child with any kind of disability. Mothers take them to an orphanage or abandon them in a public place, walk away, and never look back.'

Daugherty chose Kristen. In November 2004 a Louisville surgeon removed the haemangioma. Thin scars are healing and everything about Kristen has changed dramatically. She chatters constantly—saying 'I love you' over and over again to her mum.

In a similar way, while we were still unlovely, our heavenly Father chose us, adopted us, and gave us new life in Jesus. Today, we can only love him because he gave us the opportunity, and he amazingly continues to love us. As Christians, we must and do love God as our Father.

Count your blessings

Our salvation finds its springs in God himself. And I agree with the Puritan Thomas Manton that 'waters are sweetest and freshest in their fountain.' God is the source, the origin, of our salvation. Behind it all, there is God! Before it all, there is God! Beneath it all, there is God!

Everything about our salvation, whether past, present, or future, has God's hallmark on it. There are many transformational benefits and blessings from this enterprising doctrine that have an ongoing input in our daily life.

- It crushes human pride (cf. Titus 3:5).
- It exalts God (cf. Psalm 115:1).
- It produces unsurpassed joy (cf. 1 Peter 1:1-2, 6, 8).
- It grants unimaginable privileges (cf. Ephesians 1:3).
- It promotes holiness of life (cf. Colossians 3:12-13).
- It provides security (cf. Philippians 1:6).

The reality of God's electing love is manifest in our life by the Holy Spirit and his unique ministry of sanctification. He is the one who sets us apart from sin to live a life that is pleasing to the Lord; he is the one who encourages us to pursue righteousness and to embrace the will of God for our life (cf. Romans 15:16; 12:1-2).

He is actively engaged in this role from the moment of our conversion to Jesus Christ and it is something that he keeps on doing until we are glorified at the end of life's journey. His desire is that we might reflect the beauty of Jesus and that we might radiate something of our heavenly Father's attractive goodness to those who know him not. We need to be free to be in love with Jesus in front of people—and to be an ambassador to them, through whom Jesus can introduce himself.

A vote for Jesus

There is nothing airy-fairy about our relationship with God for it all began when we positively responded to the gospel message—the day and hour, as Paul put it, when we believed in the truth. In a multifaith society, pluralism and 'diversity' are presented as the be-all and end-all of religious experience. It needs to be said that there is no other route for a man to take in order for him to be right with God than through trusting the absolute truth as we have it in Jesus Christ. It is exclusive! It is crucial. In Christ alone!

The Puritan Richard Baxter (1615-91) noted: 'If the gospel were a fable or human device, and if the word of God were not true, ministers have the most unworthy employment upon earth.'

- There is one way—Jesus.
- There is one door—Jesus.
- There is one message—Jesus.

2:14 GOSPEL AND GLORY

He called you to this through our gospel, that you might share in the glory of our Lord Jesus Christ. Knowing Jesus Christ is a two-way relationship—we are called to him and he shares his life with us. When we cast a vote for Jesus, we are on the winning team. When we came as sinners to Jesus, he certainly did not back a loser in his eyes. We did not whistle for help; he did the calling first! We come to him as the result of his love. He does not come to us as a result of our love. Our love for him results from him calling us, and our acceptance of that call.

This is God's effectual and irresistible call (cf. Romans 8:30); it is an intensely gratifying experience for it leads to a life of fulfilment and blessing that is way beyond our wildest dreams. This is what Charles Wesley (1707-88) had in mind when he penned:

267

> *Long my imprisoned spirit lay*
> *Fast bound in sin and nature's night;*
> *Thine eye diffused a quickening ray—*
> *I woke, the dungeon flamed with light;*
> *My chains fell off, my heart was free.*
> *I rose, went forth, and followed thee.*

When we experience grace, we enjoy God.

Glory is on the horizon for all of God's people. It is something that we share the one with the other and, throughout the countless ages of eternal ecstasy, we will never grow tired or weary of being in the presence of one who is all-glorious.

We share in his glory but we never take it to ourselves, nor do we detract in any sense from his unrivalled, untarnished splendour. It is just that we savour and relish that eternal moment with his majesty. We bask in the limelight of his resplendent loveliness, and we are enraptured with his appealing charm and dignity. We are 'lost in wonder, love, and praise' when we peer into this load of theology. We reflect his glory back to him as we praise him.

2:15 BE STRONG!

Great counsel! In other words, do not go running after some new doctrinal fad, some exotic teaching. This is not the time to explore novel ideas about theology. This is the time for God's people to dig their roots down deep and ride out the storm. Back to the Bible.

Paul's appeal to these weary pilgrims is an impassioned one for he wants to see them going on with the Lord. They felt steamrolled, crushed, and deflated on the cold, hard concrete. For him and for them it is always too soon to quit—there is no point in them walking off site when the job is still not finished. A call to stickability, to persevere, to keep plodding on! They have so much to lose if they throw the towel into the ring and, quite simply, it is just not worth it when the final whistle (or trumpet) blows.

Paul writes, *So then, brothers, stand firm and hold to the teachings we passed on to you, whether by word of mouth or by letter.*

The apostle's desire is for them to be strong in the face of relentless opposition. He wants them to dig their heels in, hold their spiritual ground, and keep a firm grip on the truth, rather than being weak or vacillating. Be men! Bold. Strong. Our resolve is in God. 'At every turn,' writes Philip Greenslade, 'God's sweet, fresh, bracing air of truth blows away the fog of lies and propaganda.' The truth goes marching on!

2:16-17 BE ENCOURAGED!

May our Lord Jesus Christ himself and God our Father, who loved us and by his grace gave us eternal encouragement and good hope, encourage your hearts and strengthen you in every good deed and word.

When the believers in Thessalonica wondered was it worth all the hassle, Paul gives them a double booster—not only is the Lord with them, so too is Father God. Both are on their side! Yet another convincing reference to the deity of our Lord Jesus Christ—he is fully equal with the Father in person, power, and respect.

In the midst of all the ups and downs of life, there is Jesus! He offers a clear-eyed perspective on the here and after. He speaks calm into a troubled heart. He whispers words of encouragement and hope to those who are struggling to keep going. Paul prays for God to graciously undertake for them, not to circumnavigate the storms for them. He asks God to strengthen them, not for him to spare them.

The reality is, they have known and felt his bounteous love and intimate closeness; they have experienced and enjoyed lavish outpourings of his generous grace; they have an abundance of hope in their heart. With all this, surely they can smile in the storm. Their life will be inestimably richer through this harrowing experience. For, as John Ruskin says: 'The highest reward for man's toil and trouble is not what he gets for it, but what he becomes by it.' By God's grace…all things work together for good (cf. Romans 8:28).

At the 2002 Winter Olympics American Apolo Ohno hoped to win his second gold medal in the men's 5,000-metre short track speed skating relay. During one of the turns, an American skater fell but quickly got back into the race. While the fall and recovery only took a few seconds, it essentially put the American team out of the race. What was interesting was that the American team began to skate slower and slower, eventually being lapped by the gold-medal Canadians. Why did they slow down? Because the hope of doing well was gone!

On your bike…

What a fantastic pick-me-up benediction Paul has just shared with them. An unshakeable promise of present help and future glory. He gives them hope! Fragile hearts are made brave hearts in the courage and hope that God supplies. If that does not do the trick, I have no idea what will! By God's grace and with God's help, our best intentions are made good, our good deeds are made better, and our best words are made flesh. Yes, it is difficult and demanding, it is hard going, but there is so much in Christ to really brighten each and every day.

In 1851 when C. H. Spurgeon pastored his first church—Waterbeach Baptist Chapel—in England, he visited one of his parishioners in the country. Over his barn the brother had a weathervane with the words 'God is love' on the top. The young pastor questioned the wisdom of that message on the weathervane. He explained: 'That leaves the impression that God's love is as unpredictable as the wind.' The dear countryman responded: 'What I mean by it is that no matter which way the wind is blowing, God is love!' Amen.

This is the hour for us to get busy for God. We should 'be up and doing for Jesus' is how John Wesley expressed it. We need to use the powers and energy and gifting that he has sovereignly entrusted to us. Maximise the time. Cash in on opportunities. For one of the goals of a Christian is not only to go to heaven, but also to take as many people with him as he can!

CHAPTER EIGHT
I OWE, I OWE, IT'S OFF TO WORK I GO

'If a church wants a better pastor, it can get one by praying for the one it has.' (Merrill C. Tenney)

Paul begins this chapter with one word that makes a world of difference to the average congregation on a Sunday morning—it is that long-awaited moment when the preacher, nearing the end of his third point, eventually says, '… finally!' What does it mean when a preacher says 'finally'? Absolutely nothing! Or maybe fifteen more minutes…. And everyone heaves a tangible sigh of relief! A slight exaggeration, but you know what I mean. The problem some communicators face is that they have finished their sermon ten minutes earlier, it is just that they could not get stopped! Not the case with the maestro Paul.

At the end of this cordial, constructive, and challenging letter the apostle wants to give them a few more take-home guidelines for Christian living as well as soliciting their fellowship in prayer on his behalf. True to form, he has packed a lot into this epistle—distilled wisdom on handling people and dealing with complex situations, straight-from-the-shoulder teaching on essential truths, remarkable insights on endtime events, plus lots more.

3:1 A STANDING IN THE NEED OF PRAYER

I suppose Paul could have pleaded with them to do a lot of things on his behalf, but his main request is for them to intercede for him—*Finally, brothers, pray for us.* Prayer is a good barometer of our dependence upon the Lord and Paul's writings reveal that he was so dependent on the Lord that he asked others to pray for him. Their prayers galvanised him.

Above all else, he is increasingly reliant on their faithful prayers. Any preacher worth his salt needs the tact of a diplomat, the strength of Samson, the patience of Job, the wisdom of Solomon, and a cast-iron stomach! Paul depends upon his prayer partners to intercede for him on these very topics.

This is a vital ministry that everyone of us can engage in—it takes time, a high level of commitment, and a big heart to do it, but the rewards are immense. The thrill of seeing God answer prayer is one of those skyscraper experiences that lift us to new heights with the Lord. At the same time, it greatly humbles us for we realise that the living God has chosen to respond to our feeble efforts.

As an itinerant preacher of the glorious gospel, Paul values their intelligent intercession on his behalf; as a fellow believer in Christ, he appreciates the inestimable privilege of fellowship around the throne of grace; as an ordinary man facing many crises and choices, he is enormously grateful to them for their keen enthusiasm to be involved with him in this manner.

John Piper makes much of the link between preaching and prayer, between mission and intercession, when he writes: 'Prayer is the walkie-talkie of the church on the battlefield of the world in the service of the word. It is not a domestic intercom to increase the comfort of the saints…it is for those on active duty. And in their hands it proves the supremacy of God in the pursuit of the nations. When mission moves forward by prayer it magnifies the power of God. When it moves by human management it magnifies man.' Which would you rather depend on—the power of God or man?

'Knocking on doors to people's hearts is our job; opening those doors is God's. Prayer is what sensitises the occupant to hear the knock and respond.' (Charles Swindoll)

3:1B-2 CALL TO PRAYER

'Prayer changes things' is a quick-off-the-tongue cliché, but it is true. It always makes a huge difference. Incalculable. Immeasurable. It is hard work! And it works hard! Martin Luther realised that when he wrote that 'none can believe how powerful prayer is, and what it is able to effect, but those who have learned it by experience.'

- It impacts the man himself with a sense of realism.
- It influences the future course of his biblical ministry.
- It impinges on those with whom he is working.
- It invades the unseen areas of this world.
- It intimidates the enemy of our souls.
- It integrates both sides—the pray-er and the prayed-for.
- It inspires others to get on board—they see what God is doing and they do not want to miss out!

273

Each of these potentially life-changing, ministry-transforming benefits is seen in Paul's request, *Pray for us that the message of the Lord may spread rapidly and be honoured, just as it was with you. And pray that we may be delivered from wicked and evil men, for not everyone has faith.*

It is clear that Paul's ambition is for God's word to prosper in the region. Like an athlete, Paul wants the gospel to take great strides forward without being impeded in any way. It is the run-gospel-run mindset. Run well. Run fast. Run on. He is avidly looking for a groundswell of response. He knows it can happen for he has seen it before—the assembly in Thessalonica is living proof of that!

There was no evangelical witness in town when he first went there—but now, a few months afterwards, there is. In fact, it is mushrooming in spite of all the trials and troubles they have experienced thus far. Paul takes heart for he knows that the God who has done it before is the same God who can do it again!

This is still excitingly relevant in the third millennium—the extraordinary growth of the church in Asia, Latin America, and Africa strongly bears this out. The church in those continents is growing far faster than in the West. They are excited about the gospel. So much so that Christianity is truly a global phenomenon.

Danger of derailment

It is interesting to observe that Paul does not ask for evil to be wiped out or for him to be spared its onslaught in his daily life; he simply longs for God to take him through the tough, torrid time that evil presents as and when it intrudes into his life.

This is where God specialises. Paul, once a true-blue Jew, knows his Old Testament incredibly well—he is very much aware of so many take-your-breath-away stories of days long past when God performed miracles on behalf of his people. Paul reckons there is no harm in allowing God to repeat the process in his life! If he can do it for Daniel in a den of lions and for three young men in a blazing inferno then he can do it for Paul!

Paul does not bury his head in the sand and pretend there are no problems or scary situations in his life and work—he knows full well he has more than his share of challenges and at times more than he thinks he can cope with. Nevertheless, he slogs on regardless. The ministry is bigger than the man and all that matters is that the gospel progresses into previously unreached parts of God's world.

The presence of *wicked and evil men* does not dampen his zeal or cool his fiery enthusiasm to introduce people to Jesus Christ. Such folk may dog his every footstep and prove to be a pain in the neck in his public ministry, but Paul the preacher man soldiers on. The devil does not like it when we encroach on to his territory so he will do all in his power to oppose the advance of God's truth.

There are other times when the resistance movement is from within—a kind of fifth column mentality. Sometimes pastors need a bullet-proof vest when walking down the aisle to greet their members. Charles Swindoll said, 'One or two sheep with a little goat in them can butt heads often enough with the pastor to make his ministry miserable.' From an American pain reliever commercial: 'That's not helping my headache!' Behaviour like that is hard to take; but it happens.

The show goes on! —Paul

3:3 SATAN TO JESUS MUST BOW

Paul exudes optimistic confidence when he writes, *But the Lord is faithful, and he will strengthen and protect you from the evil one.* The secret to winning the battle is to focus our gaze on the Lord Jesus, the victorious Son of God. If we eye up the enemy too much and give him more space than we could, it can have a debilitating and devastating effect on our outlook; it breeds a real sense of fear and alarm in our heart. We are destabilised. As and when that occurs, we have taken two steps back, rather than three steps forward.

We need to realise that God is bigger than all our problems and that Satan to Jesus must bow. God is with us through thick and thin and he will protect us with the shield of his 24/7 presence. When our legs turn to jelly and we have butterflies in our stomach, the Lord enables us to keep on going for he is our strength. In our moments of weakness we are deeply conscious of his empowerment and enabling.

E. M. Bounds tells the story of rising early one morning and being confronted with an unforgettable scene. He relates: 'I heard the barking of a number of dogs chasing a deer. Looking at a large open field in front of me, I saw a young fawn making its way across the field and giving signs that its race was almost run. It leaped over the rails of the enclosed place and crouched within ten feet of where I stood. A moment later, two of the hounds came over and the fawn ran in my direction and pushed its head between my legs. I lifted the little thing to my breast and, swinging round and round, fought off the dogs. Just then I felt that all the dogs in the West could not and would not capture that fawn after its weakness had appealed to my strength.'

An all-strong God is attracted to all human weakness.

Through all the changing scenes in life and ministry, the Lord is magnificently faithful—in all honesty, he cannot be anything else. He never lets us down. He never lets us go. He draws us and holds us tightly to himself. Brian Doerksen was thinking along these lines when he penned:

Faithful One, so unchanging;
Ageless One, you're my rock of peace.
Lord of all, I depend on you,
I call out to you again and again,
I call out to you again and again.
You are my rock in times of trouble,
You lift me up when I fall down;
All through the storm your love is the anchor—
My hope is in you alone.

In other words, this God is able to do what we have decided in our mind is impossible, or impregnable, or improbable—the more we focus on his unswerving faithfulness, the more faith-filled we become. Deep stuff!

Moody memoir

This principle is superbly illustrated in the life of D. L. Moody. On 23 November 1892 he and his son Will boarded the ocean liner *Spree* on a journey from Southampton, England. Mr. Moody had just finished a series of evangelistic meetings in London, including eight days of services in the famous Spurgeon's Tabernacle, and now he was bound for New York. Foremost in his mind, besides seeing his family and students again, was the upcoming campaign he had scheduled for the Chicago World's Fair in 1893.

On the third morning of the trip, passengers were startled by a loud crash and a shock going through the ship. Will hurried out on to the deck. He quickly returned to say that the shaft of the vessel was broken. 'The ship's sinking,' he exclaimed.

The disabled ship, carrying hundreds of passengers, drifted helplessly away from the sea lanes. She was taking on so much water that her pumps were useless and ineffective. The crew prepared lifeboats and provisions, but they realised that the small boats would soon perish in the rough seas. So they mustered passengers into a main saloon and waited, hoping to be discovered by a passing vessel.

On the second evening of their torturous wait, Moody led a prayer service that calmed many of the passengers, including himself. Although he was sure of heaven, the thought of his work ending and of never again seeing his family had unsettled him.

One biographer includes another angle to the incident. Prior to the trip a doctor had found irregularities in Moody's heart and urged him to ease his schedule; if Moody did not, he would die early. Mr. Moody determined to slow down and, while sailing homeward, decided to scale down plans for the World's Fair campaign.

During the crisis at sea, Moody perceived that God confronted him with a decision: Would he press on with all his might to deliver the gospel or would he be cautious, allowing fear to diminish his fervour? Facing death, Moody decided that if God would spare his life, he would work with 'all the power that he would give me.' And if he should die this year or next, that decision was in God's hands, not his own.

The following morning, however, the steamer Lake Huron discovered the stranded ship and towed it one thousand miles to safety. D. L. Moody pressed on with his World's Fair campaign, six months of unceasing labour, from which, in Moody's estimate, 'millions…heard the simple gospel of Christ' and 'thousands [were] genuinely converted to Christ.' Evangelist D. L. Moody died in the midst of his work—seven years later! He now lives with his Lord.

3:4 KEEP IT UP!

We have confidence in the Lord that you are doing and will continue to do the things we command. Again, Paul expresses the fact that he has no hangups about their ongoing commitment to the fundamental truths of Scripture. He has no reservations lurking in the front of his mind that lead him to think otherwise—his confidence is in the Lord. Sure it is; if it was anywhere else, it would be seriously misplaced. Ultimately, this is God's work, not his!

'Faith and obedience are bound up in the same bundle. He that obeys God, trusts God; and he that trusts God, obeys God.' (Charles Spurgeon)

3:5 STEADY AND STEADFAST

Paul's aspiration for the believers in Thessalonica is beautifully summed up when he writes, *May the Lord direct your hearts into God's love and Christ's perseverance.* What a benediction! Super. During a visit to a children's Bible class, the preacher looked into their smilingly serious faces, and asked: 'Why do you love God?' After a few moments a small voice came from the back: 'I guess it just runs in the family!'

This is vintage Paul as he harks back to the impeccable character of Christ—he persevered and, with his enabling, so can we! Divine stamina. It gives us consistency as we participate in the marathon of life. He also includes the unconditional love of Father God in his all-round prayer, a God who keeps on loving despite the odds, a God whose love endures for ever—and, again, with his gracious touch upon our life, we can do the same! It gives us security.

The bottom line is that our life will then be God-centred, God-focused, and God-oriented. The by-product is a life that is God-blessed and God-thrilled. The top line is that God in the person of his Son is totally committed to us. In him alone is a rock-solid reality.

'We are called to an everlasting preoccupation with God.' (A. W. Tozer)

3:6 HI HO...I OWE

In the fairytale, *Snow White and the Seven Dwarfs*, the seven little fellows go marching off to work each morning singing, 'Hi ho, hi ho, it's off to work we go,' with a spring in their step and a lilt in their voice. Just think—if we were going to where they were going I think we would have much more than a spring in our step—a trampoline-style bounce is probably more realistic! You see, they owned a diamond mine!

Max Anders has commented: 'According to the Disney comic book I read as a child, their mine was a cave-like tunnel with golf ball sized diamonds, already cut and faceted, sticking halfway out of the sides of the shaft. What a job!

'But most of us are not bouncing jauntily off to a diamond mine every morning. Instead, we chug off soberly with a bumper sticker that says, "I owe, I owe, it's off to work I go."

'In fact, for many people, work is drudgery, a meaningless necessity. With little connection between their workplace and the rest of their life, their life slogan is TGIF (Thank Goodness It's Friday).' Our slogan should be TGIS—Thank God It's Sunday—and we should be striving to make every day a virtual Sunday of worship to God.

An illustration like that brings a smile to our face, but for many folk in what is called the 'underclass' there is more than a dozen grains of truth in that comment. They are struggling to make ends meet; every day is a financial challenge to them to put another meal on the table and to keep the kids in decent clothes and shoes. Another day, another dollar!

The lot in life for those people is mega tough. For some, it is through no fault of their own, it is just the way the dice have rolled in their upbringing and life experience. For others, it is an entirely different story because they milk the social security system for all it is worth—some of them have never done an honest day's work in their life; they view 'work' only as a four-letter word—some of them probably cannot even spell 'work'—they are freeloaders and are happy and content to live on handouts from the State and other charitable sources.

The bad old days

There is nothing new under the sun and, believe it or not, there were even spongers back in Paul's day. They certainly did not have a government sponsored benefits system in the first century. So many of these folk were, literally, living from hand to mouth. Some people were banned from their place of employment because of their faith in Jesus Christ—they lost their job when they committed themselves to wholeheartedly following Jesus. For them, it was an exorbitantly high price to pay, but they felt it was worth it in the long run. They discovered a new dimension in God's character that they had not been fully aware of before—his faithfulness as the God who is enough. The church flourishes under persecution.

Other folk, sadly, downed their tools when they embraced the apostolic teaching on the Second Coming of Jesus Christ. They stopped work so that they could spend their time looking and waiting for the Rapture! Work fascinates them so much that they can watch it all day long. Better, they reckoned, to be ready for Jesus when he breaks through the clouds—it is the mindset that says, we cannot keep him waiting! These guys much preferred to spend their time lounging in tee shirt, jeans, and trainers rather than slogging it out in the construction industry or whatever calling the Lord moved them to undertake. Talk about pushing your luck! For them, it was a cushy wee number.

As Christians, they are no better than leeches!

Steer clear

The lunatic fringe—these are the individuals that Paul is referring to when he writes what he does in this section, which runs through to verse 13. It was obviously a big issue in Paul's day otherwise he would not have spent so much time talking about it. These lazy individuals needed to hear the truth straight from the horse's mouth, and the church needed clear-cut guidance on how to deal with it.

So Paul declares, *In the name of our Lord Jesus Christ, we command you, brothers, to keep away from every brother who is idle and does not live according to the teaching you received from us.* Nothing ambiguous about that statement of intent!

Typical Paul, when confronted with a situation such as this, he goes for the jugular—no point, he reckons, in pussy-footing around and treading softly-softly on the boards. Best to go for it, say it, get it over and done with! On that premise, everyone knows where they stand—they know what is acceptable and what is a non-starter—the parameters are set.

Can't work. Won't work.

These are the individuals Paul specifically refers to in this paragraph, and to make matters worse, they are believers—brothers who sit with us in the worship service and with whom we break bread on a Sunday morning. These guys are part of the family of God, members of a local congregation of believers. But, says Paul, we have to give them the cold shoulder. If they are not prepared to buckle down and earn a living then we have no alternative but to isolate them.

A tough penalty? Yes. A harsh measure? Yes. It may appear to contradict other parts of Scripture where we are encouraged to help those in any kind of need. Not so! There is a huge difference between those who for legitimate reasons are not able to work, and those who have no desire or interest in dirtying their hands from nine to five every day. The first group need our commitment, love, and support—the second group need to learn a salutary lesson the hard way. From Paul's perspective, that means having nothing to do with them!

'There is not a thing on the face of the earth that I abhor so much as idleness or idle people.' (George Whitefield)

3:7A A WORD ABOUT WORK

Paul sees himself as a role model to these believers and especially in the whole area of work. It is obvious that Paul was a hard worker himself and, leading by example, he expected others to follow suit. In that sense, the preacher-cum-tentmaker was exemplary. It was Thomas Edison who said that 'there is no substitute for hard work.' He also said that 'genius is one percent inspiration and ninety-nine percent perspiration!' Right. My mother used to say that hard work never killed anyone!

For you yourselves know how you ought to follow our example. Having said that, Paul's theology of life and work was based not only on biblical principle, but also on the unchanging character of God. If anyone knows a thing or two about work, it is God. He has been at it from before day one and he has not stopped since. God is not a workaholic—he rested on the seventh day—but he is a great believer in work. So much so that he gave Adam a job or two to do in the Garden of Eden, even before the Fall (cf. Genesis 2:15).

Big ideas and good intentions are great; a vision of the future is awesome; five-year projections are inspiring and wonderful, but none of these on their own put a square meal on the dinner table for a family of four! To quote Henry Ford (1863-1947): 'You can't build a reputation on what you are going to do.' When it comes to setting an example, says Paul, roll up your sleeves and just do it! Like the old adage—I'd rather see a sermon than hear one any day; I'd rather someone walk with me than merely tell me the way!

'A good example is the tallest kind of preaching.' (African proverb)

3:7B-8 BURNING THE CANDLE AT BOTH ENDS

We were not idle when we were with you, nor did we eat anyone's food without paying for it. On the contrary, we worked night and day, labouring and toiling so that we would not be a burden to any of you. These words inform us that Paul was a great believer in paying his own way. The thought of him sponging on other people was abhorrent and there was no way that he was prepared to do it.

That is not to say that he did not receive monetary gifts and other generous tokens of love from people and from churches, for he did (cf. Philippians 4:10-19); but he lived frugally and he so lived his life before the Lord that he did not want to be in debt to any man. Again, there is a difference between being a burden to folk in terms of cashing in on their hospitality and us depriving believers of the genuine privilege of sharing their resources with God's people.

For Paul, tent making paid the bills and kept the wolf from the front door—for us, it pays the mortgage. Sounds a bit like the irrepressible Mr. Spurgeon to me. Apparently he was often on the go for eighteen hours a day. Famous explorer and missionary David Livingstone once asked him: 'How do you manage to do two men's work in a single day?' Spurgeon's response says everything: 'You have forgotten that there are two of us!' Spurgeon was never on his own with God at hand.

Many years ago a pastor friend told me that we have three choices in life when it comes to work and ministry—we can rust out by being lazy, we can burn out as a workaholic, or we can live out and serve our God by working hard and working well.

3:9 PEOPLE WATCHERS

'For the watching world, we ourselves serve proof that God is alive. We form the visible shape of what he is like.' (Philip Yancey)

In other words, people are looking and they miss nothing. If we are lazy and whittle the hours away, they see it (and talk about it behind our back)—if we are diligent and industrious, they also see it (and talk about it to our face)! The first group drops a bombshell of criticism, the other gives a bouquet of appreciative comment.

As Paul discovered, there are times when we have to abandon protocol, put ourselves out, forget about our own rights, and do what is best for others. It may cost us an arm and a leg but if that is what it takes for them to see an authentic message then it will be immensely worthwhile. Hence Paul's comment, *We did this, not because we do not have the right to such help, but in order to make ourselves a model for you to follow.*

As the pastor's wife opens the door and lets out the family pet—a Dalmatian—she is overheard to say: 'Remember, Spot, you're the pastor's dog; all the other dogs will be watching you!' Poor dog. That is putting him on the Spot!

Paul set the pace and he wants them to follow in his footsteps. There was no point in him exhorting them to engage in work if he himself was not prepared to lose some sweat at the coalface. When Paul preached or wrote on the subject he was not talking about some other man's experience. This guy worked himself to the bone—one shake of his hand gave the game away. Big, rough, callused hands.

In a different context, but no less challenging, Stephen Freed tells the story of watching his father slowly deteriorate from an incurable disease. That posed all sorts of questions in his mind. One such question he shared with his 15-year-old daughter Elizabeth. He asked her: 'What will you do if I end up like your grandfather someday?' Her response took him by surprise—'I don't know, Dad, but I'm watching you to find out.'

Like mama used to do...

Anthusa lived from around 330 to 374 AD in Antioch. Widowed at the age of 20, she is remembered for her influence in the life of her son, John Chrysostom, one of the greatest preachers and leaders of the fourth-century church. Her contemporaries tell us Anthusa was cultured, attractive, and from a wealthy family. Yet she chose to not remarry after her husband's death, deciding instead to devote herself to rearing her two children, John and his sister.

John later wrote that his mother not only taught her children to know and love the teachings of the Bible, but also that her life was an excellent model of grace living. A student of law, rhetoric, and the Scriptures, John was made a deacon in 381 by Meletius and later became Bishop of Constantinople in 398. A zealous missionary himself, he inspired numerous others to serve the Lord in this way. And he always emphasised that a crucial factor to effective evangelism is for Christians to be living examples of Christ-centredness. A lesson he learned from his godly mother, Anthusa.

283

3:10 NO WORK, NO EAT

For even when we were with you, we gave you this rule: 'If a man will not work, he shall not eat.' Drastic action. The average postmodern person tells us that rules are made to be broken—try telling that to Paul! Be prepared for him to go ballistic and hit the roof.

So far as he is concerned, if an able-bodied individual refuses to work then that person deserves to starve. There is no room for manoeuvre in an instance like this—if the guy does not work then we have no option but to steer clear of him. It is his problem, and his alone. As the people of God there is no biblical reason why we should feed his awfully bad habit.

A mother walked in on her six-year-old son and found him sobbing. 'What's the matter?' she asked. 'I've just figured out how to tie my shoes,' he said. 'Well, honey, that's wonderful.' Being a wise mother, she recognised his victory in the struggle of autonomy versus doubt: 'You're growing up, you're a big boy now; but why are you crying?' 'Because,' he said, 'now I'll have to do it every day for the rest of my life!'

Too much like work for little Johnny!

3:11-12 THE IDLE MINORITY

'Laziness travels so slowly that poverty soon overtakes him.' (Benjamin Franklin)

We hear that some among you are idle. Paul said what he did because he knew that some folk in the church in Thessalonica were only coming along for the ride. They wanted all the perks that were going but without any responsibility resting on their shoulders to help cover the costs. They would take everything coming their way, and still some, but talk to them about doing an honest day's work and you would not see them for dust.

One summer day a man was driving on a lonely road when he came across a car with a flat tyre. The car had been pulled over on to the hard shoulder and a woman was standing beside it. She looked flustered and appeared greatly dismayed by her situation.

The man decided this was a good time for him to play the Good Samaritan so he pulled over and offered his services in helping her change the wheel. She gratefully accepted.

The man grew hot and sweaty in the bright sun as he did what he had to do. The nuts were difficult to loosen and his shirt was covered with grime and grease by the time he helped dig the jack and spare wheel out of the boot (or trunk for our American motorists!), wrangled the offending wheel off, and got the new one securely mounted on the car.

The dear woman watched him with great admiration and appreciation and gave what encouragement she could. She thanked him repeatedly as he neared the end of the job, and then said: 'Now, let the jack down carefully. I don't want to waken my husband, he's asleep in the back of the car!'

Talk about laziness and idleness. An appalling example of someone sound asleep while others do their dirty work. Paul has no time for that attitude, and neither should we.

Busy body or busybodies?

They are not busy; they are busybodies. How true it is that the devil finds work for idle hands. This is the key point that Paul is making. What a fantastic difference it would make to them and to their situation if these disruptive guys got their act together. Even the Romans had a saying: 'By doing nothing, men learn to do evil.'

Charles Swindoll hits the nail on the head when he says that 'busybodies flit from house to house taking little nectar drops of gossip with them, leaving behind their own residue of irritating pollen.'

Someone has said that those people who are willing to work are like mules—when they are pulling they cannot kick and when they are kicking they cannot pull. Another good reason for men doing something to earn their keep! Howard Hendricks was right when he said that 'the average layman has the idea that his vocation is his penalty.' That really is sad when people see work as a giant life-sucking machine. Such folk prefer their vocation to be a vacation!

That ties in with Paul's exhortation in verse 12 where he says, *Such people we command and urge in the Lord Jesus Christ to settle down and earn the bread they eat.* The apostle brings God into the equation thereby lifting it to a higher plane; it also raises the stakes. Even former First Lady Barbara Bush acknowledged: 'You don't just luck into things as much as you'd like to think you do. You build step by step, whether it's friendships or opportunities.'

If it was merely his injunction, then he could understand them sneering and sniggering and not taking him seriously. But this command has come down from above—it is God's word into their situation, and they would be daft if they did not do something about it.

3:13 TIRED OR RE-TIRED?

Paul gives the believes a push when he suggests to them, *And as for you, brothers, never tire of doing what is right.* In their situation where some folk are not pulling their weight it would be so easy to become despondent and discouraged. Paul wants them, instead, to seize every God-given moment and make it count for eternity. There is a display of raw passion in his appeal to them not to quit. It is tiring, sure, but let us not tire in our pursuit of what is right.

Some folk I meet are tired doing nothing. When we are down to less then two millimetres of tread, it is time to re-tire, says Paul! Life is for the long haul; we will need maintenance along the way. We are not talking here about a sudden rush of adrenaline through the veins, but of someone who will pace themselves, keep going, and still be there at the end. This is not a sprint with a dash to the finish line—this is a journey of marathon magnitude. We cannot run a marathon as if it were a sprint. We must pace ourselves and maintain our spirit in Christ.

It is all about doing what is right. No whining or boasting. That is what kept classical composer Franz Joseph Haydn (1732-1809) going even when he felt like calling it quits. He wrote: 'Often when I was wrestling with obstacles of every kind, when my physical and mental strength alike were running low and it was hard for me to persevere in the path on which I had set my feet, a secret feeling within me whispered: "There are so few happy and contented people here below. Sorrow and anxiety pursue them everywhere. Perhaps your work may, some day, become a spring from which the careworn may draw a few moments rest and refreshment.'"

3:14-15 CAUTION WITH COMPASSION

If anyone does not obey our instructions in this letter, take special note of him. Do not associate with him, in order that he may feel ashamed. Yet do not regard him as an enemy, but warn him as a brother. When it comes to exercising discipline, there is a proper Christian way to do it!

The wise old preacher advises these dear folk that there is more than one way to skin a cat. If someone fails to toe God's party line, that individual should be noted and left to get on with life on his own. We should not socialise with them in any way, shape, or form. We have to remove ourselves from them. It is not because we do not like them or cannot stand them as individuals, it is to reinforce the stance that Paul is advocating we take.

If cracking the whip is going to have any effect at all, the person on the receiving end must be made to realise that he is losing out and missing out in so many different ways. Hopefully, he will also have a sense of shame and more than a tinge of regret when it finally dawns on him that people are no longer coming round to his place, and he is no longer welcome on their patch either.

Irrespective of what they have done or (in the case of work) have not done, we must still remember they are part of the family of God. Paul tells us to give the miscreant a warning; we must not tear him down in front of others. The offending person is still our Christian brother, and as such, we have a solemn responsibility toward him. We do not treat him as an enemy. We walk away, but only with a very heavy heart and with a firm commitment on our part to uphold him in prayer. In situations like that, it should be our earnest endeavour to pray the individual believer back into a place of usefulness and fruitfulness in the kingdom of God.

3:16 PEACE AND PRESENCE

The final verses in the chapter are an opportunity for Paul to tie up a few loose ends and to ultimately commit these dear people to the God of peace—a God whose peace is available all day, every day, anywhere and everywhere. Such is the awesome ability of our heavenly Father to come to us in our hour of deepest need and give us the wherewithal to keep going on. Even our darkest hours are brightened with his presence—it does not take much.

We not only enjoy a very real sense of his peace in our heart and mind, we also benefit from his companionship and presence on the journey from here to there, and to crown it all, we are blessed with the Psalmist of old in being able to say that the Lord is the portion of his people. Wonderful words—*Now may the Lord of peace himself give you peace at all times and in every way. The Lord be with all of you.*

- Yes, we have his peace.
- And we have his presence.
- And, perhaps, best of all, we have the Lord himself as a supporter.

No moan from Don Moen

Tens of thousands of Christians across the world love to sing Don Moen's praise song, *God Will Make A Way*—a song that affirms the sovereign involvement of God in our life. However, most of us who sing the lyrics do not know their origin.

Late one evening Don Moen received a phone call with devastating news: his wife's sister had lost her oldest son in an automobile accident. Craig and Susan Phelps and their four sons were travelling through Texas on their way to Colorado when their van was struck broadside by an eighteen-wheeler truck. All four boys were thrown from the van.

Craig and Susan located their sons by their cries—one boy was lying in the ditch, another in an area wet from melted snow. Nearby was his brother who landed by a telephone pole. All were seriously injured, but when Craig, a medical doctor, reached Jeremy, he found him lying by a fence post with his neck broken. There was nothing Craig could do to revive him.

When Don received news of this tragedy a few hours later, he recalls: 'My whole world came to a standstill, but I had to get on a plane the next morning and fly to a recording session that had been scheduled for several weeks. Although I knew Craig and Susan were hurting, I couldn't be with them until the day before the funeral.

'During the flight the morning after the accident, God gave me a song for them: "God will make a way where there seems to be no way. He works in ways we cannot see. He will make a way for me." The song was based upon Isaiah 43:19 NASB – "Behold, I will do something new, now it will spring forth; will you not be aware of it? I will even make a roadway in the wilderness, rivers in the desert."'

This song would bring comfort to Craig and Susan when all hope seemed lost. It touched the hurt in their hearts with hope and encouragement. Don received a letter from Susan in which she quoted Isaiah 43:4 NASB – 'Since you are precious in my sight, since you are honoured and I love you, I will give other men in your place and other peoples in exchange for your life.'

Susan wrote: 'We've seen the truth of that Scripture.' When Jeremy's friends learned that he had accepted Jesus into his life before he died, many of them began to ask their own parents how they could be assured of going to heaven when they died. The accident also prompted Craig and Susan into a deeper walk with the Lord as well as into new avenues of ministry. Craig began teaching Sunday School at their church and Susan became active in Women's Aglow, sharing with various groups her story and the Lord's provision in her time of sorrow.

She has since said: 'The day of the accident, when I got out of the van, even before I knew our son was dead, I knew I had a choice. I could be bitter and angry or I could totally accept God and whatever he had for us. I had to make the decision that fast. I've seen fruit come as a result of that choice. If I had to, I'd do it again. It's worth it knowing others will go to heaven because of what happened to Jeremy. God really did make a way for us!'

Soon after God Will Make A Way was recorded, people from around the world began to write and call, sharing with Don how they had experienced similar tragedies. All of the calls and letters had one great theme—God had made a way for them when all hope seemed to be lost! God had carried them through a shattering situation, and by his grace, they were emerging with stronger faith, renewed hope, and increased courage on the other side of heartache and loss.

The truth of God's word is always that he will make a way for those who rely solely upon him. The exact path is of his choosing. The exact methods are of his design, but he will bring us through to greater wholeness every time we place our trust in him.

God will make a way
When there seems to be no way.
He works in ways we cannot see,
He will make a way for me.
He will be my guide;
Hold me closely to his side.
With love and strength for each new day,
He will make a way.

3:17 SIGNED BY HIMSELF

I, Paul, write this greeting in my own hand, which is the distinguishing mark of all my letters. This is how I write. Seems like a most unusual comment for any man to make at the end of a letter to some friends—and yet, when we recall what Paul said earlier in the book, this note is absolutely essential. This statement is effectively his signature.

It clears the air once and for all that this is an authentic item of correspondence. It has his thumbprint smudged all over it—the Pauline imprimatur. This is how he writes. This is how he lives. This is how he will be remembered.

In the normal course of events Paul usually dictated his letter to a secretary—an amanuensis—who travelled in his ministry team. No problem there. That makes a lot of sense for it shares the load in terms of administration and it makes life an awful lot easier for the preacher on the road. It means he can think about other things.

At no time, however, did the scribe ever put into his own words what Paul was saying. He never amended anything—that is where verbal inspiration comes into the frame. His responsibility was to write down what Paul told him—a bit like a PA taking down her boss's memos in shorthand.

One pastor, overheard extolling the virtues of modern technology to a colleague, said: 'I use my laptop to write all my sermons—it's a personal computer!'

3:18 AMAZING GRACE...

What a resoundingly positive way to end a letter—*the grace of our Lord Jesus Christ be with you all.* Well, the reality is that when we have grace, we have God. Our blessed Lord Jesus is grace personified. Or, in the timely words of J. A. Motyer: 'Grace is Jesus being gracious.' A life that is mercy-filled and grace-soaked. We are a people saturated with God's grace! Wow!

The great Victorian preacher J. H. Jowett made the right connection: 'Grace is more than a smile of good nature. It is not the shimmering face of an illumined lake; it is the sunlit majesty of an advancing sea.' It is God's unmerited, unlimited favour that shines upon us all the time along all the way. Grace upon grace! And then some....

Grace that makes us ready for anything and grace that means we lack for nothing. It was grace that set our feet on the highway to heaven. It is grace that keeps us company all the journey through. It is grace that will see us safely home at last. We sing with John Newton:

> *Through many dangers, toils and snares,*
> *I have already come;*
> *'Tis grace hath brought me safe thus far,*
> *And grace will lead me home.*

This astoundingly, amazing grace will keep coming on us and to us until the Lord Jesus Christ comes for us. Hope and Glory.

STUDY GUIDE
COMPILED BY JOHN WHITE

1 THESSALONIANS 1

1. How and why in verse 3 does *faith, love, and hope* produce *work, labour, and endurance*?

2. How does it make you feel to know that God has *chosen* you (verse 4)? What do you think should be some of the practical consequence of knowing this?

3. What does verse 5 tell us about the process of sharing the gospel?

4. What does it mean to be *imitators of us and the Lord* (verses 5-6)? Paul was not shy about being a role model—what can we learn here about the importance of personal example? Who would you look to as a role model, and why?

5. The Thessalonians were a powerful witness, apparently as much by what they were as by what they said (verses 7-8). As one writer put it: 'We need to look like what we are talking about.' Think of some ways that you and your church could be a better visual witness to your common love, joy, peace, righteousness, and hope.

6. From verses 9-10 what were the three ways that the Thessalonians behaviour was affected by their conversion? Do we emphasise the need for changed behaviour today? If not, what could we do differently?

7. How does serving God now and waiting for Christ to come in the future help us keep the right balance in life (verses 9-10)?

8. What do you understand by *the coming wrath* (verse 10), and how will Jesus *rescue* us from it? Does this mean that some will not be rescued and if so, what will happen to them? What do you think of this and how does it affect the way you live?

1 Thessalonians 2

1. What encouragement is there in verses 1-4 to go on sharing the gospel when it is hard to do so? (See Acts 16:22-24 for what happened to Paul and Silas immediately before reaching Thessalonica, and 17:5-10 for opposition in Thessalonica itself.)

2. What qualities made Paul and his companions *approved by God* (verses 3-4)? Is there evidence of these high standards in your own life? If not, what can you do about it?

3. What qualities of motherhood (verse 7) make this metaphor an appropriate one to describe Christian service? And what complementary attributes are suggested by the *father* metaphor in verses 11-12?

4. Verses 8-9 demonstrate Paul's love, while elsewhere (verses 2, 13) he writes of sharing God's truth. Why are these two essential ingredients of pastoral ministry?

5. What do we learn from verse 13 about *the word of God* and its effect?

6. Some folk regard verses 15-16 as anti-Semitic. Do you agree or disagree, and why? Are these words incompatible with the compassionate picture we get of Paul earlier in the chapter?

7. What do you think Paul meant in verse 18 when he said *Satan stopped us*? How was Satan able to do this, and what was Paul's response (see also 3:1, 10, 11)? Is it true that every setback in life is due to Satan?

8. What are the values from verses 19-20 that Paul lived for in this life? In what ways are you prepared to live for the same values?

1 Thessalonians 3

1. We know from verses 1-5 that Paul could have sent money or some other kind of support to the fledgling church. Instead he sends his young assistant. What good could Timothy do for the Thessalonians?

2. Verse 1 seems to reflect the anxiety Paul and his friends felt for the Thessalonian church. How can we reconcile that with Paul's advice elsewhere to not be anxious about anything?

3. In living out our Christian lives, what encouragement is there in knowing that we are (a) a *brother*, and (b) *God's fellow-worker*? What are some of the implications of that latter phrase in particular?

4. The *gospel of Christ* (verse 2) is also the *gospel of God* (2:8) and *our gospel*. In what sense is it all three?

5. How does suffering fit into a Christian's life, and how can we respond to it, according to verses 2-4?

6. Paul, Silas, and Timothy seem to have spent no more than three weeks in Thessalonica before leaving the believers to get on by themselves the best they could in difficult circumstances. Yet to judge by Timothy's report they are doing well as a church. How do you think it was possible for the church to flourish like this? Does that tell us anything about the way we run our churches today?

7. From verses 6-10, what good did Timothy do for Paul?

8. What ambitions of Paul's for the Thessalonians are reflected in his prayer for them in verses 11-13? Why did he want them to have these qualities in particular?

1 Thessalonians 4

1. Paul talks about *instruction* and *authority* in verses 1-2, in other words being told what to do by someone above us. Do you think this kind of language still applies in our 'equal' society, and does it matter? Why?

2. Based on verses 3-8, what arguments could you use to try to dissuade a Christian friend who is involved in adultery?

3. If someone read verses 3-8 and said that God was just a killjoy where sex is concerned, how would you answer them? What are the sexual positives from a Christian perspective?

4. Why bother working? How would you answer that question from verses 11-12?

5. From verse 14, how does what happened to Jesus guarantee what will happen to us?

6. Describe in your own words, and in detail, the sequence outlined in verses 15-17 concerning the world's end. How convinced are you that what is detailed here will really happen?

7. How does knowing that this world is heading to a final climax where Jesus will take centre-stage affect your view a) of the world, and b) of your purpose and work in it? See verse 17.

8. How are the words in this section (verses 13-18) an encouragement to those who grieve?

1 Thessalonians 5

1. What is the balance outlined in verses 1-4 about our attitude towards Christ's return? How can we keep this balance?

2. Paul contrasts Christians and non-Christians as people of the light and the darkness, of the day and the night (verses 4-5). What does he mean by this, why is it true, and what are its implications (read down to verse 11)?

3. In what sense are *faith and love* a *breastplate*, and the *hope of salvation* a *helmet* (verse 8)? How can we *put them on*?

4. *Encourage* comes up a few times in this letter (verse 11). Why is it so important? What practical steps could you take to be a better encourager? Are there any tips from Thessalonians to help you?

5. What principles for church leaders—and our attitude towards them—can be gleaned from verses 12-13?

6. In verses 19-22, what do you understand by *the Spirit's fire* and *prophecies*? How are the injunctions in these verses being applied in your church?

7. What image does the word *sanctify* conjure up in your mind (verse 23)? What is it, how does it happen, and why does it matter?

8. Our Lord Jesus Christ is both *coming* and *faithful* (verses 23-24). Spend some time praising him that a wonderful future awaits us at his return and, in the meantime, he will keep us and make us ready for that great day.

2 THESSALONIANS 1

1. As in his first epistle, Paul refers in verses 3-4 to the flourishing faith of the Thessalonians and to their suffering, and these often go together. Why is a suffering church often a healthy church? How would you respond to such?

2. We are used to being told that our salvation does not depend on us but on God, that we do not earn it in any way (verse 5). How then can we be counted *worthy*? Does that not imply some sort of merit?

3. Verses 6-7 seem to be talking about retribution. Do you agree? And if so, how do we square that with our picture of a God of love?

4. How do you feel when you think of Jesus *revealed...in a blazing fire with his powerful angels* (verse 7)? What can you do to get yourself and others ready for that day?

5. How would you explain the link in verse 8 between *knowing God* and the *gospel of Jesus*? Is it possible to know God as an unbeliever?

6. Verses 8-10 are sobering verses when they tell us that those who *do not know God and do not obey the gospel* will be excluded from God's presence. Does that seem fair to you? Can we still hold on these days to the traditional view of hell?

7. What can we learn from verse 11 about the way we make progress in our Christian lives?

8. What does it mean that the name of Jesus is *glorified in you*, and that *you [are glorified] in him* (verse 12)? Is there anything you could do to make this more of a reality?

2 Thessalonians 2

1. False teaching has a long history and is still with us. What guidance is there in verses 1-3 about how to handle it?

2. What do verses 3-4 reveal about the nature and destiny of *the man of lawlessness*? What is your opinion on his identity?

3. What do you think is *holding…back* this individual (verse 6)?

4. What is the *secret power of lawlessness* that is *already at work* (verse 7)? Can you give some examples of how this power expresses itself today?

5. Jesus and the apostles did miracles, signs, and wonders. Should we still expect these phenomena today? If so, from verses 9-10, how can we distinguish between what is real and what is *counterfeit*?

6. There is a fivefold progression in verses 10-12 that ends in people being *condemned.* Can you spot it? And what is the effective protection against it?

7. Verses 13-14 have been called a 'theology in miniature.' Read them and say where our salvation originates, how it began, how it progresses, and where it will end. Or put another way, how are all three Persons of the Godhead involved in our salvation?

8. If the Thessalonians are rooted so deeply in God and his eternal purpose, wouldn't they be perfectly safe already (verses 15-17)? So why does Paul need to tell them to *stand firm* and to pray for them?

2 Thessalonians 3

1. What guidance is there in verses 1-2 for our prayers for those engaged in mission work? And what do we learn about the essence of what mission is?

2. How are verses 3-5 an encouragement to us as we try to be engaged in mission or personal witness, perhaps not very successfully—or so we think?

3. *Command* (verse 4) occurs three times in this chapter. Is there a place for this kind of authoritative direction in today's church? And if so, in what circumstances?

4. Does verse 6 really mean we are to have nothing to do with some Christians because of the way they live? Can you think of some examples where this might be true today?

5. What is Paul's attitude towards idleness in verses 6-13, and what reasons does he give the Thessalonians for following his advice? Are there any circumstances where you are prone to idleness? What can you do about it?

6. The idea of church discipline is not popular today but verses 14-15 seem to teach it. Do you think it is right for churches sometimes to discipline their members? Together with verse 6, what do we learn here about when this might be necessary, what form it should take, who is responsible for it, the way it should be done, and what its ultimate purpose is?

7. What is the threefold blessing invoked in verses 16-18, and what do they actually mean in day to day experience? What is the link between *peace* and *grace*?

8. Why did Paul insert verse 17, and why does it matter?